The Rhode Island Short Story Club
presents a Collection
of Short Stories, Essays and Poems
written by Present and Past Members of
The Rhode Island Short Story Club

ISBN 13: 978-0-615-14324-8

Printed in the USA September, 2007
Second Printing November, 2007

Published by The Rhode Island Short Story Club

FOUNDED 1894

The Rhode Island Short Story Club
PO Box 136
Barrington, RI 02806

www.RhodeIslandShortStoryClub.org
info@RhodeIslandShortStoryClub.org

*This book is dedicated to the
high-spirited and courageous women
who founded The Rhode Island Short Story Club
and to the devoted men and women
who kept it alive since 1894.*

TABLE OF CONTENTS

Present and Past Members of The Rhode Island Short Story Club

Past Presidents

**President*

Publishing Details

Publisher:
The Rhode Island Short Story Club

Creative Director:
Frances L. O'Donnell

Book Design:
Melissa Hallock

Web Site Design:
Jennifer Balch

Editorial Board:
Patricia J. Gerstner
Frances L. O'Donnell
Charlann Walker
Ingrid Wild Kleckner

ACKNOWLEDGEMENTS

THE FOUNDERS
We honor them by creating this book as a remembrance of their perseverance, determination and hard work. Their spirit and wisdom gave us this moment in time.

It is with a grateful heart that The Rhode Island Short Story Club thanks the following people and celebrates them for their unending hours of work and their invaluable knowledge, talents and labor of love. We appreciate your help in making our dream come true.

FRANCES L. O'DONNELL
Thank you Fran, for your innovative spirit, the unflagging energy and enthusiasm with which you planned and coordinated the publication of our book. Your dedication, hard work and talent made it happen.

MELISSA HALLOCK
Thank you Melissa, for your exceptional vision in creating our book and the many hours you spent bringing it to life.

JENNIFER BALCH
Thank you Jennifer, for developing an outstanding website and exuding enthusiasm while working out the details for it.

Patricia J. Gerstner

Thank you Pat, for your support and dedication during the production of *The Rhode Island Short Story Club* presents in your final year as president. Your commitment and hard work were greatly appreciated and will be remembered.

Ingrid Wild Kleckner

Thank you Ingrid, for your ongoing support, loyalty and continued encouragement in the publishing of our book.

Marie C. Russian

Thank you Marie, for your steady support and help during the making of our book.

Members of The Rhode Island Short Story Club

Thank you members, your efforts made this book possible.

And for all those who supported us, we thank you.

OFFICERS OF THE CLUB

President:
Frances L. O'Donnell

Vice President:
Charlann Walker

Treasurer:
Marie C. Russian

Recording Secretary:
June Smith

Corresponding Secretary:
Patricia J. Gerstner

FOUNDERS

Founder:
Fanny Purdy Palmer

PRESENT AT FIRST MEETING MAY 29, 1894

Fanny Purdy Palmer, *Founder*
Katherine H. Austin
Lucy Gaslin
Caroline Hazard, *President of Wellesley College*
Sarah F. Hopkins
Elizabeth P. Kendall
Mary E. Pratt
F. A. Reynolds
H. P. Richardson
A. J. Spencer
Mary C. Wheeler, *Founder of Wheeler School*

WE HONOR FANNY PURDY PALMER

Fanny Purdy Palmer was one of the most accomplished women of her time in Rhode Island. Born in 1839, she married a physician, William Henry Palmer, whom she accompanied to the Civil War battlefields from where she sent war reports to northern newspapers.

After the war, the Palmers joined *The Freed Men's Society*, an organization that helped the former slaves with their integration into a new life. Mrs. Palmer became a monthly contributor to *The True Flag* for 20 years and continued publishing short stories, essays and poetry in *Home Journal*; *Putnam's* and *Peterson's*; *Harper's Monthly* and *Harper's Weekly*; *The Galaxy*; *The True Flag*; *The Woman's Journal*, the publication of the Suffrage movement; *The Continental*; *The New York Weekly* and *The Parthenon.*

For the *Rhode Island Women Commissioners of the World's Columbian Exposition*, she wrote *A List of Rhode Island Literary Women (1726-1892)*, and a number of her books were published widely in the U.S. and England which she visited often. After her husband's death Mrs. Palmer and her daughter Henrietta lived in England for two years.

An inveterate traveler, she wrote about her trips to Italy and her four-year stay in California and still found the time to get involved in civic affairs at home.

She became a member of the *Providence School Committee*; involved in *Centennial Exposition* in Philadelphia; Chairman of project representing women as Rhode Island's contribution to *Chicago World's Fair*; was elected to the Executive Committee of the *Rhode Island Women Suffrage Association*, served as Secretary and remained as Honorary Vice President through the passage of the *Susan B. Anthony Amendment* to the Constitution and its ratification by the State of Rhode Island; President of the *Rhode Island Women's Club* for almost 10 years; President of the *Women's Educational and Industrial Union*; Director of the *General Federation of Women's Clubs*; Secretary of an organization trying to secure educational privileges by Brown University for women—achieved 1892 when she led a small group of her peers to a conference with Brown President Andrews; Factory Inspector of the State of Rhode Island to insure compliance with the new child labor laws.

In May, 1894, she invited a group of women to her Providence home to foster personal acquaintance among Rhode Island women engaged in literary or journalistic work—and so founded *The Rhode Island Short Story Club*, which continues to this day.

She was the author of and well remembered for *Dates and Days in Europe by an American resident in London (1914-1915)*. Mrs. Palmer wrote *The Outpost Messages* in the last four years of her life.

Fanny Purdy Palmer died in 1923 in Providence, Rhode Island.

INTRODUCTION

POEM
The Bringing Of The Sword

SONNET
Vikings

INTRODUCTION

From Dates and Days in Europe
By an American resident in London (1914-1915)

Arriving in England during February, 1914, I stopped for a month in Dover and from there came up to London.

I recall the early warmth and charm of that Spring and Summer which now seem very far away, and, with them, that sense of repose to which one who has lived—as I have—a rather long and busy life, feels, for some unexplained reason, entitled.

Then, one August morning, there appeared a brief headline in the newspaper whose import every startled reader understood at a glance. There were only five words: *Britain will not desert France*, but they seemed to alter the aspect of the universe. Henceforth ease and repose, for the mind or for the body, might be suited to the inhabitants of some other planet, not, certainly, to those of our own.

A year has elapsed, and on this anniversary of the beginning of the War I am dwelling, in common with the multitude whose interests I have shared from day to day, on emotions which have touched the foundations of feeling, and on sentiments, hitherto undreamed of in our philosophies, which have now become a permanent part of them. And when I ask myself what are the qualities which I shall forever associate with the England of the year just ended, I think of her sustained and self-forgetful hospitality to the refuges from a despoiled country, of the faith and charity with which occasions have been met, and of that imaginative outlook that has already given birth to the new type of courage.

London, August 4, 1915

THE BRINGING OF THE SWORD

From Dates and Days in Europe
By an American resident in London (1914-1915)

To lives at peace, enamoured of content
While prosperous tides break on a sheltered shore,
The world seems changeless, and men's aims ignore
Its spinning pace. But when an Age is rent
By storms of acquiescence and dissent,
By wild emotions never felt before,
By swift destructions—mate with mate at war—
And by alarm, and wonder, and lament—
Then, as from strings responsive to no hand,
Which chord or discord yield as we elect,
There sounds a strain whence souls at birth are stirred;
And from this rhythm—hard to understand,
And from these measures—idle to reject—
Life to the Law adds its compulsive word.

September, 1914

VIKINGS

From stormy shores, red-bearded Norseman bold,—
From stormy shores over an unknown sea
Thou cam'st,—yet left not to futurity
Record of conflict fierce for power or gold;
No lands despoiled, no captives sought to hold.
Soul stirred with novel joy! elate with free
Dream of illimitable liberty,—
Thou cam'st,—and went,—thy story strange untold.
Yet still while poets sing they'll celebrate
The fair-haired crew who roamed Rhode Island's shore;
Still with their haunting presence consecrate
Wild Vinland and bleak coast: and, evermore,
On reckless bark which to the gale puts forth,
See phantom Vikings steering for the North.

History *of the*
Rhode Island Short Story Club

KATHERINE PATRICIA TUCKER

Kay Tucker was a 1939 Brown/Pembroke graduate, and over the years, always faithful to her alma mater and committed to many Brown organizations and the Rhode Island Historical Society. However, *The Rhode Island Short Story Club* was her passion. Her history of the historic Club was published in *Rhode Island Women Speak* in 1998. She was a stalwart member working toward the life and longevity of the Club.

Each summer she loved to visit the Inn at Watch Hill, and we like to think of her sitting on the veranda, rocking, watching the sun set over the ocean.

A HISTORY

In 1894 President Grover Cleveland was in the White House; Governor D. Russell Brown was in the Rhode Island State House, and Mayor Frank Fuller Olney presided over the Providence City Hall. The same year witnessed the publication of Rudyard Kipling's *The Jungle Book* and George Bernard Shaw's *Arms And The Man*.

Here in Providence on May 29, 1894, Mrs. Fanny Purdy Palmer, writer and lecturer, invited some women interested in the literary field to her home at 272 Rugby Street to discuss the formation of anorganization of writers. The idea originated with Mrs. Palmer while she was chairman of the project representing women as part of Rhode Island's contribution to the Chicago World's Fair the previous year. At that time she compiled a brochure on 165 literary women of Rhode Island.

Fanny Purdy Palmer was born in New York on July 11, 1839. She married Dr. William H. Palmer. Mrs. Palmer served as a State Inspector of Factories and Workshops and was the first woman member of the Providence School Committee. She was also active in Rhode Island's share of the Centennial Exposition in Philadelphia in 1876. The literary ladies who met at Mrs. Palmer's home on that memorable May day agreed to form a club "to foster personal acquaintance among Rhode Island women engaged in literary or journalistic work." The club would also include "a representative of each of the arts, education, law and medicine and occasionally of the ministry."

According to the minutes as recorded by Fanny Purdy Palmer, Secretary, pro tem, "the meeting adjourned to meet on the fourth Friday in June when Miss Caroline Hazard agreed to present some production from her pen."

The next meeting was held on June 22. There were sixteen charter members. By unanimous vote, the club adopted as its official name, *The Short Story Club*. Mrs. Palmer was elected President and Miss Campbell, Secretary. A committee was appointed to draft a constitution. Caroline Hazard read her poem, *A Seventeenth Century Episode,* which related the Great Swamp Fight between the colonists and the Indians in South County. A letter was read from Mrs. Julia Ward Howe, author of *The Battle Hymn Of The Republic,* accepting an invitation from the club to read a story at its August meeting.

The third meeting was held in July in Peacedale where Caroline Hazard was the hostess. Katherine Austin read her story, *Mrs. Brown's Crisis.* The members and two guests, Mrs. Pierce of Philadelphia and Mrs. Easbee of Baltimore embarked on the 2:10 p.m. train from Providence and were met at the Peacedale station by carriages which conveyed them over country roads, arriving at their destination at 3:30 p.m.

At the August meeting, Mrs. Palmer again was the hostess and Julia Ward Howe read her play, *Hippolytus, The Son Of Thesus,* which she had written about thirty years before for production with Edwin Booth in the title role and Charlotte Cushman as Phedia, the heroine, but the play was never produced.

Marianna Tallman was a girl who was in the right place at the right time. From Mount McGreger, New York, she wrote a descriptive story of the cottage on the mountainside, the sorrowing throngs and the mournful note of church bells which proclaimed the news of the tragic death of President Ulysses S. Grant. Mrs. Tallman sent her story to Martin Day, at that time the editor of *The Providence Journal.* She became a roving reporter for that newspaper and was known in journalistic circles as a "talented descriptive writer." She was one of the first women reporters in the country. She wrote special feature stories for Alfred M. Williams, then editor of the

Sunday edition. Mrs. Tallman wrote a story about Rhode Island Lighthouses and about a stage coach trip to Danielson, Connecticut. In addition to special articles, she authored many books, including *Pleasant Places in Rhode Island.*

Mrs. Tallman wrote a poem, which was read on June 9, 1926 at a dedication ceremony at Roger Williams Park for 100 Japanese cherry trees, which were presented to the City of Providence by Mrs. Allardice in memory of her sister Irma, a musician. The ceremony was held just before sunset and two trumpet melodies were played. The theme of the *Memorial Poem* was 'remembering one who loved all loveliness.'

Marianna Tallman was a charter member of *The Short Story Club.*

Sara Hopkins, a pioneer journalist and an author was also a charter member of *The Short Story Club.* A descendent of Stephen and Esek Hopkins, she was born in Warwick in 1838. She originated the Women's Department of *The Providence Sunday Journal.* Her first newspaper assignment was to cover the Mardi Gras in New Orleans. In 1899, Sara Hopkins went to Cuba with Mrs. Emma Shaw Colcleugh to investigate conditions of the poor suffering from the effects of the war.

Emma Shaw Colcleugh, a Rhode Islander and a famous world traveler, wrote vividly of her adventures in areas ranging from the Arctic Circle to the South Seas. On October 18, 1920, Mrs. Colcleugh, while a member of *The Providence Journal* staff, was "specially commissioned to make a daring and perilous trip into the heart of Central Africa by way of Zanzibar"

Mrs. Colcleugh, a popular lecturer as well as graphic writer, was an honorary member of *The Short Story Club.* She also inaugurated a department for Club women in *The Providence Sunday Journal.*

Another honorary member was Maud Howe Elliott, the daughter of Julia Ward Howe and Dr. Samuel Gridley Howe, who founded the Perkins Institute for the Blind in Boston. Maud Howe married John Elliott, an artist. She campaigned actively for Theodore Roosevelt in the days of the Progressive Movement and worked for the cause of women suffrage.

Dr. Howe served as Surgeon-in-Chief to the Greek Army during that country's War of Independence. An ardent admirer of Lord Byron and his devotion to the Greek cause, Dr. Howe prized the poet's helmet, which he had acquired. Maud Howe Elliott tells the fascinating story in her book, *Lord Byron's Helmet*.

Maud Howe Elliott was awarded by the Greek Government "the beautiful decoration of the Order Of the Golden Cross of the Redeemer" in recognition of her return of the prized helmet to Lord Byron's "dearly beloved Greece."

Mrs. Elliott published in 1904 *Beata Roma*, a compilation of letters sent from Rome to several American papers, thus earning for herself the distinction of being the first woman syndicating journalist in America. In 1917, Mrs. Elliott was awarded *The Joseph Pulitzer Prize* by Columbia University.

Anne Crosby Emery Allison, Dean of Pembroke College in Brown University, wrote the popular column, *The Distaff*, which was published daily for nearly six years in *The Providence Evening Bulletin*.

Caroline Hazard, President of Wellesley College, continued *The Distaff* after Mrs. Allison's death. Her book, *Anchors of Tradition*, won for the Yale Press the medal of the Society of Graphic Arts as The best printed book in 1925. In an autographed copy, the author noted: "The stories in this volume were first read in *The Story Club* in the 1890's."

Caroline Hazard presented to the Wellesley College Museum a collection of the love letters of Elizabeth Barrett and Robert Browning and the door to the Barrett's at 50 Wimpole Street. *The Providence Journal's* story about this gift was under the by-line of

Myra Blosser, a member of *The Short Story Club*.

A story also in *The Providence Journal*, about Carl Sandburg's visit here and his appearance on February 28, 1930 at Moses Brown School was bylined by Elsie Lustig, a member of *The Short Story Club*. While lecturing at Brown University, Robert Frost was a guest of *The Short Story Club* and that story was written by Grace Bird, a member.

Lillie Chace Wyman's stories on the human phases of factory life in her native town on the Blackstone River, first attracted attention when published in *The Atlantic Monthly* and later in 1886 in her book *Poverty Grass*. She also wrote a comprehensive biography of her mother, Elizabeth Buffam Chace, long time President of the Rhode Island Woman Suffrage Association.

On May 20, 1935, *The Providence Evening Bulletin* printed a story about *The Short Story Club's* plan to gather records of women writers as its project for the Rhode Island Tercentenary. According to the article, "women who have written Rhode Island's name into literary Americana are being Honored by their successors."

In 1944 to celebrate its 50th Anniversary, *The Short Story Club* held a contest and awarded a $50.00 War Bond for the best story written by a Rhode Islander, who was not a member of the club.

Gertrude Hughes received the prize for her story, *You Can Get So Lonely*. The author became a member.

In 1947, an interesting story appeared in *The Providence Journal* about Sarah A. Chandler, a Providence poet and a member of *The Short Story Club* on the occasion of her 103rd birthday. According to the article, "Henry Clay was running for president the year she was born."

Annie Laney, author of *Never Let The Fairies Go* was awarded the $50.00 prize offered by the Poetry Lovers of New York for the best definition of poetry in poetry and containing thirty-five words.

For the contest, over forty-five hundred definitions were submitted from all parts of the world.

Among the members representing art were Mary C. Wheeler, founder of the Wheeler School, and Mabel Woodward who designed the Club's bookplate. Music representatives were Ruth Tripp, pianist and critic and Mrs. Florence Newell Barbour, talented musician and gifted writer, and wife of the President of Brown University. Drama was represented by playwright, Dorothy Allan, a member of the Hope High School faculty.

The Club proudly numbered among its members Margaret B. Stillwell, Curator of the Ann Mary Brown Memorial and author of scholarly articles on bibliographical research; Professor Magel C. Wilder of the Biology Department of Brown University, who wrote learned scientific papers; Elizabeth Nicholson White and Alice Collins Gleeson, writers of interesting and colorful historical stories and Mabel Neikirk, noted author of children's books.

The Rhode Island Short Story Club has a rich and wonderful tradition with high ideals and sensitive creativity. Only some highlights are set forth in this brief chronicle. The great debt of inspiration can never be fully repaid.

A History by Katherine Patricia Tucker

BATTLE HYMN OF THE REPUBLIC

By Julia Ward Howe
1819 – 1910
RISSC Member August, 1894

Mine eyes have seen the glory of the coming of the Lord.
He is trampling out the vintage where the grapes of wrath are stored.
He hath loosed the fateful lightning of His terrible swift sword.
His truth is marching on.

Chorus*

I have seen Him in the watch-fires of a hundred circling camps.
They have builded Him an altar in the evening dews and damps.
I can read His righteous sentence by the dim and flaring lamps.
His day is marching on.

Chorus*

I have read a fiery gospel, writ in burnished rows of steel.
"As ye deal with My contemners, so with you my grace shall deal.
Let the Hero, born of woman, crush the serpent with his heel,
Since God is marching on."

Chorus*

In the beauty of the lilies Christ was born across the sea,
With a glory in his bosom that transfigures you and me.
As he died to make men holy, let us die to make men free,
While God is marching on.

*Chorus
Glory, Glory, Hallelujah
Glory, Glory, Hallelujah
Glory, Glory, Hallelujah
His truth is marching on

BATTLE HYMN OF THE REPUBLIC

Written for Centennial Celebration 1994
By *Douglas Phillips Whitmarsh*, RISSC Member

Some lines to sing to the tune of "The Battle Hymn of the Republic" upon the occasion of the Centennial Celebration of the Rhode Island Short Story Club (1894-1994).

Mine eyes beheld the crowning of one hundred fruitful years
Of a tiny band of women who haven written of the tears
And the blood which flowed unceasingly both here and there abroad
And all in the name of Liberty and God.

Chorus*

The War Between the States was not the last one by a shot.
There was one they called The Great One, and the Second they
   did not.
Then we sent our youth to die upon the Asian land and sea
and all in the name of God and Liberty.

Chorus*

In a city named for Heaven, in a land we took by force,
we continue to endeavor to record the human course.
If the written word can help us sing a Truthful history,
then we must keep writing what we do and see.

Chorus*

The woes of life are lessons learned by every girl and boy.
But equally important are the triumphs and its joy.
We have witnessed and have written until Nineteen Ninety Four,
and, if it please the Lord, we will write a hundred more.

*Chorus (As per Julia Ward Howe, *RISSC* member, August 1894)
Glory, Glory, Hallelujah
Glory, Glory, Hallelujah
Glory, Glory, Hallelujah
His truth is marching on.

Our Town
RI Short Story Club Will Note 75th Birthdate

By Mary McCaughey
May 18, 1969
Providence Journal

PROMINENT AUTHORS, educators, poets, librarians and play-wrights, all residents of Rhode Island, have over the years been members of *The Rhode Island Short Story Club* which will observe its 75th anniversary on May 29.

Recognition of their ability has often extended far beyond the state. There was Caroline Hazard, a charter member and president of Wellesley College from 1899 to 1910; Mary C. Wheeler, who founded the girls' school which bears her name; and Marion S. Cole, vice president of the White and headmistress emerita of Lincoln School; Adelaide Patterson, author, was a member of the faculty at Rhode Island College of Education.

The late Julia Ward Howe of Middletown wrote, *The Battle Hymn Of The Republic* and Mrs. Daniel W. Knowlton of Bristol, immediate past president, wrote Longfield, based on her home, *Butter Balls And Finger Bowls;* a technical book entitled, *My Turtle;* and a novel *The Innocent Cause.* Mrs. Knowlton is the sister of Charles Dana Gibson, famed for his illustrations of the Gibson Girl.

The former librarian of the Ann Mary Brown Memorial Library, Margaret Stillwell, is currently working on a book based on the 15th and 16th centuries. She is the author of *While Benefit Street Was Young,* and *The Pageant of Benefit Street Down Through The Years,* and makes

REMINISCING. Mrs. Frank L. Hinckley, president of *Rhode Island Short Story Club*, holds book with minutes of former meetings. L-R, Miss Ethel Blaisdell and Miss Louise H. DeWolf, recording secretary.

her home in Greenville with Miss Dorothy Allen. Miss Allen, a former member of the faculty at Hope High School, is the author of a great many plays which have been presented by churches, schools, and amateur theatrical groups.

A partial list of others, whose names will reawaken memories of long ago and who were well known in the social, literary and civic life of the community includes, Mrs. E. Nicholson White, author and former president; Miss. Alice Comstock, Mrs. Morris Phinney; Anne Allison, former columnist for the *Journal Bulletin*; Grace Sherwood, state house librarian, Grace Slocum of the *Journal Bulletin* staff;

Charlotte Tillinghast, Club secretary; and Mrs. Marion Nicholl Rawson, author of a number of books on antiques.

Mrs. Frank L. Hinckley is club secretary, and in addition to Miss Cole, vice president, the other officers are Miss. Louise H. DeWolf, recording secretary; Mrs. Paul W. Fletcher, corresponding secretary; and Mrs. Lorrin A. Riggs, treasurer.

The spark that lit that long ago enthusiasm, continues to burn with current members submitting their work to publishers. Mrs. Hinckley has had numerous articles published in the *Journal Bulletin* and the *Rhode Islander Magazine,* and Miss Ethel F. Blaisdell of Bristol is the author of *And God Caught an Eel,* the biography of the Rev. Charles S. Thurber, for 33 years chaplain at the Seaman's Chapel, New Bedford.

Among those whose work has appeared in the *Rhode Island Yearbook* are Mrs. Fletcher, Mrs. Virginia C. Catton, Mrs.William Slater Allen Jr. and Mrs. Knowlton. Miss DeWolf and Mrs.George E. Wilson Jr., prize winners at the club's annual spring short story contest, have also had their works published in the *Yearbook.*

At the 75th observance, which will take place at noon at the home of Mrs. O. Griswold Boynton on Arnold Street, the winners of this season's contest will be announced. Nine stories have been submitted and these are currently being read and graded.

It all began when Mrs. Fanny Purdy Palmer, writer and lecturer, invited a group of women to her home on Rugby Street on May 29, 1894 to organize a club to "foster acquaintance among Rhode Island women engaged in literary work."

Short Story Club Marks Century of Creativity

By Maria Miro Johnson
May 29, 1994
Journal Bulletin staff writer

Compared to the suffragettes who founded *The Rhode Island Short Story Club* 100 years ago today, the current crop of members—how do we put it?

"A bunch of pansies," says Dorothy G. McCarten, who at 67 is among the younger members, but at an age where one tells it straight. "I mean, boy, they were girded for battle."

The club's founder was Fanny Purdy Palmer, who fought for women's right to vote (and lived to see them win it) and for child-labor laws. She was the first woman factory inspector in Rhode Island and the first woman on the Providence school board. She had her daughters apply to then-all-male Brown University, which rejected the women, but within 10 years, Pembroke College for Women was founded.

Literary Life RI Short Story Club Makes History with Prose

This same spirit of dedication to women's intellectual development, and the written word, prompted Palmer, on May 29, 1894, to gather some women at her home at 272 Rugby St., Providence, to form a club. Its purpose: "to foster personal acquaintance among Rhode Island women engaged in literary or journalistic work."

Over the years, the membership has included Julia Ward Howe, who wrote *The Battle Hymn Of The Republic* and invented Mother's Day (originally Mothers' Peace Day); Howe's daughter, suffragette Maud Howe Elliot won the *Pulitzer Prize* for her biography of her mother; Emma Shaw Colcleugh chronicled her travels from the Arctic Circle to the South Seas to the heart of Africa; in 1899 Sara Hopkins went to Cuba with Colcleugh to investigate the conditions of the poor suffering from the effects of the war; Lillie Chace Wyman wrote about the human face of factory life on the Blackstone River for the *Atlantic Monthly*; several college deans and many trailblazing women journalists.

These days, says McCarten, *The Short Story Club* is "not as focused on public activity," but its members are nonetheless accomplished in other ways; an exhibit of members' drawings, paintings and other creative work will be displayed around the state throughout this centennial year.

McCarten also points out that whenever individual members have embraced a cause, the club has backed them. "There's that feeling of fellowship," she says.

("Fellows," by the way, have been allowed to join since the 1970's, when the by laws were rewritten to include men.)

CHAMPAGNE ANYONE?

The club's May meeting took place, as it usually does, in a back room at the Providence Art Club. As a steady rain fell outside the gallery windows, members enjoyed johnnycakes, quiche, asparagus and strawberry shortcake. "Are you sure you won't have some champagne?" Ellen Burchard of New York and Little Compton asked a reporter.

Soon, the president, Joseph W. Abraham, called for the chatter to end and the meeting to begin, for the agenda was long. This would not be a typical meeting, with workshops on writing or talks by authors. Instead, the writing contest winners would be announced; the final details for the centennial celebration, down to the design of the cake, would be decided; and new officers would be installed.

- - - - - - - - - - - -

The meeting ended with the winners reading their works aloud. Afterward, Mary Frye, who won second prize for her story about the anticipated return of an old flame, dashed up to Phebe Chase and congratulated her on her winning poem, *Crib Animals,* which was inspired by stuffed animals washed up on the beach.

Frye was so moved by the poem, she gave Chace a big hug.

- - - - - - - - - - - -

'THEIR INTEREST AND INVOLVEMENT IS REALLY INSPIRING'

Ann Harleman, another local author who's spoken to the club about writing and has judged their contests, says, "I love 'em. I think they're just wonderful."

The women, particularly, are "role models" for her, she said, no matter whether they've been published or not. "It's more the degree of their interest and involvement that's really inspiring. I don't think you have to have produced a lot or have produced for money in order to be serious."

To join the club, one must be invited by a member. Candidates then submit three pieces of writing, and are voted on by the full membership.

"I was delighted when I was asked to join." says Evelyn Doherty of Rumford, who wouldn't exactly call herself serious. At age 85, being serious about writing would be too strenuous, she says. She writes mainly for herself and her family, and because it's fun. A few months ago, she says, she wrote a funny story about the adventures of three sisters, who were bars of soap—Jasmine, Violet and Rose.

A 'NEAT THING'

For Douglas "Douggie" Whitmarsh, 62, of little Compton, the incoming president, 'joining the club is one of the neat things that's happened to me in my later life.' She never finished college, lost a young son to a brain tumor and has been caring for her invalid husband since 1977. So, for her, writing is a release and the club an escape. When she thinks about the club's long history and distinguished membership, she feels honored. "I hope I don't preside over its demise," she says. "We've got to get it going a little more. People are very busy these days."

Whitmarsh wonders how those very accomplished founding mothers managed to make time for everything. She'd like to think the club is carrying on their goals, "if not precisely as they did."

The founder's great-grandson, Stephen Palmer, has no complaints. He is deputy treasurer of the state and the former chairman and CEO of Shawmut and Peoples Banks. He is not a member—"I wish I had the talent"—but says, "I think it's wonderful that the women have, over 100 years, banded together to keep this alive."

In an age when "the media is dealing in nano-seconds and impressions on the screen," he said, it's important that people devote time to writing poetry and prose. "One of the real messages of *The Short Story Club*," he added, "is while these women were gathering together to give each other support, and mentor each other's writings and encourage each other, they really were helping to create a written history of the events of their times."

Governor Sundlun and Providence Mayor Vincent A. Cianci Jr. have issued proclamations establishing today as *Rhode Island Short Story Club Day*, Exhibits of the club's history and creative work will be up through June 30 at the Providence Public Library, 225 Washington St., and at the Providence Athenaeum, 251 Benefit St.

Also, beginning Tuesday and running through June 30, there will be an exhibit at the Barrington Public Library, 281 County Rd, from August, 1-31, at the South Kingstown Library, 1057 Kingstown Rd. Peacedale; the first two weeks of September at Rogers Free Library, Hope Street, Bristol; and from Sept. 20 to Oct. 22, at the Rhode Island Historical Society Library, 121 Hope St., Providence.

SHORT STORIES, ESSAYS AND POEMS
WRITTEN BY PRESENT AND PAST MEMBERS
of the RHODE ISLAND SHORT STORY CLUB

JOSEPH W. ABRAHAM

Joe Abraham's stories always surprised and entertained; stories which were published and won awards. His energy and enthusiasm was so apparent during his *Rhode Island Short Story* presidential term as a leader and later as a friend to all. When calling Joe, his answering machine greeted us with one of his famous, clever limericks.

SHORT STORIES
> The Man With the Duck
> A Fairy Tale
> Roger

THE MAN WITH THE DUCK
With gratitude to Anton Chekov's *The Lady with the Dog*

It was said that a new person had appeared on the lakefront: a man with a duck.

Katerina Wit, bored with riding the strip around The Plaza in downtown Elmwood and with the night clubs and bars and cocky young studs, jaded scions, and overweight businessmen, had taken to strolling the beautiful grounds of the Roger Williams Park and around the lake, where ducks swam in long, sensuous glides until someone threw bread into the water and they lost all sense of caution or reason in their haste for the delectable morsels.

As a saleswoman for a national lingerie company, she traveled around the northeast, sometimes overnight, thus finding it easy to explain her absences to an indifferent and alcoholic husband.

She wondered why a man with a duck would be walking along the lakefront. Why not a dog or even a pig? But a DUCK!

He wore a yellow beret, almost the color of the duck's bill, with a small, white duck's feather curving out of the side like a duck's tail.

How men strive to attract their opposite gender, and in what outrageous ways! How foolishly puerile they are in doing so. But their innate, all consuming drive to mate carries them heedlessly towards their goal, and they lose all sense of caution and reason in their haste to get the sweets of love.

She was already thirty-nine, or somewhere past that, but the number was hidden in the sands of forcibly-forgotten time and in an unyielding refusal to celebrate her birthdays.

She took great pride in her apparel and grooming, exuding an air of suppressed sensuality and subtle invitation, which had produced numerous short-term affairs with a variety of suitors.

Although men were easily drawn to her, few met her demands for intellectual as well as physical stimulation: her pleasure and self-satisfaction derived from the thrill of the chase, for once her prey was snared, she lost interest and always managed a rapid disengagement without pain to either party.

But there was something about the man with the duck that both attracted and repulsed her. He was young—but portly with a projecting rear end. His walk was slow and unhurried, in synchronous step with the companion waddling behind.

She saw him often after that, always along the path that bordered the lake and never without his white-feathered companion goose-stepping, unruffled, behind or beside him. Sometimes the duck, in a moment of rare assertion, would take the dominant position ahead of his master.

On the fifth day, a day of soft, warm sunlight and a light, soothing breeze, when the ducks on the lake had drifted somnolently to the further shore, and a mesmerizing quietude had hushed the park, she determined to meet him.

Stepping forward as he passed, she spoke boldly, "My, what a beautiful duck you have."

"The better to meet with you, my dear," he whispered impulsively, but she scarcely heard it, for she was startled to see, close up, how much his face resembled that of his escort: broad, slightly upturned nose, bright, beady eyes and light, silver-dyed hair feathered thickly over his forehead.

They met often after that, for an aperitif or coffee, or just to sit by the water and feed the ducks, her initial repulsion slowly diminishing, new and confusing feelings emerging. What was happening to her? Where was the anticipation and excitement of the thrill of the chase?

She was calm, and comfortable, and at peace in his company: in another world, free of the past and her life outside the park, safe and secure in the arms of the man with the duck.

It was two weeks later that she learned his name, Joseph Joseph, and that he was married, and that he and his wife were childless, and that his spouse was a termagant beyond endurance, who had thrown him and duck out of the house, and had sworn never to give him a divorce.

And despite this, he was deeply shy and tender, and vulnerable.

Joseph Joseph was also concerned about his ultimate destination after death, about his salvation. As a young altar boy, he had been intensely devout, and much of that religious fervor had carried over into manhood.

So Katerina knew the barriers to her goal of capturing Joseph Joseph: his strong religious convictions and a wife, and always the duck, the inquisitive, intrusive, quacking duck, her annoying, vexatious rival for the affections and attention of Joseph Joseph.

"You will hate me in the morning, I know," he said, a tiny solitary tear easing its way downward. "I've committed a mortal sin. I will suffer in hell for what I have done."

Katerina looked at him in disbelief, thoughts of 'what am I doing here with this wimp?' weighted her mind. But the memory of their frantic hour of unflagging passion drew her close, and she comforted and reassured him until his sobbing ceased and they rejoined again in fervid expressions of love and desire.

Their affair continued for the remainder of the summer: by the lake, behind the boathouse, within the old unused carousel, in the secluded lakeside area. The only witness to their lovemaking was the man's duck.

So as the summer and fall ended, and the cold winter drew close, they knew that their romance must end, for the park could no longer offer its warmth and protection—and his wife had demanded his return.

So they said good bye for what was to be the final separation, kissing passionately by the shore of the lake. They were oblivious to all and everything except an occasional quack from their constant companion.

But a week later, they met again for one last time inside the boat-house. They had to find a way to be together for the rest of their lives—had to find a solution to the multiple quandary affecting their happiness and peace of mind. They must be together, but without shame or pain to themselves or to their families and must sever the bonds which held them to their spouses, and to the duck.

As the sun went down, they held each other as if for the last time. Covering themselves with a down blanket, and alternately crying and laughing, they searched desperately for solutions.

His face reflected the pain and indecision affecting their relationship. How could he divorce? What would become of the duck?

"I can eliminate one problem rather easily," thought Katerina Wit, "A surreptitious roast duck dinner for one."

But how to remove the other barriers to their love?

And at that instant, she recalled how when she had first seen him walking by the lakeside, and how one week ago, they had said their final goodbyes on a cold, blustery day and thought they would never meet again.

And as they clung together in passion and love, it seemed "as though in a little while the solution would be found, and then a new and splendid life would begin; and it was clear to both of them that they had still a long, long road before them, and that the most complicated and difficult part of it was only just beginning."

A Fairy Tale

Once upon a time, on the seventh hill of the seven hills, there stood the castle of King Joseph the Wordsmith, grand ruler of the kingdom of Adjectivia. With him lived the richest jewel in his crown, Princess Desirable. She was beautiful, enticing, captivating, alluring and charming, with a loveliness, elegance, and pulchritude beyond all description, portrayal, definition, depiction, delineation, characterization, or even explanation. Her subjects viewed their princess with great reverence, adoration, idolization, glorification, exaltation, laudation and even veneration...

And so it was in the kingdom of Adjectivia.

Now, the arch-enemies of the Adjectivians, across the Great Divide, were the monosyllobs. Ruled by King Vacuua, a direct descendant of King John the Minimalist, who, centuries ago, had decreed that his subjects speak only in monosyllables...but unfortunately, over the years, the language degenerated into a raucous aggregation of grunts, groans, moans squeals, ohs and ahs, and one-sound expletives.

Even the handsome and virile Prince Veegor, despite his broad education and astute knowledge of other languages, uttered only the speech of his country...except, we are told, during his secret meetings with the stunning and sensuous Princess Desirable. And, certainly, during those times, even the harsh Monosyllabic must have achieved an uncommon dulcification.

Now the Adjectivians and the Monosyllobs were at war most of the time, but since the Great Divide was difficult to traverse, the adversaries engaged in endless battles of words, hurling insults through enormous loudspeakers across the chasm...the din was unbelievable... mono- and polysyllables clashed and clamored in a bizarre cacophony of noise and nonsense.

But the Adjectivians were a refined and well-bred people whose ears were weaned on the exquisite milk of fine language...and the abhorrent assault on their sensibilities was beyond acceptance, beyond tolerance...so they retreated with their loudspeakers several miles from the edge of the Divide...and a vast wasteland was created thereby...a void without sound or song, except for the distant malevolence impinging from the other side.

But suddenly, peace came to the warring countries: both kings, weary from incessant conflict, relinquished their thrones to their impassioned and irrepressible offspring...and the prince and princess were married, and combined their countries into one, and lived happily ever after. But eternal peace was achieved only after exhausting and interminable argument and debate. By adopting a new language: the original Minimalism, which was spoken before its decline into Neolithic grunts and groans...and everything thereafter was...fine, good, o.k., great, the best, grand...and nothing ever again...was exciting, magnificent, beautiful, phenomenal, unprecedented—or even extraordinary.

ROGER

It was cold, dark, and gloomy, that late autumn night long, long ago when two teenagers, Roger and I, decided to walk across Memorial Bridge, which spanned the Connecticut River from Springfield to West Springfield.

I can still remember the penetrating chill, the overpowering darkness with only a faint, reflective illumination from the city behind us, and the black, foreboding water swirling far below.

I can still feel the cool, chilling breeze which flowed silently across the bridge, every now and then gusting unexpectedly with a sudden, rushing, pushing wind.

Roger Tourigny was the kid in our childhood gang everyone else laughed at or laughed about because he stuttered and had a foolish, self-deprecating grin. He had poorly-formed teeth, and when his lips parted, you could see them framed behind two, long, protruding incisors, which gave him the appearance of a puppy dog doing tricks for his master. His hair was thin and sandy-brown, and it fell Hitler-like over his forehead and on his upper lip he had several long and lonely hairs, the ludicrous semblance of a mustache.

I liked Roger and felt sorry for him...resented the abuse he had to endure. And I knew why he stuttered: three years before, the neighborhood bully had set off a cherry bomb next to his left ear, causing not partial, but permanent loss of hearing, and imposing a long-term, psychological imprint.

I was Roger Tourigny's only friend at that time, and he responded deferentially, gratefully.

Roger and I did some crazy things in those early days, like most thirteen-year-olds, I guess. I was constantly daring him to do this or that. He always took up the challenge, determined to impress me with his courage and fearlessness...as if our friendship depended on it.

So on that long-ago "night of the bridge," as we walked along, saying little, oppressed by the darkening gloom and anesthetizing cold, I suddenly blurted out, perhaps to relieve the tension, "Hey, Rog, I betcha can't walk the rail!"

In a quick Pavlovian response, Roger answered, "I can too!" and climbed carefully onto the concrete bridge railing. He crouched on all fours and then brought himself to a standing position. He stood there, grinning down at me.

"Hey, Rog, I was only kidding...get down from there," I pleaded nervously, "Please!"

Like a metronome in slow motion, Roger's body swayed to the

left and to the right...then steadying itself, took a few halting steps towards the beckoning blackness ahead.

In a fog of fear and guilt, my lips formed a slow, tortured, "Hail Mary, full of grace...please God, don't let him fall, please!"

Roger continued, slowly but with more confidence now, oblivious to my pleas, the narrowness of his deadly footpath, and the black-shrouded death that waited patiently far below.

My legs were so leaden with dread and apprehension that I could hardly walk, scarcely keeping up with Roger as he moved wraithlike into the swallowing darkness.

Suddenly there was a tremendous gust of wind as the breeze abruptly changed course, intensified, and swept over the rail. Roger tottered for a few frightful seconds, and then, arms flailing in frenzied futility, fell forward, my scream following him down...

No, I have not forgotten Roger Tourigny, even after forty years.

Yes, I do still feel some guilt over what happened that night.

And, of course, I thank God that Roger was thrown off the rail onto the bridge instead of into the water.

Dorothy C. Allan

Dorothy Carter Allan, a long-time member of *The Rhode Island Short Story Club*, was the author of many plays written to be performed by high school students and published by *Baker's Plays*. She taught English at Hope High School in Providence, Rhode Island from the 1930s, well into the 1950s. Although considered quiet and even shy in everyday conversation, in the classroom she was a dynamic lecturer, who brought literature to life and made good writing an attractive goal. Several of her students through the years later became members of *The Rhode Island Short Story Club*.

Poem
New England Granite

New England Granite was written on the occasion of the retirement of a faculty colleague after 48 years of teaching. The poem appeared in the May 23, 1944 issue of the student newspaper paper, *The Hope Log*.

Dorothy C. Allan

NEW ENGLAND GRANITE
A Tribute to Miss Bessie S. Warner

New England rests on granite; from the great
North hills of Maine, down through each southward state
Into Connecticut, New England farms,
Villages, cities, all the varied charms
Of crowded mart or open country side
Stand firm on granite rocks that have defied
The storms of years long past and will defy
Those yet to come. Oh, to the passerby
New England shows a quiet, placid face,
A form whose life moves at a gentle pace
Day after ordered day: this village street,
Under an arch of elms; that field of wheat
Rippling beneath the cool salt breezes; there,
Perfume of lilacs in the clean May air,
And here, like solemn finger raised on high,
A slim white church spire pointing to the sky—
A land conservative in deed and dress;
Helpless, you'd say, in its rare gentleness.
But let the stranger never dare forget
New England rests on granite; all the fret
And stir of living, all the rains that beat
And winds that blow to flood that village street,
Level that wheatfield, beat those lilacs down—
All touch the surface only; skies may frown
Or smile. New England Granite stands unmoved,
Its strength unshaken, its endurance proved.
She is New England—she whom now we praise—

New England in her birth, in all her ways
Of daily living. The Elm-shaded street
Where honest business thrives and good friends meet
And talk a while–this is her heritage;
This is a part of her. From youth to age
She is New England–all its gentleness,
All its reserve of manner and of dress
Are hers.
But let no stranger dare forget
New England rests on granite; never yet
Has raging blizzard, howling hurricane,
The numbing frost of grief, the heat of pain,
Troubled the solid rock that underlies
Her life, shaken the granite that supplies
Her strength; granite of cheerful fortitude
To do each task and find the doing good;
Granite of faith that meets both rain and sun
Serenely as contrasting threads of one
Eternal pattern; granite of kindliness
That uses discipline and rule to stress
The greater freedom of the ordered mind.
I say let him take heed who hopes to find
New England easy prey to foes. This land
And she who calls it home will ever stand
Together in my thought as being one
At heart. Under the warm New England sun
The granite strength of mountains, and in her
The greater granite strength of character.

Justine K. Armington

Justine graduated from Rhode Island School of Design in 1939. Her passion was art. She taught art and had many shows over her lifetime. Poetry and short stories came later and she published her semi-autobiographical novel, *Trust the Heart* in 1989. We remember Justine with fond memories and valued her friendship to *The Rhode Island Short Story Club*.

POEMS
    Flowers Like Jewels
    Bells

PAINTINGS
    Teapot with Flowers and Fruit, *watercolor*
    Irises, *watercolor*
    Irving Avenue Rooftops, *oil*

Teapot with Flowers and Fruit, *watercolor*

Irises, *watercolor*

FLOWERS LIKE JEWELS

Flowers, my dears are like
jewels to me. Close your eyes,
take a few flowers, cup them in
your hands. One red for a ruby,
one white for a diamond and feathery
green leaves for emeralds. The blue
sky illuminating everything
—sparkling with turquoise.
The jewels, when put on a table
make a gorgeous still life. Looking
at the "still life" arrangement makes me
want to paint a colorful abstract painting.
So I gather my tubes of paint together
—squeeze the brilliant colors on my palette.
Now I want wide brushes, stubbed brushes,
thin brushes- am I ready? I think so.
The flowers now jewels, in my mind,
come even more alive as I put paint
to paper. Sparkle—shine—colors leap
out from the paper into my heart,
before my eyes. Flowers, my dears are
like jewels to me.

Bells

Bells, bells, bells
Bells to the front of me.
Bells to the back of me.
Bells coming from all sides,
hammering in my head.

Bells every day for five days
here in the hospital.
No sleeping allowed.
Now I hear and remember
all the bells through my life.

A big metal school bell
with a walnut handle
that my mother clanged
to call me home from play.
It was so shrill and loud
I could hear it a city block away
calling me home.

The scratchy, scratchy
bicycle bell
warning people that I would
be pursuing them.
I didn't want to bump into them.
How can anyone ever forget
that special sound?

Door bells from the front and back doors.
Each with their own distinctive tone,

Soprano and alto voices.
We could decipher the difference immediately.
So could the animals.
The canary mimicked them.
The cat slunk under the bed.
The dog ran to the correct one,
barking greetings and warnings
to one or the other.

The telephone with a mellow,
yet prodding demand.
Easy to hear and easy on the ears,
an alert to answer the phone

before the phone stopped
its determined ringing—hurry!

The full tone of the bell
in the church belfry.
Calling to worship!
Come—come—meditate and pray.
Thank God from Whom
all blessings flow.

Wedding bells of happiness and bliss.
ringing brightly to invite
people to join in
in a lovely celebration
of the couple being married.
Pealing gleefully, announcing
the vows of the couple's

new united life together.
Sleigh bells ringing,
tingle—tingle tingling.
Jingling as only they can.
Full of laughter and cheer.
Greeting another new year.

The somber tolling
of the bell in ponderous tones.
Surely a remembrance and tribute to
 a life that has left this world.
Don't sound those gloomy,
heavy tones for me.
Give me bright and heaven high
Accolades
and the introduction
to a life of adventure
and newness in another dimension.

Irving Avenue Rooftops, *oil*

CLARA I. RIVERA BANCHS

Clara was born in Puerto Rico, grew up in Rochester, New York and moved to Rhode Island in 1979. She has three children, four grandchildren and one on the way. She's the oldest of seven; has four brothers and two sisters. Both of her parents are living. She holds a Bachelor of Arts Degree from Rhode Island College; major in Spanish. Her favorite hobbies are clay sculpturing, collecting rosary beads, and visiting historical places. She has a great interest in museums, architecture, and particularly likes to travel. She has visited many countries such as Spain, Israel, Egypt, Greece, Italy, Colombia, Mexico, Portugal, France, Canada and hopes to visit more in the future. Clara is a great believer in miraculous healing and she prays often. She began writing in her teens and finds joy in it for it gives life to her thoughts. She looks forward to many more years of writing.

SHORT STORY
  Making Love to the Pharaoh

POEMS
  There is No Such Thing as Slavery
  A Grandmother's Love
  So Bring Me a Rose
  Dearest True and Gentle Love
  Essence

Making Love to the Pharaoh

The flight was not long, but it seemed like forever to Sól. The anxiety and suspense of finally fulfilling the fantasy she had since fifth grade had overtaken her. The books she read and stories she heard about far away lands always intrigued her. Those memories remained vivid in her heart. Traveling to a mysterious land of antiquity seemed unreachable for her days long ago. Sól had said that the word Egypt gave her goose bumps. She was hoping that a cruise down the Nile River and four days at Al Medina Al Qahira, meaning The City of Cairo, would be the adventure of a lifetime. This trip was a much needed remedy to sooth away loneliness of missing her loved ones back home in the U.S. She flew from Barcelona by herself not once thinking she would be alone in a faraway land. She had often said that Barcelona was the most charming and exhilarating metro city she had ever lived in.

The Hilly City of Gerona was one of the reasons she chose to go to Barcelona to study. Gerona was the birthplace of Sól's mother's grandfather. Gerona was an hour away from Barcelona. She went there only once and always lamented not going again. Sól's great grandfather was a slave owner, and as told by her grandmother, he was a very harsh man and not in favor of her grandparents marrying. Sól's grandmother was mulatto and not accepted in the family although her five children were.

During that one trip to Gerona, Sól stopped at the Dali Museum in Figueres. She enjoyed the flamboyant artist's work and was taken by the sketches of his jewelry designs. As she read the displays, she observed that there were no acknowledgments or names of the jewelers who had actually made the beautiful jewelry pieces he designed. Her favorite piece was a ruby red stoned pin shaped like a heart, that when opened, a mechanical object mimicked a human heart beat. The artist's pencil sketches were the ones that she stopped to look at and admire most. She said that "a pencil sketch is an artist's mastery in conception."

In Gerona, everyone walked towards the old plaza, but Sól stayed behind. Someone later asked her why and she said, "I loved the feel of that place, it bewitched me, it felt as though I had been there before." She was amazed at the historical events that had taken place there during the Middle Ages. One of the places they visited was The Call which is the legendary medieval Jewish quarter in Gerona; a city buried and hidden under the city with the intent to hide its past and historical facts. Gerona was the birthplace of the 13th century Sage and Rabbi Moshe Ben Nahman, also known as Ramban, whom she found to be very interesting. He was a mystic, Kabalist, philosopher, physician and one of the most famous Jews of the Middle Ages.

Ramban believed that wisdom of the truth was in learning the mysticism of the Bible. Sól was an avid Bible reader. A friend, whom she often traveled with and trusted, once told Sól that she should keep a journal as she does, but she never listened. Sól always seemed well prepared and knew what she wanted to see when they traveled together. She saved receipts, tickets, foreign currency, coins, maps, and brochures. She always made sure that she visited churches, temples, mosques, historical sites, and bought rosary beads on her journeys. She had a great sense of humor and could keep a short term conversationalist in a trance for hours, which some would often say seemed to last only minutes. She was a dedicated mother and friend who was never judging and was always willing to help. The colorful stories she told never ceased to amaze anyone. One of her friends once said that it was fun traveling with her because Sól was never too tired to attempt one more adventure. She loved staying up late especially on the last day of a vacation because she knew she would sleep on her way home.

As soon as they were over the Egyptian airway, the captain announced that right below them was the Sahara Desert just waiting to be admired. The Sahara Desert, keeper of much mystery and awe inspiring secrets was staring back at her. The captain also announced that the town of Aswan, the landing destination, appeared below the flaming sun. It was a small airport and the group seemed to be the only attraction there. The airport personnel were very helpful in directing everyone to have their documents processed. The airport security soldiers were handsomely tanned and dressed in military attire carrying riffles and machine guns. Everyone seemed delighted to have arrived safely. Finally at her destination, the thrill seemed surreal to her. She met some really great people on the bus en route to the cruise boat. As a welcomed gesture, they were all greeted at the cruise boat and invited to go to a nearby café that night. She settled in her room, freshened up and went to dinner. The group she met on the bus all went out into the gentled breezed evening in Aswan, and rode on a horse buggy called a Caléche. On the way to the café they stopped to see the beautifully lit mosque that stood out above all other structures in the skyline of the small town. They were escorted to see the interior of the mosque by two keepers. The next stop was the towns' suq, an Arabic name for bazaar, where they all got off. She was immediately attracted to the spice stand which seemed to have had an absolute embalming effect upon her. She had never seen so many exotic spices before. The store keeper kept bringing her different spices to smell, and she would close her eyes and breathe in the deliciously invigorating aromas.

Natives walked by dressed in exotic attire and stared, some smiled and others said things in Arabic. Habibi was the most common word they would say to her. Writing pens were a big commodity in Aswan as she soon found out. Natives would ask for a pen everywhere she went and she soon ran out. They finally arrived at the café where they all ordered mint tea and the customary hookah pipe filled with aromatic tobacco. Some smoked rose and some smoked a sweet fruit mix. This was the first time she smoked aromatic tobacco in a hookah pipe. After returning to Barcelona she continued to smoke the hookah at an Arabian Moroccan restaurant.

When she returned home to the U.S., she continued to smoke at a Lebanese restaurant and hookah bar off Thayer Street in Providence. Her favorite preferred tobacco flavor was apple.

She had difficulty falling asleep on her first night on the boat. The pink room was very comfortable and the white bed covers were soft and warm. She brought reading material for times like these. She bookmarked page fifty three where it read, "A man who cannot love is useless, much like an angel that refuses to sing in heaven, and if

God so wishes could cause its wings to fall off." Will God keep His promise? Instead, she chose to read the Bible that night, followed by her usual ritual of nightly prayers. She walked up to the big window in her room and pulled the curtains wide open to look out. All she could see was a huge expanse of total darkness which seemed like a black hole. A knot of fear and suspense entered her and she immediately yanked the curtains shut. Her heartbeat racing, she stood there holding her chest motionless in the middle of the room, as she caught her breath. Her eyes were startled as she stared into space. It was hard to imagine living by the river bank on such dark nights when the moon had totally hidden itself from site. When told the story of huge monstrous man eating crocodiles and all types of vicious wild beasts, one could believe that parades of evil spirits were also lurking around the Nile River, ready to devour and destroy anything in its path. It only seemed reasonable that the Pharaohs built colossal temples to honor the gods for protection.

Her only wish after that frightful moment, which drained her of all energy, was to relax and watch TV. After fussing with the blurry channels, she turned it off and lit up a cigarette. Only the sound of her breath, as she smoked, could be heard. With her fear subsiding, she trusted that everything was finally resting in the hands of the Nile.

A slight scent of diesel fumes from the boat made its way into her room during the night, giving her a headache and making her nauseous by morning. Several of her friends walked with her to the nearest drug store. The pharmacist prescribed pills for the ailment which was soon relieved. Her friends said that the water used to wash the fruits and vegetables is usually what makes people ill. They walked down the busy street as natives stopped to stare, as usual. The sun was blazing hot and she kept blotting the sweat off her forehead and drinking bottled water. They stopped by the pier to watch people get on the felucca to ride down the river. That night they contracted with a taxi service to take them to Abu Simbel the next day. She looked for Pharaohs under the stars on the way to Abu Simbel.

The road trip was a long six hours of unexpected grueling bumpy riding through the desert in the wee hours of the morning. She fell asleep in the back of the old passenger jeep. She was startled and awakened by a loud noise as the old jeep flew over a big bump on the road. As she opened her eyes she was breathtakingly spellbound by the beauty bestowed upon her sight. Her head faced the dark sky in pure amazement. She had no words to describe the sensation she felt gazing at so many bright shining stars all together in one place.

The stars all appeared much closer to earth, all brightly shining amidst a lone and abandoned desert. No wonder the Pharaohs were so in awe of the heavens, the beauty of God's creation, having no motive or explanation for it just is. She mused until becoming sleepy again, rolling into fetal position and covering herself with an old beige wool rug which was on the floor. It was all she could find to keep her body warm from the cold desert air which penetrated intensely into all the open crevices of the old jeep. There was a couple in the jeep that huddled together to stay warm. The other woman shivered as she dug her arms and feet into the clothing she was wearing. Both the driver and his friend listened to Arabic music seemingly not bothered by the cold. The Pharaohs marched along side of the road one by one through the desert, some staying behind to guard the Nile with their eyes of blue. Finally, they arrived at Abu Simbel. Much to her delight, the white tee shirt, jeans and sandals she wore was perfect attire for the morning sun.

In the background, native musicians played their exotic instruments sounding captivatingly alluring. Many people came to admire the colossal statues of the Great Temple of King Ramses II. Sól found King Ramses II to be the most interesting of the Pharaohs that she had read about. His name meaning born of the Sun-god Ra and he is also known as Ramses The Great. He was ruler of Egypt for 66 years and thought to be the suspected Pharaoh in the Exodus Bible story. There are many other interesting theories about the Exodus Bible story still being investigated by scholars. Abu Simbel was built over 3000 years ago. One of the men traveling in the old jeep was 6 feet 7 inches tall. A photo of him near the foot of one of the colossal statues revealed the mammoth heights of these figures.

The Pharaoh's belief in an Almighty Creator evident as the rays of the sun still continues to penetrate the rocks of the Holy of Holies in the temple. He dedicated the smaller temple at Abu Simbel to Hathor, the goddess of love and happiness, and to his wife Nefertari. It was his romantic gesture of love and honor. The captivating art, the dedication, and the meaningful reasons for creating these temples is proof of the highly sophisticated gift of intelligence from God to natural man. The next site she visited was the Temple of Kom Ombo, dedicated to the god Haroeris or Horus The Elder, the good doctor.

The temple is also dedicated to Sobek, the crocodile god of fertility and rebirth and creator of the Nile. Crocodiles were feared and respected in ancient Egypt. Sculpted on the walls of the temple were ancient surgical tools, bone-saws and dental tools. The cult Temple of Edfu is also dedicated to the falcon headed god Horus meaning "he who is above." The myth of Horus was that the sun and moon were regarded as his great eyes, which was a symbol of spiritual ability. The right eye was the symbol of the sun Ra and believed to be "the father of the gods." The right eye controlled by the left brain represented the male oriented. All factual information, anything that deals with words, letters, numbers, sentences or complete thoughts are represented in the left brain. The left eye of Horus was the symbol of the moon and considered a very powerful and protective amulet. The left eye controlled by the right brain represented the female oriented; intuition and feelings. Sól was fascinated by the myth of Horus. The ancient Egyptians believed that all the senses in the human body were controlled by the eyes.

The day before leaving to Luxor, the group went to a local suq to shop for native outfits to wear to a masquerade party being held on the cruise boat that night. Sól stopped to look in a shop and she and the store keeper began talking about many things. One of her friends called out to her to hurry up for the group was heading back to the boat scheduled to leave port soon. The store keeper and Sól said goodbye hurriedly as she ran off. She had not realized she was carrying an outfit draped over her arm that she had not paid for but it was too late to go back. The masquerade party that night was fabulous. They played many games, won prizes, and there was lots of great Arabic music playing for dancing. As she was leaving the boat, she stood and contemplated the Nile River as the sun kissed its fresh and lush beauty in the early morning hour. She became teary eyed admiring the true silence and peace of the river as she looked through the camera lens taking her favorite and most captivating picture of its essence at that very moment.

They arrived at the temple at Luxor which was constructed for worshipping the god Amon Ra, called the king of the gods. Two obelisks preceded the temple, one of them is still there and the other one stands erect in Concorde Square in Paris. Sól had previously visited there with a friend. The obelisk was a gift from Egypt to France. As they continued their tour in Luxor they visited Karnak Temple which is a massively scaled complex that covers a hundred acres of land. Its ancient name was Ipet-isut which means the most sacred of places. About thirty Pharaohs contributed toward the construction of the complex. Its entrance, The Avenue of the Rams, was built to protect the temple. There are twenty rams on each side of the avenue that seem to greet everyone that enters the temple.

Beneath each rams' head is a small statue of King Ramses II. Next on the list was the Valley of the Kings and Queen. She was disappointed for not being able to see the tomb of King Tut Ankh Amon in the Valley of the Kings because it was temporarily closed due to archeological work. King Tut's gold mask and fabulous exhibition of his treasures are housed in the Cairo Museum; which she later saw. The tombs she saw in the Valley of the Kings and Queen were extensively decorated with detailed art work and painted in undying colors still vivid after 3000 years. Queen Hatshepsut's was the only woman to ever rule Egypt in the Pharaonic era. The temple built in her honor had been moved to its present location. There were many excavations and research projects going on in the vast areas of the valley. She said that the sun felt as though it had eyes and was watching as it saturated everything with a steady overpowering beam of energy as the sand harmoniously rested under its siege.

Sól arrived in Cairo at 9 p.m. The airport was quiet and barren. The group was greeted by courteous tour guides and a presentation given about things to do or not do in Cairo. She sat by the window of the bus looking at all the city glitter on the way to the hotel. She recognized many of the well known big names and chains from corporate America written on many high rises. A countless number of people walk the well lit streets in the lively metro city. The massive fast moving traffic made it almost impossible for people to cross the wide roads. There are not many pedestrian crossings or traffic lights in Cairo. The five star hotel in Giza where she stayed was very elegant with a king size bed to die for. The view from her room was limited. All she could see from her balcony were the swimming pool patio, the bar and other people's balconies. Voices could easily be heard coming from all directions by an echo. She met up with friends for breakfast the next morning to begin another fast paced day of sight-seeing. The itinerary was to see the Pyramids at Giza, the Sphinx, and visit a papyrus museum. On the same day they visited a sheik that specialized in magic and essential body oils. The sheik told Sól she had a virgin spirit that attracted younger men to her. She blushed wondering how he knew that younger men seemed to always flock to her. She thought that at her age she needed to meet a mature man and settle down. The group entered the Pyramid at Giza and half way down the stairway to the tombs the lights went out. Total chaos broke lose as people became panic stricken yelling and screaming. Sól became a bit nervous and immediately put her hands in her black raincoat pocket, pulling out her cigarette lighter which she lit.

Standing in front of her was the old woman from Argentina, of room 318, hanging on to dear life on the handrails. As soon as she saw Sól she ran to her and told her that she was scared and wanted to get out of there. Sól told her to stay close to her. Minutes later, the lights came on and she convincingly took the old woman down to the tombs. Sól later said that the old woman thanked her and told her that the tombs were sites one should never miss. The camel ride was gentle and beautiful and Sól was amused. Sól laughingly said that The Sphinx looks like a mammoth sized stuffed animal. Their first night in Cairo, she and friends relaxed at a nearby café enjoying their favorite pastime of mint tea and hookah smoking.

The next couple of days they hit the streets of Cairo in full force. There wasn't a place hidden they didn't walk to, run to, or taxied to. They visited the Christian Church of Saint George which dates back to about the 7th century AD. He is Sól's patron saint and is the most popular warrior saint in the Middle East. It is not Saint Peter but Saint George that is believed to have miraculous powers to cure the demon-possessed and paralytics. They visited the Ben Ezra Jewish Synagogue which dates from the 12th century AD. Sage Rabbi Ramban of Gerona worshipped there while living in Cairo.

They shopped at the Khan el-Khalili market considered to be the most historic market in the world which was founded in the 1300's. Back at that time it was considered the biggest market for trading products from around the world. This market may have been the reason Columbus sailed to the New World. Sól and her friends toured the whole City of Cairo in a taxicab, ate Arabic food on a boat on the Nile River, and visited countless mosques around the city. They visited The Citadel complex, a military fortress which houses ancient mosques and museums. A beautiful view of Cairo can be seen from the terrace. That day they waited outside The Citadel for three hours to see a spectacular show by a Sufi Muslim dervish dance group. The dancers attracted such huge crowds that people were running inside as soon as the gates opened to find seating. The musicians played drums, tambourines and other instruments sounding rhythmically exotic as the dancers performed. The audience watched silently as the dancers magically swirled for long periods of time without falling or passing out.

They planned to visit the Cairo Museum the day before leaving but most decided not to. Sól packed and safeguarded her flight ticket and passport in her luggage, then went to lunch with a friend and ate native Egyptian food one last time. She went to the Cairo Museum even though she was exhausted from having stayed up late the night before. The museum was extremely crowded with many school groups and families. The exhibits and antiquities were all superbly magnificent. A person would need endless weeks inside the museum to appreciate everything under its roof.

At 7:00 p.m. the old woman from room 318 called Sól to remind her about dinner at 8:00 p.m. She said that they would wait for her in the hotel lobby. Sól told her she was going to pass up dinner for she needed to rest before going out with them again that night.

Before laying down for a nap, she decided to shower and get dressed so she would be ready when her friends returned. Sometime later, Sól heard a little girl's voice screaming but she was asleep and in a dream like state. The screaming continued persistently and finally it awakened her. Sól immediately got up to look out her balcony and saw people running wild in all directions. The little girl was screaming, "help the hotel is on fire, help the hotel is on fire!" Sól ran to the door to look down the corridor and saw that it was filled with smoke. She was grateful that she could still see the floor so that she could get out. At the same time, a man was running up the corridor with a fire extinguisher in his hands. She yelled to him "where is the fire?" He just looked at her and did not respond as he continued running down the hall. She closed the door immediately and she put on her black raincoat. She picked up her purse, a white prayer scarf that her friend had given her that day as a gift and wrapped it around her face and head. She attempted to get her ticket and passport but she was so nervous she couldn't get the luggage unlocked. She ran out closing the door behind her, while trying to avoid smoke inhalation. She paused briefly at room 318 and knocked very hard several times to be certain no one was still there. She continued to run down the stairwell to the hotel lobby which was saturated in smoke.

Everything was pure pandemonium. She was unable to detect any sign of where the flames were coming from. People were being carried out on stretchers. Many were coughing, bleeding, running, tripping, screaming and crying as they rushed out of the hotel. She ran out as fast as she could and stood across the street looking. The left side of the hotel burned like a towering inferno when suddenly all the lights went out in the building. Thick white smoke was rising to the sky while the fire trucks sounded their sirens loudly. The street was mobbed with onlookers and people running everywhere. In order to prevent the onlookers from stopping, policemen used big thick wooden sticks to hit people, trucks, buses and cars that passed by. She thought her friends were at dinner and later learned that they were across the street the whole time. The group was grieving, wondering if Sól was still asleep inside. Sól felt truly blessed as she cried on her last night in Cairo.

She noticed a big crowd of people and began walking toward them to see what was going on. She ran into a friend and they hugged each other. She told Sól they were all worried sick about her and that the man on the ground seemed like he was dying. She had managed to sneak by the police to look. They both snuck their way through the crowd that surrounded the man. He had a frozen gaze. It was him, Sól recognized the man. She had seen him earlier running down the corridor with a fire extinguisher in his hands. They both immediately tried to make some room for him. Very saddened, Sól looked at him and touched his soot covered face and forehead.

They turned him over onto his side. Her friend supported his head and neck as Sól began hitting him hard on his back trying to revive him. Every so often she hit him on the chest and also would move his arm that felt lifeless. He was a strong man becoming weak in their care. His lungs probably collapsed from inhaling so much smoke. Sól's friend kept on screaming and begging for someone to get an ambulance. At one point, Sól felt like giving up on him but she felt his sweat going down on his neck. She said out loud, "come on breathe! Oh please God revive this man!" When suddenly his eyes fixed in hers and his neck and back stiffened as he came up and purged a great mass of yellow thick phlegm from his mouth and began coughing. The ambulance never came because they were too busy helping the hotel guests first. Someone managed to stop a taxi and four men picked the man up and put him inside the taxi.

He sat there coughing, his face still covered in soot. Sól cried as they took him away. He was driven away from all the chaos to the nearest hospital breathing on his own. She hoped that the unknown man she had been called upon to love on that clear November Cairo sky was going to be blessed with countless rejoicings. She and her friend looked at each other and hugged for a while both crying. They walked away together to join the others who were waiting. Making love to the Pharaoh at 9:00 p.m. Cairo time.

- - - - - - - - - - - -

Upon returning home, Sól was asked, "Do you have any regrets after visiting Egypt Sól?"

"Yes."

"And that is?"

"I wish I had not fallen asleep in the Cairo Museum."

"What?"

Sól, who was also laughing responded, "Well, I was standing in front of a glass enclosed display reading about the exhibition inside it. Suddenly the words began to hypnotize me and I began to doze off. I felt my head tilting forward when suddenly I realized I was about to land on the glass enclosure. I immediately awakened and knew that I had to get some rest. So I left. I did not see the mummies. You cannot visit Cairo and not see the mummies at the Cairo Museum because it is unforgivable!"

"How does it feel to have finally seeing Egypt Sól?"

"Exhilarating. I can not find words to describe the magnificence of the temples built by Pharaohs to honor and respect a superior Creator or Power. Believing in an unseen Creator and doing so only by faith is remarkable. They built Pyramids that kiss the sky in awe of its beauty. They have Funerary Tombs to honor the dead in the hopes of eternal rest and glory. Since my return home, I remind myself each day to recall all that has been gently carved deep within my heart and soul. There is nothing more important and sacred than to love."

Clara I. Rivera Banchs

THERE IS NO SUCH THING AS SLAVERY

There is no such thing as slavery.
For no one can chain my heart
nor tie my soul against my will.
No one can jail my thoughts and my phrases
nor enter in to arrest my senses.

There is no such thing as slavery.
For no one can fight against my spiritual defenses.
No one can trespass my dreams and intentions
nor walk through my God given nature.

There is no such thing as slavery.
For no one can take away my liberty
to gaze at the moon and the stars,
the trees, and the birds, the green blades of grass,
the sun loving flowers of pinks, reds, yellows, purples and blues.

There is no such thing as slavery.
For no one can take the smell of the rain as it falls on my face,
the rush of the sea as it melts with the sand,
the whistling of the wind as it kisses my cheeks and fondles my hair.
For no one can take away the innocence of a child
as they smile and they play.

December 18, 2001

A Grandmother's Love

As I look into the tiny happy faces
of my beloved grandchildren,
I can not imagine living my life
not loving the shine that is of you
and lives in them forever brightly.

And as their tiny heads
are nestled sweetly in my arms,
so ever gentle near my heart,
I know that you are also here.
Oh so near, my sweet, my dear,
to remind me of whom you are.

Smiles from their innocent tender lips
fill a room with a purity I can't resist.
Bless them with your love my Lord
and all my beloved tiny happy faces keep.

Deep down inside my heart you'll find,
a treasure filled with lots of love.
Each day it fills up more and more
with thoughts of you my sweet
that I keep safe to eternally adore.

May 1, 2007

So Bring Me a Rose

So bring me a rose
to whom I can tell my sacred woes.
Innocent unrehearsed words.
The feelings of a hidden story.
Your blind unforgiving spirit.
How soon must you go?

So bring me a rose
for all the time that has expired
as I was growing with desire.
Shock and awe quite unexpected.
May I forgive you, or shall I
let your love inter me?

So bring me a rose
of stems bent and dried.
Petals gently on the mantle falling
when there is no one there to notice
the one who has been forgotten.
Love divine once there waiting.

So bring me a rose
scented with the smell of my repose.
Blooming in old forgotten gardens
of dewy eyes and stunted promises.
Don't pity my broken soul
as it rests when is time to let go.

May 1, 2007

DEAREST TRUE AND GENTLE LOVE

When I look into your face
my eyes evaporate into my soul
with the pleasure of knowing you.

Dearest true and gentle love...
...once again be whole.

As you are through me, I am through you.
Touch so weak and distant,
    yet so pure and delightful.
Wandering eyes dimmed by life.
Poor hearts aching, silently waiting
for the embryo of love to grow within.

Dearest true and gentle love...
...once again be whole.

Sweet names born from light
of perfect peace and love divine,
singing and declaring unity and beauty.

Dearest true and gentle love...
...in harmony we are dancing.

October, 2006

ESSENCE

I was never waiting for you to love me,
that was never my intention.
My only desire was that you would promise
that your words would not deceive me.
Guard all my poems as proof of my love.
If you can think of me again, do not believe in me,
believe in your own true heart instead
for I have stopped writing to the angels.
"Clement daughter."

You forgot to tell me,
and died without saying a word.
To whom do I give thanks?
Crazy they all will think.
The tiny yellow house underneath one tree?
When it rains?
If the Holy Land had wings
I would let it fly to another place
where it could rest in peace.
I love you so much that
I am going to give you my only treasure.
Oh my dearest children to you I give my love.
Tears discover happiness and
the last contemplation is saying goodbye.
Some will say that they don't care.
Can it be true that you are thinking of me today?
If you want please tell me so.
With your overworked fingers please play me ever so slow.
From heaven they look at me, the saints,
for sometimes I fall asleep calling their names.
"Don't cry."

I learned to look beyond your delight.
Mother's love has no comparison.
Up to the stars oh how intense the universe.
How many colors can heaven be?
It is not my fault that I do not know.
Why do you blame me?
My effort is incomplete.
Plenty it will be! Everything is timing.
Confused but not defeated.
Green book longing for words.
Cleanse my conscious,
I am becoming cold my Lord.
I soothed myself one day realizing the truth.
You want so much from me that it aches my heart.
I know that you follow me for here you are.
Do not leave till I am finished.
You went away without completing your last sentence.
All was written but God had a different plan.
I believe it is my turn tiny head of white.
Children the fruit of my heart, flower of my love.
The farther I am from you the more I love you so.
I leave you my whole being.
"Verses only for you."

The day you were born, continued my mirror.
Your father did not know how to love you,
but I loved you with all my soul.
Simple pure Mary my dearest Virgin.
From my skin gushes blood now I know love.
I will go for I want to think of you.
Bless my fingers for it is the only inviolable thing I have.
Your face brings me joy, the delicate sighs of my soul.
Compose yourself for I will sustain you.
A love between two continents is my pretty ashen maid.

Clara I. Rivera Banchs

I am happy to see you labor
as you always reveal your struggle.
Go to the other side of the earth and you will see
a beautiful mountain that waits for thee.
From its peak you will look and see
how different the stones all are; some big some small.
Do not exhaust yourself maidservant, do not weaken your strength.
Save your stamina for tomorrow when you will be most awake.
Breathe for I sustain you with love between two continents,
"As you arise!"

May, 2003

LIESELOTTE BOWEN

German-born, Lieselotte Bowen first visited *The Rhode Island Short Story Club*, intending only to accompany a friend who was a member. Persuaded to join in the writing exercise, she surprised herself and pleased us with what she wrote. She joined the Club, continuing to write short, sometimes whimsical descriptions. Now living on Cape Cod, she visits occasionally and we love her friendly presence. Following is a poem she has given us permission to include.

POEM
Not Yet

NOT YET

All right, here we are
  Outside now,
    on the bench.
Oh this moment!

Flowers around me.
Blue sky above.
Breathe
  deep,
    relax—

A beautiful world!

Ok now the best,
the promising book.
Here we are—
  no,
    not yet,
Eye glasses!

How could I forget them
again
  and again
    and again!

Into the house—
Look for the glasses—
  Where?
    Down cellar?

Have not been there!
Pocket of robe—
No—
Goodness,
     what did I do
          last night?

Ringing telephone!

I thought not to be home...

"Yes-yes this is she.

Hold it.
     I must write
          that down."
Without glasses?

"All right, all right.
I will be there.
Bye."

Now, what time is it?

Sun has gone—
     it is cloudy.
          What?

Time for lunch
     already?

It cannot be!

CAROLYN BRAY

Carolyn Bray has been a writer since winning a short story award at nine from her school in England. She has degrees in writing and film from Brown University and Boston University. An award-winning poet, her professional roles have included: instructor of writing, film and English as a Second Language; media consultant for causes and campaigns; director of human rights and peace organizations; editor of books and newspapers; and recent journalist/photographer. Carolyn has authored scripts, books and numerous stories she occasionally tries to get agented, sold or produced. International affairs—both political and romantic—are recurrent themes in her work, as are her devotion to animals and colorful past as a San Francisco hippie activist.

SHORT STORIES
> Rigal
> Eleuthera
> At the Bar, Providence

ESSAY
> Chapel Near the Sea

POEMS
> Celtic History
> Paula's Moving Sale
> Under Mimosa
> To Rhoda 1980

Rigal

Dedicated to Ricky Lee, who turned out to be right when he said Saro had always loved him.

The road was lit up by the sun when he appeared at the door, the sky almost bleached behind him. Maybe it was a trick of the light. The streets ran gold and her love tumbled out into memory that would haunt more than 25 years.

Or that's how I keep trying to begin my novel.

I am called Rigal for madrigal, so the story goes. I think my mother just liked the sound and the play on words (pronouncing it "Regal"), being a woman descended from Irish aristocracy who could be heard at odd moments singing throughout the house. My childhood was filled with Astrud Gilberto, folk songs, and lessons from a displaced European on my right to a princess's place in life. Or my mother would simply put down the hated vacuum cleaner, dance the samba and laugh. Is it any wonder, than, that I dreamed of very grand husbands-to-be, beautiful places in Europe, and prepared for the most romantic of fates. Unlikely I might first find it in a hot town in the Midwest, most American of Americas.

But there he was, coming into the courtroom with the sun making his hair yellow, carrying himself like a prince in disguise if ever there was one. He honed his absurdly incandescent smile in on me like a bee to angular, golden honey. I was a dreaming, passionate girl of 18 just waiting for the trap to be set—primed to seek love but not to recognize it.

I had been passing through town on my way to the Coast, detouring for the trial of the famous GI civil rights activists. I was even contemplating law at college, until I saw their trial. David was the star, the most beleaguered and eloquent. After that first stunning stare in court, I nearly lost the gist of the proceedings—but not enough to overlook that David and two well-meaning cohorts were facing years in prison for being leaders of a peaceful protest march held on an Army base. The looks he kept tossing off to me drove me out to a dusty bathroom hallway, to think. Well, I was actually pirouetting when he got the guard to take him back to the bathroom too: I do that when overcome with emotion sometimes. He smiled, I swear lovingly, at the sight of me twirling in my slippy white dress, grasped my hand, whispered, "You are beautiful"—and my fate was indefinitely sealed by a 24-year-old political prisoner.

But the Army had their own plans for David's future: he was convicted of mutiny and given 6 years in prison. There followed nine horrible months of waitressing in a saloon-style restaurant in town, sleeping in a like-minded supporter's home, and visiting David in military prison—with almost daily letters going and coming on the five days of each week we couldn't meet.

There were continual episodes of harassment from a few military police and 'intelligence' investigators who'd show up at the house or work. I dragged the women attached to the other two convicted 'mutineer' soldiers to press conferences with me, making as much noise as possible about the men as part of exhaustive attempts to free them, and keep them from being tortured by cruel jailers. Once David lay near death for days, from an overdose of drugs the Army had administered to him. If I close my eyes I can still see him on that hospital bed, with me holding his hand and murmuring to him for long hours.

Then suddenly they were freed by the Secretary of the Army. David said my support and talks to the press had saved his life. We sold our respective cars, bought a beat up VW bus and began caravanning across the U.S. towards San Francisco, followed for the first week by another freed activist and his wife.

When we passed through a town David said looked exactly like the California one he'd grown up in, he suddenly wanted to talk about his relatives. He told me his late father's side of the family had money, but had not been heard from during his ordeal; the other side, his mother's, were embarrassed by his notoriety and his politics, so had also remained almost completely silent. My parents admired our activism, and just resigned themselves to a love affair they couldn't stop, trusting my allegedly level head.

I would waitress here and there as we slowly trekked West. David would make and sell art, and also sing guitar on the street well enough to get paid by passersby. I wrote some poems, and helped collect items for his collages, which brought in sums that surprised us both.

One day I came back from a 12-hour shift at work to find flowers all over our mattress and a romantic mural of my face and long hair across one inside wall of the van. David appeared, got down on one knee with uncharacteristic nervousness and raised riveting eyes to mine. "When I found you, a soul found its mate. Please, will you have my baby?" he asked softly. Piercing sweet joy like that is so rare, even then it felt like I was dreaming my happy ending.

When David had nightmares about his gruesome moments in military jail, I would rock him and promise I was still there and would never go. Often consolation would turn into love-making, and he would murmur with overwhelming intensity: "You saved me, every day you save me just by loving me."

It was love all right: core-deep, tight-around-your-heart love. We wept for two days when I miscarried. I could see nothing in the world but David—his magic, tender, demanding self took up that much space.

I did begin to notice too much hanging around by other charmed women. But I knew David's commitment was forever, his love inseparable form the essence of idealistic David himself, so I didn't worry much about it. His hours became erratic in a town just out-side Carmel where the VW broke down, but I thought he was just off smoking dope with a fellow musician.

I was knocked around the planet when he disappeared. One brief call to my latest restaurant to say he was off, and—poof! I tried to find him, loitering forlornly there and in San Francisco for several months before finally giving up and coming back East. We were supposed to get married. But aren't we all.

Oh, I went on and had a life, college and all. But no marriage, no family. Still, I was busy doing many things, and had myself all sorts of interesting times, some with men, most without. I worked as a reporter, a photographer, a restaurant manager—even a human rights activist for a bit. Somehow I kept attracting men who smelled like love, but usually turned out to be more like skunks masquerading behind good cologne. One image kept catching me off guard, about twice a year, when I was alone. It was of the moment David came through the swinging door of my restaurant in that Midwest town, having unexpectedly been freed a day early. The sky seemed bright as a searchlight behind him, his dancing green eyes glowed with absolute joy...

Ten years ago I got curious and launched a search for David—made easy by the fact he left his Social Security card with me. When I found him across the country via telephone, he was humbly grateful. He also waxed romantic, even wistful. But that couldn't erase the trail of women and children he seemed to have accumulated, including the recently-married mother of his latest kid, who was undoubtedly trying to listen to our conversation. I gathered he was still making and selling art, and also taking medication for epilepsy fits apparently brought on by one too many beatings in that long-ago military jail.

When I learned he'd fathered a son not long after leaving me to run off to Hawaii, that sore place for the child we didn't have opened, and I choked up for a minute. I could hear that he was weeping too. As David and I stumbled through slightly-conflicting memories, he appealed to me for patience and took my breath away with a Thornton Wilder quote: "Even when memory is gone, the love will have been enough and will return to the person who made it." We had some back and forth by mail and phone, exchanging photos too, which caused sighs from him and heart-lurching in me. I criticized and forgave—though he never could explain why he left me, only that he was a mess then and that he was sorry.

David even claimed he called my father's house when his travels brought him near it, just two years after his disappearance, but he got no answer, there were no answering machines then, so he ran on. He wanted me to go to Seattle to meet him, and I wanted him to come here to see me, noting that I'd gone far enough for David in my life already. I was afraid his family would get disrupted if I showed up at his home—you can feel chemistry that powerful is still there, even on the phone. No one budged; a few years back silence fell.

They told me last month that David died of lung cancer, after a prolonged battle about which he'd said not a word. I kept seeing his cigarette-stained fingers holding mine in that prison.

I won't go on about the two weeks of devastated sobs I just got through, bitterly resenting that David had tossed me around the globe again with a surprise of the most final kind. But the bigger shock was the bequest I was notified of just the other day. Right before he fell ill, David inherited a number of things from his wealthy uncle, including a small cottage on a piece of land in Europe. This he was leaving to me: "To make up for the home I never gave the woman who saved my life."

How my mother would dance, knowing her Rigal finally became European landed gentry. I'm flying out tonight to claim my inheritance. I've promised myself to leave the crying behind with the country. When I remember David now, coming through that door as if sent by the light behind him, I can smile...and pirouette too. After all, some people say getting the castle without the prince can be its own sort of happy ending.

ELEUTHERA

Ellie needed this day off, this Saturday. If one more tourist winked and asked her where the nightlife was in Blackpool she might do a mischief. Normally she enjoyed the tours coming into the little office off the pier. But lately, what with things at home, her patience was wearing thin and the colors seemed to have gone out of life.

More and more now she realized that taking care of her dad had helped keep her from making her own family, with husband and maybe a kid or two. Ever since Mum had died she'd been checking up on Dad, and now his hip had broken and left him with an odd walk, she had to go more often than ever. Oh he was nice enough about it usually, giving her bits of money to buy herself something she needed by way of a thank you. But she felt like a 60-year-old lady sitting there watching telly with him many nights, instead of getting out with friends. She would look at his downcast face, think of how her mother had told her she was named Eleuthera for the place in the Bahamas where her parents honeymooned, and wonder what had happened to that fun-loving fellow.

Today, instead of stopping in on him, she had a plan just for herself. She had called to tell him she wouldn't be over, and he'd taken it fine, only asking her to come on the Sunday at 2 p.m. when the gardener would do the flowers, as he wanted her opinion.

She tied up her long pale hair in a black band, and checked the make-up she'd applied to her light blue eyes. Next she put on her new black trainers, black gym pants and top, and petted her dog, Roan. This time Roan wasn't coming on her walk.

I'm going to chat up that man I see every Saturday, she told herself silently. I'm going to ask him for tea or maybe drinks at the pub later if it goes really brilliantly.

Ellie followed her usual power-walking trail, pumping her arms and enjoying the breeze off the water. Just as she approached the beach, at her usual Saturday time, she saw him. He had an easel up again, and seemed to be finishing the seascape he was sketching. As she stopped to watch, he turned his head and smiled at her, as if coming back to consciousness. He pushed his brown hair out of his friendly face with its crooked, endearing smile as she slowly walked up to him.

"Hi, I'm Ellie." He extended his hand to grasp hers, his smile growing bigger.

"Pleasure to meet you. I'm Eric. I've seen you here before...last Saturday was it, with a big red dog?"

He remembered—this was a good sign. "That was me, and Roan." His smile was so sweet, she was almost sure he fancied her a bit. She was just summoning up the nerve to ask him for tea, when a car pulled up behind her and he waved to someone in it.

"That's my ride," he said, as he hurriedly gathered up his sketching tools. "I'm off for a match—football—but it was nice to meet you. Maybe we'll meet here again?"

"Maybe, yes," she said, feeling they'd made a good start anyway, until she turned and saw the woman in the car Eric was getting into—thirtyish, attractive. Of course he was too nice to be single. She should have known.

Feeling dejected, Ellie wandered over to her dad's house like a homing pigeon. As she let herself in the front door of his semi-detached, she was startled to hear a woman's voice. She walked into the parlor, calling hello to her father, and there was Mrs. Burbridge from two doors down, clearly settled in for the evening, sitting very close to her father.

"Hello Ellie, sit down," her dad said. "Margaret is joining me to watch that movie I told you about."

"Hello luv," said Mrs. Burbridge, as Ellie caught the distinct odors of ladies' perfume and men's cologne. Her father was having a date! How nice for him. But she wouldn't linger.

"Really nice to see you Mrs. B.," Ellie said brightly. "I was just checking in, but I see all's well here. I'll be off than."

"You have plans?" asked her father.

"Yeah, right Dad, bye you two," and she darted back to the door, as her father called out a reminder about Sunday. So much for her exciting Saturday. She spent the rest of the night chatting with her married friend Jeannie on the phone, and washing a smelly Roan, who'd gotten into something on his evening walk.

Sunday at 2 p.m. Ellie turned up at her dad's, dressed in her white gym outfit this time, as she was going to walk on the beach later. She went around the back to look at the garden. A man was crouching over the flower beds with secateurs in hand, and stood to smile as she came up to him.

"Ellie! Great to see you. My mate's wife picked me up for the game yesterday before I could think to ask for your number. Do you live here?" asked Eric.

"My father does. Nice to see you too Eric. Where is my dad?"

"Oh, he said he had to do something down the road, but he'd be back. He said his daughter would tell me what was wanted this time with the flowers."

Dad had set her up to meet Eric—normally he would never have left a decision about his garden completely up to her, or anyone else. He had noticed her loneliness, and gotten himself and her dates. And he'd picked just the someone she would like too, showing a far greater perception of her tastes than she'd ever have guessed.

Suddenly Ellie's heart felt so free, she wanted to sing. She'd not only been presented with an interesting man to get to know, but she'd gotten her father back—the thoughtful, life-loving fellow her mother used to tell her about, who'd taken his bride to Eleuthera.

At the Bar, Providence

It was the summer of 1985. Providence was sweaty-hot that night—though the city abuts a nicely polluted river, it is not surrounded by the ocean that graces places like Newport, 45 minutes away, and cools things down.

Dorothy was on the prowl this particular evening, in her rollicking, sweetly friendly sort of way. She seemed to try harder and jump quicker than most when it came to men, probably because she's a big girl—heavy women are so very appreciated in America.

We had already been to the Swot Club, the hotspot on the river that had started attracting creatures from the depths of Rhode Island, from towns south and west of Providence we won't name. Place was now a wall-to-wall meat market of bad accents and worse attitudes. So we stopped into this nice little bar attached to a university, where you could gaze out large plate glass windows onto a grassy nook that looked as cool as the blessed air-conditioning.

He spotted us right away, and ambled over to the group of vinyl chairs where we sat and gratefully sipped cold beers. This freckled pretend-hippie with lank red hair seemed to focus on me for a minute, but I turned on my man-repellent look instantly. I had seen this guy around the neighborhood, and my radar told me: No Good. I whispered a warning to Dorothy, as he sidled over to her and smiled down into her pretty face. My Loser sensor was in high gear now.

Dorothy, of course, married him.

And he turned out to be the worst guy—on coke (not the cola), hiding knives under the pillows, sucking up money she earned, eventually leaving her and their kid for a woman more willing to coddle this bad boy than Dorothy, finally, was.

When Dorothy and Lank Hair married the New Year's Eve following that ill-fated summer meeting, hardly anyone came. A handsome artist I met there nearly ran off with me. He was a friend of the groom's grateful ("He's off our hands!") parents, who held out little more hope for the couple than I did. The air of despair hanging over the whole affair made you want to seek comfort fast: we all got drunk. But over coffee the next day I learned I would be joining a triumvirate if I tangoed with Mr. Handsome Painter, as he already had a wife and lover. In the same house. Friends even. Providence strikes again.

I just had a little e-mail flame-throw exchange with the man I met that same summer of 1985 at that same bar, and did briefly consider marrying. A dear male friend of mine was to dub him Vlad the Impaler. He was Yugoslavian, ponderously patriarchal, but capable of dashing Euro-charm and quiet attractiveness when he wanted. He was also a scientist mad enough to be sure his work would one day surprise the world, but I didn't find THAT out until later, late one night in bed to be precise.

Vlad also came with hidden baggage, in the form of an ex-girlfriend: an earnest, ordinary sort of man-hunter, who couldn't stand his relationship with me, and did what she could to bring it down. She even planted herself at our table once (uninvited) when we were out at a dance. Any relationship will hit the bricks sooner or later, and you don't want a loiterer there to catch him when he's in the mood to fall.

Dorothy met Vlad, at that same university bar we had all taken to frequenting, and was impressed. She admired me for holding out for a peer—a man who was smart and cultured, with good earning potential, who also worked hard to romance me into his life. I just liked Vlad, he was funny and affectionate and terribly serious about me. (Maybe all that youthful beer affected my eyesight.) He would even make me lunches to take to my PhD studies.

But Vlad could also turn on a dime, like a sudden flash of lightning in what had seemed gentle dusk. He was a real Jekyll/Hyde in the emotions department. My friend started calling him the Impaler because he heard us arguing one day and recognized Vlad's special gift for mental torture. By the time it was all over, I was writing poems about being a Yugoslavian war victim (ahead of my time there), and wondering if I might be capable of beating up a man. With what Vlad told me about his home, and what he was, I was not surprised the Balkans exploded.

Right before he left town for a job, Vlad married the still-loitering ex, who was by then one of the few people left in Rhoda Island who liked him. Through an oddly providential chain of events — a letter from the loitering ex in a Providence-produced magazine I still get — I recently found out that they divorced shortly after leaving Providence.

After allowing myself a few good guffaws, I looked Vlad up on the Net and dropped him a line to see if he'd grown up to be sorry about the past. He was very glad I would speak to him, but upon being reminded of what a colossal ass he had turned into years ago, he began the old annoying dance that used to mesmerize me, like a rabbit with a stoat. Vlad's only real hold on me had been the traffic-accident fascination of seeing someone turn sense completely upside down — sometimes treating me like I was nothing much, when I was generally viewed as quite something by our circle and others outside it.

This time, in e-mail, as Vlad subtly taunted me with alternating flirtation and unkind reminiscences, I wouldn't play. But it sure was nice to realize he was just a boring old Mr. Wrong I wouldn't be interested in now. Providence is probably better off without him. Although its citizens should be even more thankful Dorothy's ex got out of Dodge.

A visiting girlfriend of hers once remarked that Dorothy was attracted to men who had loser written on them with red magic marker. I attracted awful men too, of course, but mine were good at looking and seeming to be all the right things, and a damn sight better at concealing their deadly weapons.

After Dorothy recovered from her marriage to Lank Hair, admittedly one of her worst excesses, the reign of terror ended. Dorothy and I both stopped going to the bar which held such tumultuous memories for us both, and which is now an office space. Dorothy is living in another state with her daughter, happily remarried to an old friend from her youth. She got wise, and safe. It might have helped that she also got clear out of Providence. I know she thinks so.

Chapel Near the Sea

We would meet there on the weekends and after school, my friend and I. Down Waterway from Barrington beach, inside the gates of the cemetery where my brother lay, getting us in the door so to speak.

But it was not a sad place, indeed the ancient sun-bleached stones greeted us like serene old friends, and the rhododendrons—one remembers Barrington for those flowers—and sweet-smelling white-flowered bushes we could not name seemed to dance with us as we pranced and swayed and dreamed through the woods at the bottom of the hill.

There were always lush flowers to spread upon special graves just before they began to wilt, no doubt flourishing because of the sea air close by we could smell and feel in the breeze. Perhaps in the child ways of coltish young girls we knew something then we may have since forgotten: the intensely gentle restfulness of a land where people reside who will never scream or cry again. I felt the same thing years later when at the small burial ground in the middle of the Tower of London, which had known such violent deaths.

My friend and I, 18 and 14 respectively at this time, would plan our escapes from the human troubles of the pretty town where we roamed the beach and rested against sand grass, when not in our friendly cemetery. We would enter Forest Chapel (which we never knew by its name then), greet my brother, then wander among the stones, pondering the possible stories behind the oldest graves of young people we found. Later we would slip into the trees, whose heart held a small cleared circle and a stump like an altar, and preside like fairy queens over our personal woods. Maybe the Celt that runs so strongly through us both brought us naturally into communing with woods: I had been brought to the tree in Ireland where my mother told me the Little People lived.

It wasn't too long after our cemetery sessions that I did escape from Barrington, out to San Francisco. My friend would follow later, but we barely met there as I was swept into events so colorful and demanding that I was on the move a lot. Used to the beauty of a seaside village, to me the Bay Area was just an extension of verdant sea-blessed splendor on a much bigger and more magnificent scale. But there too, I would wander naturally with friends into the many parks, roaming Golden Gate like it was another Forest Chapel.

My friend and I both returned to Rhode island some years later, to the surprise of each of us, having been raised to feel, and finding some reason to believe through hard experience, that we were far too unusual and cosmopolitan for the place ever to embrace us. She lived in Barrington for a time again, in her mother's home—her father long since having joined my brother in Forest Chapel; and I settled, unwitting, into the heart of Providence. We would both, separately, visit the cemetery to say hello, and roam the beach often, sometimes together, cherishing it even more now for all the uglier, less peaceful places our travels had shown us.

The next time we met at Forest Chapel, we were burying my mother, an insurmountable loss. But we swayed together then, arm-in-arm, still looking very like the waifish, light-haired girls who had moved so much more gaily in that place. Maybe our long ago experience in what had become a crowded and denuded ground— Barrington's upward mobility striking even here—made the graves and the visits to them as adults much more bearable. It did for me: I could go and talk to my mother, and see her dancing in the old trees so like those among the hills of her beloved Ireland.

The restrictions and ceaseless noise of life in cities bother me now, even the tame and elegant East Side of Providence where I lived for years—I was meant always for the trees and seas, and have begun relocating in that direction. My childhood friend now lives on an island in southern Rhode Island, with a son, and a daughter who looks very like the girls who used to roam Forest Chapel, and speaks of wanting to avoid cities for her whole life if she can. I understand.

My friend's mother and my father have now joined the crowd at Forest Chapel, as no doubt we will one day. Although I only go to Barrington very occasionally, to visit the beach and the graves, I think I'm all right with ending my journey there too, under a still-standing tree, sea scents permeating the air.

Celtic History

Lambent light danced over hills of brown
and whisper green, older still than Celts who left
their stones upon them, stones of love and faith

you and I were there once, young and wildly
dancing in and out of light and shadow, we fell
then rolled along the hill and into one

it's in the bones, in tilting eyes that meet
and dialogue begun that feels it's always
been, like arrowheads the moors reveal

we know we've been somewhere before
together, made of some same cloth
and blood that sings beneath our stilled skins

we're quiet now, if meeting gently
stories played before us so no action asks
for taking or forsaking—that too has been before

but if the moon, the light, the hills are right
no telling what we could create, ignite:
stones and blood and stories come to life.

Carolyn Bray

PAULA'S MOVING SALE

Her eyes reach out across
the room where she stands patiently
selling gorgeous works of luxury
—remnants of her many lives going by

Every woman in her door
for longer than ten minutes
leaves secret fears and sorrows for
graceful objects more than worth the price

Her heart and dreams are strong
as the silence and embracing that draws people
to her space, a place where listening
and the telling weaves so many women's voices

She'll make you laugh at anything
including her, and feel for you
the pain you feel yourself, but still
she's counting minutes of the last tag sale
to her epiphany.

UNDER MIMOSA

Everything
everything glistens
here, under mimosa cloud
water streaming off a lifted toe
the only part of her
he dares to know
watching from the lime tree
eyes seeming not to see

As she rises from the pool
he looks away, his twisted heart
must push and pull, body swaying
—languid boys in teak trees
guess his secret, yet don't see
it's her curving arms, wet-tendriled hair
he wakes from dreams to need

Her knowing eyes scorn,
she slides away.

Carolyn Bray

To Rhoda 1980

The past
is broken
like an hourglass

Here life begins
and will no longer
be a waiting
for the end of things.

Ellen Williams Burchard

Ellen Burchard's life was always involved with the theatre and the arts. She studied extensively and acted, produced and artistically directed productions in the U.S., Rome and London. She and her husband John Burchard founded the *Carriage House Theatre* in Little Compton, Rhode Island in the 50s.

In later years, Ellen began writing both prose and poetry and was published in 1994 in *A Glass of Green Tea with Honig*, on the occasion of Professor Honig's 75th birthday.

Short Story
    Portrait of Amy

Essay
    Flying Gardener

PORTRAIT OF AMY

Her name is Amy, Aunt Amy to generations of children growing up
and sometimes just plain Amy, such as the time she stood tall and
straight and young and proud at a dance while Lieutenant Governor
Roswell B. Burchard pinned a medal on her shoulder for bravery.

The dance was a festive affair held in the barn on Governor
Burchard's estate. Japanese lanterns hung in the carriage house, in
the stables and in the trees outside. They circled the pond and were
reflected in it. Those and lights from the horse drawn carriages
made the place an enchanting wonderland.

That night, as Amy stood before the guests, they wondered how
this slip of a girl could have done what she had done.

The sea had been rough that day and terrible in its fury. One of the
bathers, who had been caught in the currents was being carried out
to sea. The lifeguard immediately dove in to save him. Soon, he too,
was in need of help. It was Amy who swam out, fighting with all her
strength, to save the lifeguard and the sea's other intended victim.

She was always "just Amy" to me. She was my friend. She had sons
and daughters my age, but I never thought of her as being older. She
was always included in our parties as she was included in the parties
of all age groups. No one thought it strange. Amy was any age. She
was a thoughtful and considerate listener and a confidant of anyone
who needed a sympathetic ear. She was a charming and gracious
hostess and her clam chowder was famous; the best, by far, of any
I have ever eaten.

Then one day Amy began to change. Friends waved to her on the
beach, but she no longer waved back. People she knew well, found
her guarded and distant. This was not like Amy. 'Was Amy getting
snooty?' they wondered. 'Had they offended her in some way?' She
refused invitations and no longer drove her car. She never spoke to

people unless they spoke first. The awful truth was out. Amy, our beloved Amy, was going blind. For five years she had been losing her sight. Too proud to let anyone know, she carried on as usual. Amy, who had been so self-reliant all her life, hated to be dependent upon others. What would she do?

She used to jump in her car and go anywhere at the slightest excuse. Europe and the world were her playgrounds. For a hobby, she painted landscapes in oil and carved exact replicas of birds in wood, painting them so well, so subtly that they seemed to breathe. She loved birds and there were always quantities of all kinds, flying about in her informal garden.

Her great independence of spirit was known and recognized by everyone. That this should happen to Amy, of all people, was unthinkable. 'Oh please, not to Amy,' they prayed.

When last I called on her, she greeted me at the door. Her white French poodle, "Buttons" by her side. She looked lovely, wearing oxford grey Bermuda shorts and silver and turquoise jewelry she had picked up in Mexico. Her manner was warm and gracious.

"I do all my own housework now," she said. "It's one of the few things I can do." Her house was immaculate, just as beautiful as when the servants were caring for it.

Her house is built high on a hill. She has a round tower of grey flat fieldstone in the front with bright, red geraniums always in the high, tiny windows. It makes the house look like a castle in a fairy tale. Inside, the curving iron stairway goes up into the tower and leads into the upstairs. At the foot of the stairs a gaily painted Czechoslovakian cart is filled with colorful flowers. Vines climb up the outside of the staircase. The flagstone floor adds further to the illusion. Her living room is white with mahogany. A fire was crackling comfortingly in the fireplace. Everywhere was warmth and charm.

"I must show you what Holly did," she said, opening a drawer of her French desk. Holly is her delightful granddaughter. "She cleaned out all the drawers and put everything in packets. She also labeled them."

"Oh look, she has a rose on top of this one," I said.

"She has decorated each one of them," Amy went on, "Isn't she a darling child?"

I noticed a piece of cellophane from a package of cigarettes hanging from the crevice of the drawer. It showed on the outside, so I quickly pulled it out and threw it in the fireplace. It was the only thing in the room Amy had overlooked.

"I made some green pea soup with ham bone this morning," she said. "You must stay and have some." Knowing Amy's green pea soup, I didn't need urging.

She poked the fire, put on another log and went out to mix cocktails. These, she carried back on a tray, negotiating the step up into the living room without spilling a drop.

"This tastes great," I said, "But how do you know how much to put in?"

"Oh, I have an elastic band around the glass," she explained. I still can't figure out how she knows when the liquor reaches the elastic, but somehow Amy finds solutions. Another example of this is her green pea soup with ham, which lived up to my full expectations.

"It's getting dark," she said as she went to adjust the drapes. She senses this, but she can hardly tell light from dark and cannot see one's face. She stopped by my chair on the way back and patted my head. "My, your lovely hair shines under the light," she murmured.

That's Amy. She just refuses to be old...or blind.

FLYING GARDENER

I walked down the winding path from my house to the fields in back. Everything was green. Halfway down I noticed a white patch in the middle of the fresh field. Looking more closely, I could see it was a spray of small white flowers showcased in green, which made it even more beautiful. Tiny white clumps of flowers, their brave little heads held up strongly by long stems.

I wondered how they got there.

Could it be they were dropped by a member of the Church family upon their arrival from England during the 1600s; or maybe it was Edith Burchard, John's mother directing her gardener as to where to plant the seeds. But my heart tells me it was John on one of his flights over the property, remembering how I loved white flowers, sprinkling the seeds for my surprise.

Virginia Conroy Catton

Virginia's career began at a tender age and her entire life was involved with the arts. She studied at the John Murray Anderson School of the Theatre in New York, where she roomed with Bette Davis. She was in *Little Theatre* work, acting, writing theatrical columns and articles. She gave readings and read scripts for MGM. She always wrote poetry, short stories and plays from her earliest years. Virginia loved to make people laugh, for as she once said, "There are in life so many things to make one cry."

Essay
Crumbs

Poems
Pollyanna
New Year's Resolution
Mystery Fan
Twinkle, Twinkle

CRUMBS

This past winter, I became very ambivalent about feeding the birds
—a dramatic departure from my childhood, when I was taught
religiously to look out for these little chorusing creatures when the
snow is on the ground. Feeding them has always given me a smug,
beatific feeling, as one basking in the aura of St. Francis.

It was a bit disillusioning the previous winter, to say the least,
when a friend of mine on her way to the bird feeder with a plate of
suet slipped, fell flat on her back, broke her right wrist, and was
knocked out of commission for the winter. When you go into your
icy backyard on an errand of mercy, speak softly to St. Francis but
carry a big bucket of Halite.

My bird-feeding activities start right after Thanksgiving, when I
begin to save old bread in paper bags, possibly becoming a nuisance
to my friends—I beg for their pumpernickel heels and party sandwich
cuttings to add to my supplies. But, as I have explained to them so
many times, one must be sure that those warm-blooded vertebrates
known as Aves will live through the winter and continue to lord it
over their first cousins, the cold-blooded vertebrates *Reptilia* (derived
from *repere*, "to creep").

Of course if the truth be known, the birds I feed from my sun deck
every winter are not really a very interesting lot. Mostly those com-
mon little black fat things, some belligerent blue jays, pigeons, and
on occasional sea gull who blows in from the Bay—Hoi polloi, in fact.

A Japanese barberry planted in the backyard would, I am told,
relieve the monotony by inveigling such birds as the junco with a pink
bill or the cedar waxwing with a yellow band on the tip of its tail.
And my cousin, the bird expert, tells me that if I would stop my cheap
bread crust bumming and buy sunflower seed and other avian deli-
cacies at the supermarket, I would attract a much higher type of

bird altogether. It seems that my cousin's place is positively crawling with cardinals every winter.

But then he easily spends several hundred dollars a season on his bird table, and considers it a worthwhile output, as the birds pay him back by debugging his garden all summer. But how can he be sure that the little debuggers won't spend just as much time on the grounds of his stingy neighbor who never spares them a crust? I have given it all a lot of thought, but so far have not succumbed to his suggestion. With the proletariat already having squatter's rights, I might start a class revolution in the backyard.

It is an intriguing question, however: How would the cardinals learn that there was a change of menu?—unless birds have extrasensory perception, which I have often suspected. Indeed, it has long been my intention to suggest that the parapsychology lab at Duke University stop waving little cards in front of people and start testing the birds. If they don't have ESP, how else does a bird on a bush four blocks from my house know that I have opened my back door with a hand-out and get here in 30 seconds flat, picking up his gang on the way?

When the last big nor'easter hit, I certainly thought the birds would go away someplace and hide out for the duration. But, much to my chagrin, they were waiting for me at the crack of dawn, fluttering feebly among the flakes or huddling reproachfully along the fence. That day I held open house.

I used up all the regular rations, all my emergency storm supply of bread, a box of Scandinavian reducing crackers and a pound of bacon, cut into hors d'oeuvres-size pieces and served tastefully on a tin tray. And still the hordes descended.

In the end I crumbled up a perfectly good pound cake and called it a day. When the birds started running their relatives in from over the city line, it was too much. Birds are a thankless lot and this year I've had it. I ask myself, if I were starving in the wilderness, would the birds feed me?

POLLYANNA

In our town lives a lady
I cannot help but censor.
She is a walking greeting card,
Perennial cheer dispenser.

Upon the job of optimist
She's taken a long-term lease.
Not a soul will she permit
To be miserable in peace.

She comes with smiling visage.
She comes with jolly jingles.
She comes with twenty reasons
To rejoice in having shingles.

Fate has always shielded her
From every single blow.
She has never lost a dollar.
She has never sprained a toe.

Some day will Satan tempt me
To plant banana peel
Upon her very doorstep
There to wait her heel.

The folks will come for miles around
With cymbal, brass and banner.
A mass attack of sunshine
To cheer up Pollyanna.

Virginia Conroy Catton

New Year's Resolution

Ring in the new!
The old ring out!
Last year I was
A Stylish Stout.

All cakes and sweets
I'll greet with hisses
To shop again
In Junior Misses.

I'll live on fruit
And meat that's lean
So I can wear
A size sixteen.

I'll never slip.
I'll never falter.
My will is stronger
Than Gibraltar.

Oh pass me please
That apple tart,
To give me strength
To make a start.

The old ring out!
Ring in the new!
No diet to-day
To-morrow'll do.

MYSTERY FAN

I hardly slept a wink last night.
That book gave me an awful fright.
I dreamt I dwelt on marble slabbing,
The victim of a gangster's stabbing.
Corpses filled my room with gore.
A clutching hand came through the door.
That book—I wish I hadn't begun it,
But I *have* to go on to see whodunit!

TWINKLE TWINKLE!

Twinkle, twinkle little Star.
How wonderfully slim you are!
Though you're richer far than I,
You can't afford a piece of pie.
While you're dining on your juices,
I am gobbling charlotte russes.
I'll never be a millionaire.
Neither must I bleach my hair.
While your name goes twinkle, twinkle
I can laugh at my first wrinkle.
Little Star—fess up—agree.
Don't you wish that you were me!

MARY GAIL

Mary Gail, a *Rhode Island Short Story Club* member in the 80s, is primarily a playwright. Her plays have been published across the country. She also writes short stories because of the inherently greater freedom the narrative form allows.

SHORT STORY
   Hugh

HUGH

I'm a pretty hot item here. Only a few get really disappointed and want their money back, expecting 15, maybe 20 feet.

It started when I was 30 and threatened to sue the dry cleaners for shrinking my suits. Hell no, they said, it ain't us; it's you, you're growing—which was crazy, I told them. Height don't change at 30. Believe me, I know. I've read everything there is to read about height, 'cause then I was only 5 foot 4, which for a guy is pure hell with women who want them tall, you know, like those 6-foot studs always standing in front of you in ticket lines making you look like the shortstop for a team of midgets.

Fact is, I thought they were trying to pull one over on me, so I switched cleaners. But my feet were hurting and my baseball cap was leaving dents in my forehead. And later, I went to buy some new clothes and sure enough, my regular size didn't cut it. I even had the clerk measure me, and there I was a full inch and half taller, which made me real glad. I bought myself a whole new wardrobe.

It was a gradual thing at first, inching my way up, measuring myself every week. Things started happening to me. Girls were noticing me more, guys were more respectful, especially where I worked—driving for a sheet-metal outfit. And it wasn't just my imagination either. And believe me, I got quite an imagination.

Before, I used to go around with a kind of phantom knife, slicing the tall guys off at the waists and ankles then stitching them onto myself. Course you can't add on to yourself like that. You're stuck with heredity, and I always blamed Mom for giving me the same pygmy genes as my uncles and for feeding me fish and chicken instead of steaks full of hormones they shoot into cattle. Other things I did too, like always buying those thick-soles shoes or wearing boots or fluffing up my hair or wearing hats. Sometimes, I figured the combi-

nations gave me another 3, maybe 4 inches. Course, soon I didn't
need those things. Folks were starting to look up instead of down.
   Funny thing was, it didn't stop. The first year I grew a full 8 inches,
so I came to 6 foot even. My folks and sister couldn't believe their
eyes. They said something's wrong, Hugh, you got to see a doctor,
boy. Your growing days are long gone. So finally at about 6 foot 4,
when I started getting headaches and pains in my joints, I went to
a clinic, and they said it just wasn't possible, but hell, there I was,
shopping in the tall sizes, wearing flat shoes, no hats and getting all
the dates I wanted.
   The doctors poked and x-rayed and found a tumor on my pituitary
gland leaking hormones. They said they'd never seen the like and
that I should have it cut out right away. Hell no, I said, let me keep
her in there till I'm a full 7 feet. I always dreamed of towering over
crowds, having people think I'm some hotshot B-ball player. They
tried to change my mind, said I was crazy, risking my life. But put
yourself in my shoes; it was a dream come true. I even had this idea
God gave me the tumor—on loan to make up for all the hell I'd
gone through being short. In the U.S. of A. folks respect size. Brains
don't count for beans, believe me. How do you think I got my raise?"
Size. Size is everything!
   Anyhow, soon it became a kind of game, everybody measuring me
week to week. I passed 7 feet in five months and decided to go for
the big 8.
   Sure I had my troubles. There was the pain in my knees and elbows.
Then I started bumping into door frames and I didn't fit in cars. I even
had to buy a new bed and get my clothes done up special. And smaller
girls didn't like me being that much taller. Made them feel like kids
and that didn't sit well. Hell, I made the guys feel like kids too.
   In those days, when I walked into places like department stores
or movies, people would turn and stare. Sometimes they'd recognize

me. They started calling me Hugh Mungous, like I was one of them TV wrestlers. It really caught on. Everybody was calling me Hugh Mungous.

Sometimes kids would think I was some Hollywood superstar and ask for my autograph. Even the company I worked for took shots of me standing by my truck. All that happened at 8 feet. Eight was enough and I decided to quit for good. Trouble was, it was too damn late.

The tumor had grown too big to operate, so they said they'd give me chemicals, but the chemicals just made me sick, and they didn't stop me from growing. Then they tried radiation, and that was worse. It seemed to give me an extra spurt, and the next thing I knew I was 11 foot 7, the tallest human being on record. They had to put two hospital beds end to end to lay me under their machines.

Fact is, I outgrew everything; my truck, my house, my friends, even my underwear was custom-made. The only place I fit was the circus, and here's where I'll stay till I kick off. Already they're fighting over my body. The doctors want it for research, and the circus says I should get myself preserved so they can still use me. I haven't decided which way to go yet.

One of the doctors comes by a lot, a little shrimp of a guy about 5 foot 3 at most. He says I'm something he dreams about. Hell I tell him, I was something I dreamed about myself, but I ain't going to be dreaming much longer now, am I? He asks me if it was worth it. Hell yes, I say. I had some real fine days feeling big and mean and looking over heads like I was some kind of Hercules. And of course I'm going to make history.

I've already been on TV, magazine covers, the whole pie-in-the-sky American dream. Once, I even stood next to the president—made him look like a dwarf. I've been to Paris, Russia, Hong Kong and they say I'm going to be the star feature in *The Guinness Book of Records.*

That's something most folks don't get into, now do they?

But then I tell him—just to make him feel good—that I'd take it all back if I could fit into a store-bought bed again—with some nice warm dish who'd call me just plain Hugh.

Patricia J. Gerstner

Patricia has a husband, three sons, two daughters in law and 5 grand daughters of assorted ages. She was a registered nurse by profession before retirement and began writing in 1984. This was the year *Big Brother* was supposed to come on the scene and dominate our lives. Thank goodness, he didn't as she is not only a voracious reader, but writes, as all writers do, with freedom. She joined the *RISSC* twenty-three years ago and her portfolio contains many short stories, some of which have been given *Blaisdell Awards*. There are two unfinished novels and recently her writing also includes poetry. She has completed her sixth year as President of the *RISSC*. She says, "The *RISSC* has captured my heart and I work toward preserving its history."

Short Stories
> Echoes
> Conversations*
> Waiting for Manny*
> Memories of Love and Other Things*

Essays
> First Gifts
> A Rhode Island Day

Poems
> Truth
> Love Words

Blaisdell Award

ECHOES

The clicking of his shutter startled me from my reverie. As I turned, the shutter snapped again and again.

"Do you mind?" he said. A wide grin greeted me.

"No, but why would you want my picture?'

I had finished my walk on this perfect morning and stopped, as I always do, to watch the mountain transform with the season, to see the silent lake mirror the phenomenon.

"I'm a photographer," he replied in faultless English, "and you are a good subject. Seiichi Kato," he said, extending a hand.

I returned the introduction.

He sat beside me, careful to protect his Nikon from the bed of pine needles beneath us.

"The finest," he said, patting it like a much-loved child. "I purchased it in Japan."

"Do you get back there often?"

He looked at me through rimless glasses with serious, heavy-lidded eyes.

"Occasionally, but it's painful. My parents are now gone."

"You miss them," I said, for lack of something more profound.

"My parents, both professors, taught at the University. They were much respected, solid citizens, as you would say in the United States."

...my gaze wandered to the mountain. The pines stand forth stately, dark green-black and strong.

He continued to speak. "A blood disease took both of them. They warned me so I was prepared. It was still a shock being alone."

"No brothers or sisters?"

"There was a sister. I was born late, so I never knew her. She was in the city that day. My mother and father had traveled north to a seminar. They remembered seeing the cloud. My mother told me it was bright and fiery, but Father disagreed. He said time plays tricks on your memory."

...a maple sits on a ledge high above the lake. I glanced up and it was an explosion of brilliant scarlet.

"Your sister died?"

"Yes, she was a baby, left with an aunt that day. My mother said they tried for years to have more children and finally I was born. Shortly after, they both knew that they too were affected."

"The blood disorder."

"Yes. They had many remissions; they were luckier than most. The doctor thought it was the result of their great zest for life."

"As I grew older, my mother, as I said, prepared me."

"Was she bitter?"

He did a double take. His straight black hair swayed with the movement of his head. "I never knew her to be." He looked away, and the silence was somewhat uncomfortable.

He shifted. "They died within weeks of each other."

...the sun was behind a cloud. My eyes rested on a treeless precipice of granite. In shadow, it is dark, foreboding. I followed it down a sheer drop to the lake where the morning haze was rising.

"What did you do?"

"My uncle came from New England to get me. They took me into their home, like I was their own. I was educated here. He is so like my father, but of course, it is not quite the same."

...the haze burned off as the sun warmed. The lake, so often like glass, was marred by a light breeze, causing small waves, distorting the mountain image.

We sat together in the quiet, unique to my retreat.

"Seiichi, *Seiichi.*" His companion was returning from shooting on the far side of the lake. His call and accompanying echo broke the silence.

The man approached, carrying his tripod.

"You ready?"

Seiichi got to his feet, turned and said, "Hope we meet again."

I reached for a business card, but of course, had none in my sweat shirt. He gave me his.

As they walked he crouched, pine needles still clinging to his pants, and retrieved a stone. He fired it into the glassy surface.

...the ripples formed, first one small circle, then several, spreading, breaking, reaching far beyond the initial target.

CONVERSATIONS

I'm sitting here in Central Park again today, as I have every day for the last six weeks. Many people come and go, but a certain woman comes every day. She sits, slumped, on a nearby bench, arms folded across her chest. Now and then she mindlessly tosses bread pieces to the birds, which gather around us. She wears an ankle length red coat, which is why she interests me, I believe. Red was Mae's color —Chinese red. Throughout our forty-eight years together, the touches of red were always there, from her favorite knit Christmas dress to little scarves she tucked at her throat—and now, the Chinese red ceramic urn, which sits on a bookcase in my study and holds her ashes. It's been over a year, but I cannot part with them.

Approximately six weeks ago, we had a discussion about this. Yes, I find myself discussing things with Mae all the time. What it amounts to is I'm talking to myself. I have decided this has to stop. I feel Mae would agree. She needs to be at rest. I need someone to share my thoughts—to share my days. I have chosen this lady in the red coat.

My son, Billy and his pregnant wife, Nan live in Connecticut. They're a phone call away, so I'm not totally alone. But they have a life of their own. I need to get out and meet some new people. However, N.Y. City is not the place to meet new people. There's an army of them out there. They never look from one side to the other, giving me a chance to make eye contact. Christmas time, I got caught in a crowd in front of Macy's. We all came to a dead stop. The lady next to me continued to walk in place. Nobody spoke, just craned their necks right and left, trying to see what the holdup was. They were all hurrying along, racing to some unseen something straight ahead. "Did we ever move that fast Mae?"

I've returned to my old office where young men look up briefly from the computer screens. Young women in the halls nod pleasantly, but I'm no longer a familiar face nor are they, after three years. All the old-timers are gone to Florida, or to their children's homes. Billy and Nan have asked me to move in, but I'm not ready to give up the old place. I've taken trips across town, through N.Y. State, to Atlantic City, leaving alone and returning alone. Everyone is with someone, it seems.

The lady in the red coat had stood up. She looks at her watch and pulls her coat around her against the autumn chill. I make a decision to approach her tomorrow and strike up a conversation. She appears to be as alone as I am.

Back in my apartment, I boil water, turn on the weather channel and sit at the kitchen table with my tea. Billy stops by before his train ride home. Another plan is materializing in the back of my mind.

That evening, after I've eaten a light supper and talked with Billy, I sit in my study. "Well Mae, you're going to like this. Saturday we're going to Connecticut where you will finally rest in peace." After saying this, I sit back, hoping to get a feeling of peace myself. Mae was born and raised in the house where Billy now lives. She kept this place all these years, wanting her ashes strewn in her mother's garden. Billy, Nan and I will do this Saturday.

The following morning, as planned, I return to the park. I've dressed and shaved and talked to Mae a mile a minute. "Mae, I won you. How can I miss? I'm scared though. It's been so long. I look in the mirror and see myself as others do and shake my head. But I remember how I felt when we were dating and I don't feel much different today."

It's a perfect Indian summer day. I arrive at the park early and sit on my usual bench with the morning paper. After what seems like hours, the lady in the red coat appears and sits down on a bench nearby.

"Well, here I go, Mae!" I slowly approach her bench and ask if she minds if I sit. She shrugs her shoulders and gestures to the empty end of the bench as if to say, 'It's a free country.'

I sit for a moment feeling less than confident. The weather seems a safe subject. "A beautiful day, isn't it?" I say and open my paper. No response. After a moment or two, I face her and ask, "You enjoy the park? I've seen you here before." The lady glances at me dismissively. Soon she checks her watch, gets up and I watch her until she is scarcely more than a red blur. Disappointment wells up inside me. After a time, I make my way back home.

That evening I sit in my study and talk to Mae, reminiscing. I talk about how we filled our days with museum visits, quiet times in St. Patrick's. Some days we just walked and had a bowl of soup together in the Village. I wonder how I'll survive alone. I've made a commitment to her, however, and in the morning will follow through. I get up with a heavy heart and pack the Chinese red urn into a carton.

Saturday arrives and I call a cab, hoping the driver is a pleasant sort. He is and helps me load the urn into and out of the cab at the train station. Train traffic is light so Mae can be perched next to me on the seat. The ride to Connecticut is quiet. A baby cries at the back of the car, but I am preoccupied with my thoughts and I hardly hear him. Mae and I took this trip together many times to visit her parents. Billy would remember this well as visiting Grandma and Grandpa was a highlight in his childhood. "This will be our last trip together, Mae."

The Connecticut house is bustling. Nan is an illustrator and works out of her home, so there are pleasant looking things strewn all around. Soup is simmering on the stove and it's comfortable to be here. After lunch, we proceed with our plan. The yard is overgrown. I regret my promise to Mae and fight tears. Billy apologizes and says somehow the garden never looks as it did when Grandma was here. We clear the yard. The crisp autumn air and the work invigorate me and pull me out of my doldrums.

Afterwards, we spread Mae's ashes under the Dogwood trees, which will be umbrellas of pink and white come spring. Mae will like that.

Well, it's Monday morning and the weekend is over. Billy said 'You did the right thing Dad,' as he put me on the train. Nan hugged me with a tear in her eye. Mae's urn is in her mother's parlor and she's resting in the garden. But I'm still in Central Park. While deep in thought, a tap on the shoulder startles me. The lady in the red coat is standing there.

She says, "I was rather rude the other day and I apologize. I spend a lot of time brooding about my brother, Ed. He's got Alzheimer's. I forget to be nice to people. Can I sit?" She points to the bench.

"It's a free country," I reply, softening it with a smile.

WAITING FOR MANNY

"Have I missed Joe again?" Lila moans, as she bursts into the kitchen of their family bakery.

Sophie looks up from the dough she is rolling. She flicks imaginary specks of flour from her face and fixes her eyes on her daughter. "How many years of your life will you waste loving Joe?"

Joe has come and gone. Early every morning he appears. Plump Sophie in her neat housedress and starched apron fusses over him, filling his coffee cup, buttering his scone, patting his arm. Joe hardly notices. His mind is on other things.

As I un-wedge myself from my plumbing chore under the sink, I see that Lila has gone to the window. She looks out into the fog that rolls in each morning from the bay and says softly, "He's there again."

I don't have to look. He's been out there every morning for a year, a far cry from the swarthy fisherman he once was. He just sits on a bench, the ones the city puts there for the retired guys to sit on to wile away their time. Joe stares out to sea the whole day. He's waiting for Manny.

We all know Manny is not coming back. Last September he went out one day on their fishing boat with a crew of five. Joe didn't go that day for some reason. The crew never returned. There have been five memorial services for the others. Families are learning to live without their sons and fathers. All, that is, except Joe.

Actually, Joe never learned to live without Maria. She was his wife who died ten years ago. She was pregnant for the second time and there were complications. Joe and his boy Manny, who was ten at the time, were left to fend for themselves. After that, he was always sad.

In the evening when Joe leaves his bench, he goes to Bud's, a bar on the back street behind Sophie's. No tourists go there, just locals. I go in on Tuesday, maybe Wednesday. Tonight the place is empty. I join Bud and Joe who are exchanging small talk. Bud is telling Joe he needs a good woman, needs to get back working. Says he should get on a crew just to keep occupied. Joe gives a short laugh. He's already in his cups. Later he passes out on the bar.

Bud says to me, "Sallie and I usually take him home. My wife straightens his place a little, while I'm getting him in bed." I offer to give them a hand. Joe is a dead weight and no help at all. I wonder how Bud and Sallie manage by themselves.

At the house we struggle getting Joe into bed. I can hear Sallie in the kitchen washing dishes. I join her there and notice a casserole on the counter. She sees me eyeing it and says, "Lila was here" and puts it in the fridge. The whole town knows Lila is in Love with Joe and has been since Maria died, maybe before.

The next day, as I clean up after the lunch crowd, I watch Lila going out, as she does every day to sit by Joe. The sun catches glints of gold in her beautiful blond hair. She leans toward him slightly, un-wrapping the sandwich she's brought, talking and smiling. Joe, with elbows resting on his thighs just sits staring out to sea.

As I turn away from the window, I glance at Sophie in the yard. A somewhat dreamy expression on her face makes me wonder what she is thinking about. It could be the snapshot thumb tacked on the bulletin board in the office—the little girl, Lila with her blond banana curls, shining eyes and toothless grin, six years old and waiting for life to happen. Sophie shakes her head and returns to the kitchen.

The next morning I'm on the stepladder changing a light bulb. Inside the office I can hear Sophie. She's in a snit about something. She goes on and on until I hear a chair scrape against the bare floor. Lila's voice floats, loud and clear, out into the hall. "Mother, I keep the books. I order supplies. I'll bake your rolls and pastries, anything you ask of me, but I will not have you tell me who to love."

On the surface, things run smooth at the bakery. The customers, local and tourists, loving Sophie's delicacies, are drawn in by the smell of fresh bread. Sophie smiles for everyone. Nobody would guess at the undertones of disappointment and dissension rumbling beneath her pleasant manner.

Summer is on the wane and I'm cleaning the yard—raking, pruning. A commotion across the street alerts me. About the same time I get to the bench where Joe usually parks, the fire truck arrives—red lights flashing. A woman is hysterical and a fireman is trying to talk to her. She calms down somewhat and I recognize her now. She is the proprietor of the souvenir shop a few doors down the street. She's now pointing and yelling, "There, there," as the wet suit who has materialized from the fire truck, dives in.

The fishing boats have left for the day and I only see ripples in the empty water, spreading, and catching sunlight.

Within seconds, blue lights are flashing behind me and Lester jumps out of his squad car. I raise a hand in greeting and he gives me a cursory nod. Soon he's back guiding the souvenir shop woman, whose hysteria is bubbling just beneath the surface. The woman speaks, enunciating clearly as Lester writes. "I had a few minutes before I open for business so I sat on a bench, you know to relax. The water calms me. All of a sudden, Joe, who is sitting two benches down, jumps up and darts toward the water like he sees something. His voice is hoarse. 'Manny, you're back,' he shouts, 'where are the others? I knew you'd'... His voice was cut off as he was so close to the edge of the wharf, he fell in, flat on his face, his arms outstretched."

By then everyone on the street is here. Sophie and Lila have run across the street. Everyone is shouting. Sophie's hands are folded and she is praying. Lila, tense and leaning slightly toward the water, is dry eyed and fiercely concentrating, as if she's willing Joe to be alive.

Another wet suit has joined the first and now they both surface. With them is Joe, appearing limp and pale. An ambulance is arriving. The people are cleared away to make room and the men begin CPR. After a few attempts, Joe responds and begins thrashing. Lila runs to him. He pushes her away.

"Manny's back," he cries. "I helped him out of the boat. Where are you, son?"

He lifts his head, looking around muttering incoherently.

The attendants wrap him and put him on the stretcher. He resists the blanket. Flailing arms strike Lila as she again attempts to talk to him. I move closer. Sophie is crying. Joe is crying and babbling.

Lila slumps, but catches herself. I look into her face, once beautiful, and realize what pain has been inflicted upon her. Her skin is blotchy and pasty, eyes swollen and bloodshot, lips contorted. Her dull eyes turn and follow the ambulance. I stand there for a few moments before returning to work—with praying Sophie and vacant Lila, who has sent part of herself off to be with Joe.

MEMORIES OF LOVE AND OTHER THINGS

My mother sits on the couch in the kitchen with her legs tucked demurely under her, filing her nails, while Stan prepares supper.

You might wonder why our couch is in the kitchen. Well, we are a dysfunctional family, so it follows that our household is also dysfunctional. The kitchen counter holds a clutter of toilet articles with an 8x10 inch mirror hanging over the sink, where each morning my brother and Stan prepare for school and work. The TV stands in the corner near the kitchen table. The living room serves as a bedroom for my brothers, Alajuon and Joshua. My mother, being Queen of the Hill, has a bedroom of her own with a bureau, a dressing table and chair to match. She has a double bed with a framed picture of the Eiffel Tower overhead, because it reminds her of the trip to Paris, which she will someday make. Stan sometimes sleeps here, depending on my mother's mood, his mood or whatever. Otherwise he stays in our 8x8 foot bedroom, which holds a twin bed. If he's not there and it's cold outside, I sleep there. Otherwise, being the luckiest person in the family, the porch is my space. I have a day bed and three lumpy chairs, one chest with drawers, several table tops for books, my clock radio and the lamp I bought at Corcoran's Second Hand Store for three dollars. Corcoran's is next door to the Burger King, where I work, so I can watch for bargains. Tables are always too expensive, so my tables are boxes turned upside down with bright cloth covers, which I've fringed myself. My porch has thirteen windows with Venetian blinds. Mr. March, our landlord, installed them after three or four calls from me and a promise that I'd dust them every Saturday. I love my room. My best friend, Tatanisha can come over and it's private, not like Grand Central Station.

My mother shifts on the couch and looks up at Stan, who is stirring spaghetti sauce. He's a good cook and can make a lot of wonderful Polish dishes, but tonight it's Italian.

"You know, Stan..." my mother says in the thoughtful, rather theatrical way she has, index finger resting on her chin. That always alerts me to tune out whatever I'm doing and listen. I learn a lot this way, as my family is not the type that has round table discussions.

"What's that hon?" Stan replies absently.

"There was a time, way back, when I'd see you across the room and I'd get goose bumps."

"That don't happen anymore?" he says, with a wink in his voice.

My mother shrugs. "You were this big-time foot ball player in High School." She sighs.

"Well, I'm still big. I'm a big, ugly man, Cathy and I never pretend to be anything else...a big ugly man just hangin' around."

Yeah. Stan's been hanging around as long as I can remember, except for a short time when James lived here. James moved in after Alajuan was born and Stan left. James wanted my mother to cook. He always talked about the food his mother made and how she ironed his clothes. They would fight. The neighbors would call the police.

One night my mother was at Samantha's, her girlfriend, who lives around the corner and James had gone out. I was eight and Alajuan was a baby and we were here alone when the police came. They took us away. Shortly after that, Stan showed up again. When he came back, James left for good. Well, he still comes to take Alajuan for a day or so. He's actually nice now. He always says, 'Hi Stephanie. Ok if I come in the front door?' He sits on one of my lumpy chairs, kind of quiet and waits for Alajuan and when he comes in, he gives him the high five. He's real good to my brother.

We finish eating spaghetti about the same time the news ends. Joshua, age 3, blubbers throughout supper most nights because the cartoons are over and also because he can't leave the table until he finishes his milk. Stan sits with him, while I clear the table. My mother gets freshened up, changes and gets ready to go to Samantha's every night after supper.

After the boys are bathed, Stan always stretches out on the kitchen floor. He'll yawn and say, 'Long day,' 'tired.' When we hear the fake snores, the boys begin to giggle. They climb on, roll over, sit on and mess Stan's hair and he just lays there like the Rock of Gibraltar for them, while the sit-coms come and go. Sometimes I wonder why Stan lets my mother go out. Every night she spends her evenings with her girl friend, missing all this.

Stan lets my mother go to Sam's, but if she isn't home by midnight, he goes after her. Their worst arguments have occurred after Stan has gone to fetch my mother. I usually go into the small bedroom, so I can hear better, as their arguments are never loud like when James lived here. On one particularly bad night four years ago, my mother was crying and pleading, but Stan's replies were firm. I could hear bits and snatches...

'Not my hard earned money for this.' 'But I can't go thru with it.' 'You made your bed, lie in it.' 'It's not yours.' 'You never know for sure, do you?'

Several months after that argument, Joshua was born. I was thirteen and old enough to be 'little mother.' A good thing, too as my mother was hardly interested. On the other hand, Stan's spongy heart gobbled him up. Joshua will never know about the argument, of course, but sometimes when he's pale and cranky, as he so frequently is, I wonder if he senses more than we know.

The reason I say this is because I've always had a second sense about our rocker. It's an old wooden one with faded, old fashioned covers on the back. When I was little, I always told Stan that was 'our rocker' and he never disagreed or asked me to explain. If I close my eyes, to this day I'm sitting on Stan's lap and he's rocking and crooning to his girl, Stephie. I've always felt I was Stan's girl, although nobody ever told me. Of course, now I have no doubt, as I'm big-boned and tall for sixteen and the image of Stan.

Saturday is payday and I usually wander by Corcoran's and beyond to the drug store. On this particular Saturday, the Valentines Day candy has been marked down by fifty percent. Feeling very flush, I buy a three pound, pink, heart shaped box with a pink, satin heart attached to the top. I'm not sure what my plan is, but I sense one will develop.

That night we have beef and potatoes and gravy and vegetables for supper. Joshua begins his usual fussy routine. I whisper in his ear and he in turn whispers to Alajuan. After we finish, my mother starts to get up. I stand and announce that I have a treat and would everyone remain in their seats. I run to get the heart shaped box, which seems even larger in our small apartment. I offer my mother a piece first and, as an afterthought, whisper something in her ear. She shrugs and goes over to the couch. My brothers help themselves from the box sitting in the center of the table. Stan is grinning from ear to ear. My mother tucks her legs under her and picks at the second chocolate, which Stan has brought her.

She stays home that evening as I had asked her to. She watches the boys stuffing candy into their mouths, laughing, chocolate oozing between their teeth. She sees big, solid Stan stretch out on the floor, being a bridge or whatever it is that satisfied my little brother's fantasies. I sit on the floor, cross-legged, stealing glances at my mother. She looks thoughtful and less theatrical than usual. I see a tear glisten in the flickering light of the TV and escape down her silky cheek.

First Gifts

I've been giving a lot of thought lately to gifts, especially those first gifts we get from our children and ones we gave as children.

Sometimes I get good, useable things, like a shirt, well wrapped with a card signed with my daughter's "hand," which I recognize as mom's handiwork. Other times it's a picture of a stick man and a stick girl, holding hands with flowers in their path. I seem to appreciate such a gift more, but I must admit its usefulness is limited.

A gift I purchased as an eight-year-old returns to mind. I purchased it at St. Tim's White Elephant sale. It was a planter in the shape of a kitten. Mother's Day was a few days off and I couldn't believe my luck. My mother not only loved kittens, but the price of five cents was well within my reach. I think my decision to buy it was made even before I retrieved it from the shelf. In retrospect, this planter was an indescribable piece of art work or at least craftsmanship. At one time it had been in at least one hundred pieces. The "artist" had painstakingly glued each piece together again, leaving an open space here and there like missing pieces in a puzzle.

In my excitement, I remember running all the way home, into the house and slamming my bedroom door behind me. Later Dad and I found a neat box and wrapping and prepared it for Sunday, when the Mother's Day gifts would be presented.

My mother opened the gift; she opened all her gifts, exclaiming after each and following with hugs and kisses.

The ceramic kitten found a spot on the kitchen window sill. I'd check on it periodically with a self-satisfied feeling. Then one day, it was no longer there. I knew without asking it had probably been relegated to the basement with the other Good Will items.

I felt bad; I think my face flushed. But for some reason, I thought of my old toy box and how Teddy, a favorite gift of my childhood lay smashed in the bottom. I thought, well isn't this what happens to things that lose their usefulness; (Or some similar thought, appropriate to an eight-year-old). I hope my daughter will discover this when her pictures disappear from the refrigerator.

A RHODE ISLAND DAY

I arise in the dark and take measured steps to the front door. Flip on the light switch and the pavement, my private weatherman, sends its message—dry and gray, not white and sparkly or wet and shiny. Flip off the light and the moon in the western sky is signing off for the time being and millions of bright studs are following suit. Gorgeous!

The latent poet in me spouts "It's very early, but I can't be surly." How Gauche! "Erase that, God. Strike it from the record." The demon subdued, I make my way through the house to the kitchen, get the coffee brewing and gather cereal bowls, as dawn cracks in the East.

Out on the driveway, I climb to the mailbox, hugging myself as the air nips at my legs. High up, a bird chirps feebly. He may have been left behind when his friends winged south or just chose, as I did, to take his chances on a Rhode Island winter. I must remember to throw crumbs for him and the many squirrels skittering about. Returning to the house, morning paper in hand, I see the sun beginning to rise, blasting through my hilltop neighbor's be-windowed house. I catch my breath and am glad I can be home today.

Later, I pull on a sweater and go to the porch. With spring just around the corner, it needs to be tidied. But, I'm locked at the window, mesmerized by the blue, blue sky I see through leafless trees. They sway gently and cast bold shadows on the lawn, allowed to be brown on this mid-February day.

If only I were a poet! I'd have all the words and know how to say them. They would be gathered together and properly arranged in measured stanzas. They would metaphorically ring out like music.

But I'm not and I can only stumble clumsily with prose. So, I'll just steal this day and stow it away in my private self to be retrieved when I need it and sung like a silent rhapsody.

TRUTH

My child comes to me at vulnerable times.
Awakened from a dream to loss.

My child comes to me unannounced.
Once at five he rode a shiny bike,
but only in my mind.

My child comes to me in fantasy.
A man grown tall with curly beard,
smiling down at children of his own.

My child comes to me in memory,
a shadowy, laughing child
running on two-year-old legs,
blond curls ruffled in the breeze.

This is my only truth.

LOVE WORDS

Love conjures up stolen kisses,
holding hands and dreamy eyes,
dancing close to mellow music
and chocolate candies, valentines.

Soon eyes are opened to her charm.
His winning style, delightful fun.
Winsome ways so captivating.
Lovely goes beyond the young.

Supporting all the ups and downs
is bliss of marriage on the scene.
Paychecks stretched the utmost length.
Precious little ones in need.
Through it all, a disposition
blossoms indestructible
to muddle through with firm resolve
and find that they're still Lovable.

All the years of trial and error,
children growing up to leave.
Remembering the culmination
hear now the echoes in our ears.
Soon recover, plan a future,
trips and restaurants and plays.
Growing gray and wrinkled, slowing
Beloved at the end of day.

ELAINE KAUFMAN

Elaine is a graduate of Brown University and received a Masters Degree from the University of Rhode Island. She is a long time member of *The Rhode Island Short Story Club*. Elaine has been writing for many years and is a *Blaisdell* contest winner. Her working years were spent helping the poor and needy and her writing reflects her empathy.

SHORT STORIES
    Josephine
    Elsie's House
    The Satin Dress
    My Dad

ESSAY
    A Visit

JOSEPHINE

While sitting at my desk at the meal site for the elderly, I heard a faint tapping on my office door. Opening the door, I saw a timid, gray-haired woman standing there. Fright marred her lovely, sky-blue eyes. I invited her in and as she came hesitantly into the office, I realized she dragged her left leg.

Welcoming her to the meal site, I introduced myself, telling her that I was the meal site manager. I motioned for her to sit down so that I could fill out the necessary forms for new participants. The woman meekly told me her name was Josephine and sat down. Sensing her apprehension, I decided not to ask her any questions just then. Instead I escorted her into the dining room, where the people were starting to congregate for the noon meal. I sat down with her and introduced her to a few participants.

In the days that followed, Josephine came to the meal site, but remained shy and reticent.

Gradually, encouraged by the warmth of our relationship, Josephine began to reveal the strange and unbelievable story of her life. Her father had been abusive to his wife and seven children. In fact, Josephine blames her limp on her father, who kicked her mother when she was pregnant with her. When Josephine, the youngest of the seven children, was five years old, the father deserted the family. Her mother, having no job skills or means of support, was placed, with her children, in the County Home for the Retarded. There the family remained until Josephine was 50 years old.

By this time Josephine's mother, whom she relied on heavily, had died.

Since Josephine had no other income except supplementary social security, she lived in a rooming house in the poorest section of the city. She invited me to visit her. The dismalness of the crowded room faded away with her friendly greeting. A large maple double bed covered with a chenille bedspread took up three quarters of the room. She asked me to sit down at the kitchen table, which was flush against the only window in the room. A refrigerator, a bureau and a double hot plate were crowded onto the bright linoleum floor.

Feeling chills up my back, I placed my coat over my shoulders. Noticing my shivering, she apologized, saying that the heating system had broken down the week before. We were interrupted by a knock on the door. Opening it, a little old woman entered. Josephine introduced her to me as her next door neighbor. She explained that this woman had told her about the meal site and that they had become good friends.

After several weeks of coming to the meal site, I asked Josephine to fill out some forms. I realized from the puzzled look on her face that she didn't know how to read. I asked her if she would like to learn. She answered enthusiastically 'yes, yes, yes.' I borrowed a beginning reading book from my nine-year-old granddaughter and although I didn't know how to teach reading, I proceeded as best I could. Josephine appeared at my office an hour before lunch every day, eager to begin. Her mind was like a sponge. After a few weeks, she knew all the words in the first grade reader. I realized that Josephine had an innate intelligence and a strong desire to learn. She was like a budding flower opening up in the spring. Her appreciation for my help was boundless. Every day she brought in little presents for me and my granddaughter. One day there was a plant for me and a doll for my granddaughter and so on. Her sweet nature was recognized by the participants of the meal site and soon she became a volunteer. Her cheerful outlook and eagerness to help made her popular with the other volunteers at the meal site. When the meal site sponsored a trip to Newport on a bus, her joy at seeing the ocean and ships was contagious. Her delight at seeing sights for the first time was like that of a young child exploring and experiencing new things.

An annual banquet and dance is given for the volunteers in appreciation for all their work during the year. Josephine was thrilled to receive an invitation to the affair. She bought herself a new dress for the occasion. The night of the party, Josephine, entranced by the glittering decorations and the music supplied by a live band became completely engrossed in the evening activities. Her feet were tapping in time to the music. Talking and laughing with the people at her table, she seemed oblivious of all past impediments. When asked to dance, she jumped up quickly, her eyes sparkled with joy, her limp was completely forgotten. Accepting every invitation, she danced lightheartedly until the music was over for the evening.

As Josephine became more confident and self-assured, she ventured to another meal site, housed in a new modern apartment complex. Becoming increasingly dissatisfied with her present living conditions, she buoyed up enough courage to apply for an apartment in the housing complex where she ate. To her complete surprise, within a few months she was assigned one. Her new home consisted of a modern kitchen with an electric stove and refrigerator, spacious living room, bedroom and bathroom with a stall shower. Never had she dreamed that she would live in such a magnificent apartment. She collected discarded furniture from her many new friends and before long her apartment was cozy and comfortable.

She recently divulged that she bought a simple cookbook with plans to master a good recipe, adding that we, my granddaughter and I, can expect an invitation to dinner.

ELSIE'S HOUSE

My knock on the small bungalow door was answered by a frail voice saying "Just a minute." Five minutes later, a petite woman in her eighties, dressed in a cardigan, skirt and knee socks opened the door, ushering me into a spotless, comfortably furnished living room where the coffee table and the carved wooden frame of the sofa gleamed with fresh polish. She smiled at me, pointing to a chair. She told me to pull up a "car." Realizing that she had used the wrong word, she explained that after she had fallen two years ago, sometimes she had difficulty saying the right words.

I told her that I was the woman who had called her this morning and that I was here at the request of the gas company. Inadvertently, she had overpaid the gas company $300.00. If she would like me to, I could help her make out her checks. I explained that I worked for the Department of Elderly Affairs and helping people with their bills is one of our services. Seeming to understand, she took me to her highly polished desk where bills were placed neatly in the cubbyholes of the desk. Amongst her bills were many checks returned because of being made out incorrectly. As if a weight was taken off her, she welcomed my offer to help.

Proudly, she took me on a tour of the house. The kitchen was immaculate. The chrome on the stove shone and the white sink and refrigerator sparkled. If I had not smelled chicken and potatoes baking in the oven, I would have thought that the kitchen was never used. In the bedroom, the twin beds were made without a wrinkle in the bedspreads. The closet door, which was open, revealed many dresses hung up in an orderly fashion. After showing me the upstairs, she escorted me down to the basement where the same order prevailed.

She asked me to call her Elsie.

In the weeks that followed I made several visits. She always greeted me warmly and led me to her desk, where her bills were neatly stacked together awaiting my arrival. It seemed that, other than being unable to manage her financial affairs and groping for the right words, she was able to function quite well.

One day when I returned from doing her banking, I smelled pie baking in the oven. The table was set for two with her best china. I asked her who was coming. She smiled and said, "You."

As time passed, I pieced together some of her background. The youngest of four girls, she stayed home doing the cleaning and cooking for the family, while they worked in a textile factory. No household chore was too difficult for her. She was a born homemaker. She yearned for a house of her own that she could furnish to her own taste. The tenement where they lived was small and crowded. In her twenties, she fell in love with a young factory worker. Realizing how important owning her own home was to her, he tried to save some money from his pay check every week. Years flew by and many pressing obligations interfered, but when they were both in their late forties, they finally married and had saved enough money to buy their house. Elsie cherishes the house where she now lives and every item in there is treated with loving care.

Several years of happiness ensued. Elsie was content to do what she loved most in the world—keeping house. However, after ten years, her husband died and Elsie was distraught. Her sisters never married and were still living at home. Elsie asked her favorite sister to come to live with her. This arrangement worked out well until her sister developed Alzheimer's disease. For a few years Elsie took care of her sister until she had to be placed in a nursing home.

Meanwhile, her parents died and her other two sisters took sick and went to another nursing home.

Now more than ever Elsie scrubbed and cleaned her house. She lived sparingly on the small pension left her by her husband. She had no desire to leave her house except when her friends took her shopping.

Several months after I started helping Elsie, there was no answer when I phoned her. The friend who was to take her shopping, found her laying on the floor in the bedroom, unable to move. She was taken to the hospital.

When I visited her in the hospital, she seemed to be fine. No bones were broken. As usual, she was happy to see me. Her words seemed a little more jumbled, but she seemed to comprehend when I spoke to her. However, after being in the hospital for a week, the hospital psychiatrist deemed her incompetent and she was taken away to a nursing home. A guardian was appointed. Her house was put up for sale so that the money from the sale of the house could be used for her care in the nursing home. Because of her jumbled speech, she was unable to defend herself.

My next visit was to the nursing home. Elsie cried and as best as I could understand, she said 'They carried me here. I want to go home. No one will listen to me.'

To make matters worse, she was placed in the nursing home where her sisters were. When the nurse took her to see them, they didn't know her. This was very upsetting to her and she cried when attempting to tell me about it.

On my frequent visits, Elsie's hands, which had never been idle, lay limply in her lap. Bereft of all her prized possessions, she sat forlornly in the sparsely furnished room in the nursing home.

Six months later, she died.

Elaine Kaufman

The Satin Dress

Sitting forlornly in my rented beach cottage at Narragansett, RI, I was thinking about my uncertain future. October was almost over and my rent was due. I was a real estate sales person and had not made a sale in several months. Opening my front door to bring in the morning paper, gusts of tangy salt air refreshingly hit my face. How I loved living near the ocean.

The sharp, shrill ring of my telephone shook me out of my reverie. My real estate broker's deep, guttural voice pierced my ears.

"Daphne," he said, "I have a good property just listed that I am sure you will be able to sell. The price is good. The owner, Jannette Passine, is in her eighties and is now in a nursing home. She has been renting it, but now wants to sell."

"Jannette Passine, the designer?"

He replied, "Yes, that's her"

After receiving the directions to the house in Pt. Judith, five miles from Narragansett, I quickly grabbed my parka, started up my '79 Volkswagon and headed for the house.

Driving along the ocean road, I opened the car window to inhale the invigorating salt air. The sharp wind blew my hair astray. How I loved watching the white capped waves smashing against the sea wall.

When I arrived at the neat looking yellow, salt box seaside cottage, framed by the finely cut bushes, my hopes soared. This was my lucky day. Having been told by my broker that the key was hidden under a flower pot on the back patio, I went to the back of the house. My hopes vanished when I saw the condition of the house. The glass doors of the house facing the patio were completely broken. Glass was everywhere. Stepping gingerly over the broken glass, I entered the house. The house was completely trashed. Empty beer cans and garbage were strewn around every room. Flies were buzzing around the piles of garbage. Nothing seemed to be worth salvaging. Scanning the living room, I saw two cartons in one of the corners. Looking into the cartons, I discovered many pictures of a long gone era. Surely these pictures must have some meaning to the owner of the house. They weren't ordinary pictures, but of women dressed in the high fashion of the 1920s. In the second carton there were sketches of many public buildings, some of which I recognized as Rhode Island buildings.

My disappointment over the condition of the house was diminished by my curiosity to meet the owner of the house.

I called my broker the next day and described the horrendous state of the house. I also asked him if he could contact the owner to ask her if I could bring the cartons to her. This was soon arranged and the following Saturday, with the two cartons packed in my car, I was ready to make the hours drive from Narragansett.

Having called ahead, when I arrived at the nursing home, I was escorted to a private room. It was sparsely furnished with a bureau, a small table and a rocking chair.

In the chair sat a thin, hunched, old woman, hands folded in her lap and dozing.

The attendant, who took me to the room, shook her gently to awaken her. The attendant said that most of the time she sat listlessly in her rocking chair, seldom talking to anyone or participating in the many activities offered at the nursing home. After a few minutes she slowly opened her sleepy eyes. I introduced myself and told her about the condition of the house.

She sighed and said, "I suppose I can arrange to get a crew in to clean up. Perhaps the yard man can help."

In an attempt to raise her spirits, I then explained how I had found the cartons in her house. I placed them on the table near her chair. Slowly looking at the pictures inside, she opened her eyes wide and exclaimed, "I thought these were lost. How happy you have made

me!" Seeming to come out of her lethargy, she shuffled through the
stacks, telling me who the person was in each photo. I seemed to
travel back in time with her as each picture brought back happy
memories of many years ago. As she sifted through them, she told
me about her life.

From the age of ten she loved to draw, especially creating dress
designs. Her drawing pad was always with her. She won a scholarship
to the Rhode Island School of Design. At the age of twenty, she
entered a contest. The winner would win a year in Paris, studying
under a famous designer. She worked day and night, drawing many
creations and won the contest, which covered all her expenses for
the year. Under her teacher's tutelage, she progressed rapidly and
became a top designer. At the end of the year, her teacher asked her
to work for her in her elite dress salon, which catered to the rich
people from all over the world. Many of the pictures in the carton
were of well know actresses and society women taken in the 1920s,
wearing her creations.

When she opened the second carton, her eyes filled with tears. She
found sketches made by the young man she fell in love with. She said
that he was an American, who was studying architecture in Paris.
They had met at a party given by her teacher and they had much in
common because he came from Rhode Island. He had been promised
an apprenticeship with a large architectural firm in Rhode Island the
following year. Later, when he asked her to marry him, she hesitated
because she was fulfilling her dream of working for a renowned
designer in Paris. The old woman, while wiping away tears, sighed
and continued. She said that love won out and she married the young
architect and moved back to Rhode Island.

Curiosity overtook me and I asked if she would mind telling me
about her husband. "Oh yes, I'd be delighted to tell you about him.
He became a well know architect, designing several public buildings

in Rhode Island. We had many years of happiness. Our only child, a daughter, lives in England and is so busy with her own life that I seldom see her. My darling husband died ten years ago. During his last years, we lived in our lovely beach house, which you have seen. After he died, I tried to stay in the house we both loved, but because of my failing health, I rented the house and came here."

Afraid that I might be tiring her with all this excitement, I said that I would go, but would return to talk more about the business of the house.

Leaning on her cane, she stood up and said to me, "Please come with me. I want to show you something." She opened the door to the closet, which held several crumbled plastic bags, stiff with age. Proudly, with shaking hands, she unsnapped the plastic bags, revealing the most exquisitely designed dresses I had ever seen. Smiling at me with a twinkle in her eye, she asked me if I would like to try on a couple of them. She said that they looked to be my size.

Astonished, I picked out a white satin dress of the twenties with a dropped hip-line, which had come back in style. It fit me perfectly. I felt like Cinderella. Her eyes sparkled with joy, saying, "It would give me great pleasure if you will take it."

Thanking her profusely, we hugged each other. I could hardly believe that this animated woman, who was hugging me so tightly, was the same woman I had met a few hours ago sitting listlessly in her rocking chair.

It was strange that I completely forgot about my financial woes. I had put the house and its problems in the back of my mind. I had renewed hope that things would get better. I felt uplifted and now all I could think of was where I could go to wear the magnificent satin dress.

My Dad

Now, as I, an old lady, sit alone in my sunny apartment, watching some young children laughing and carefree outside my windows, memories of my own early years flood my mind.

My life revolved around my Dad, whom I loved dearly. Since my mother was confined to the house taking care of my baby sister, Dad and I spent many hours together walking down to the ocean several blocks away watching the large boats sail by, trying to guess their destinations. Dad was a sail-maker. We lived in a modest three bedroom house in a coastal city.

In the winter Dad built a big, long plank with a sled at each side called a reaches. By pouring many pails of water down the hill in front of our house, he made it slippery enough to slide down. Dad would yell, 'Abby keep your legs up, be careful.' After several hours of sliding, Dad and I skated on the circular pond over the stone wall next to the hill where we sledded. The pond was quite large and deep, with a small island in the middle where we stood many times to rest, exhausted and exhilarated, rubbing our hands to keep warm, waving to neighbors skating by.

Grandpa, who lived next door, had a span of horses, which he attached to a surrey with a fringe on top. Dad used the surrey to take me and my friends riding. We sat close together on the benches on the sides of the surrey. We stopped several times to pick up friends along the way, and off we'd go to the fair in the next town. We sang our favorite songs to the accompaniment of the local fiddler who also came along. He was a fat, jovial fellow, who could play any song we requested.

In the spring, Dad and I picked mulberries, which stained my chin and fingertips and the bushes left white scratches on my shins. Later Dad made wine from the mulberries and all the neighbors came in to taste it.

One of my fondest memories is of the time Dad and I watched the big fire at a mansion down the hill. The brightness of the fire lit the sky for miles around. We saw it burn to the ground. Next day when Dad and I went to look, all that remained was the stone basement, which housed bunks and chains where the owner had kept his slaves.

On my tenth birthday everything changed. The aging owner of the sail-making business made Dad a partner. The business prospered. Dad rejected his former life. Mother said that prosperity went to his head. He bought a red sports car with a rumble seat. Instead of spending time with me, he cruised around in his new car. Before long he made many new friends and went to parties with them. Family life no longer interested him. I was discarded like an old doll.

One spring morning Mother and I saw a strange man standing across the street from our house looking for someone. He had a big mustache and was wearing white flannel pants and a straw hat. Dad saw him too and skipped out the back door to avoid him. Later we learned that he was the father of the girl Dad was seeing.

A few weeks later a strange woman called my mother and asked her to come to her house, saying that she had something important to discuss.

Mother took my sister and me over to the exclusive section of town where she lived. The imposing house was set way back from the road. It was a large white house with columns in the front. We were ushered into an elegant living room. The woman who greeted us was dressed beautifully in a tailored suit. She glared at our shabby clothes. She explained that her young daughter of nineteen was in love with my father and that she would give my mother $2000 if she would divorce him. Mother was humiliated, refused and pulled me hastily out of the house.

I often thought afterwards that Mother should have taken the money because before long Dad left anyway.

A few months after he left, I needed a pair of white shoes for the school choir. I asked Mother if I could go down to Dad's store to ask him for money for shoes and also to ask him to come back home. Mother said, "You can ask him if you want to, but I'm sure he'll refuse to come back." I was confident that he would return if I asked him. I dressed in my best white dress which had a big sailor collar and big red bow and skipped the several blocks to the waterfront, where he had his store. The first floor of the building was rented to several fruit and vegetable grocers and the second floor housed the sail loft where he worked. I climbed the long flight of stairs trembling with anticipation. Dad seemed surprised to see me, but smiled and said that he was glad to see me. I asked him for the money for shoes and if he would come back home. He said coldly, "Your mother doesn't want me." I said, "Yes she does, she said I could ask you." He handed me a quarter for my shoes and didn't say anything else. Gripping the quarter in one hand and wiping the tears from my eyes with the other, I stumbled down the steep flight of stairs.

From then on, nothing was the same. One disaster followed another. Dad divorced mother, married the nineteen-year-old diamond merchant's daughter, and had three more children, whom I never saw. Dad's father told us all about his new life, which now consisted of cocktail parties and good times. My mother, sister and I were soon forgotten.

We moved to a small apartment in a three family house in the city away from the ocean that I loved. Mother went to work. My dreams of going to college faded away. I had to go to work at sixteen to help support my mother and sister.

Many years later, I yearned to see my Dad. I summoned enough courage to call. He only lived in the next town. He seemed happy to hear from me but said that he was busy and would call me back. I didn't have a phone. That was the last time I spoke to my Dad.

Visit

I arrived to do his shopping on a chilly September afternoon. Pushing my way through the tall, unkempt bushes and grass, which hadn't been cut all summer, I reached the door and rang the bell. After ringing several times, I heard feet shuffling slowly and bolts being unlocked. He welcomed me, his deep blue eyes sparkling under his bushy gray eyebrows. Making room for me to come in by brushing aside empty cat food tins, strewn papers and empty bags, he led me to a chair from which he had just removed a stack of unopened letters. He combed through the jumble on a nearby table for his checkbook and grocery list. Angered because he couldn't find them, he sat down defeated. He sighed, stating that his mind was not working as quickly as it once did. He said that he was frustrated by the chaos around him, but could do nothing to change it.

I interceded, helped him find his checkbook and suggested food items he had bought the previous week when I did his shopping. Saying that he felt better, he read me some notes he had written about the events of the day before — a call from his out-of-town son, being awakened during the night by a tooth ache. Then he read a note asking me to find out about a neighbor who had fallen in her house and had been taken to the hospital.

As he apologized for taking up so much of my time and thanked me profusely, I left to do the banking and shopping for him.

MARY H. KENNEDY

"I have always written," said Mary Kennedy in a recent telephone interview. She began writing stories in her childhood and went on writing them during high school, where Dorothy Allen was one of her teachers. During her working years, writing was still her hobby. She joined *The Rhode Island Short Story Club* as a young woman and continued active into her retirement. She was also a faithful member of the *Creative Writing Group* at Hamilton House Senior Center. The following selection from her "Archives" is printed here with her permission.

SHORT STORY
    Party Pieces

Party Pieces

Mr. Brown, in shirtsleeves and vest, stood at the front end of his basement Studio checking the seating arrangement set up theatre style. With upraised hand held near his face and forefinger moving slightly, he counted the rows of unmatched chairs. The lighting, in his opinion, was adequate, reflecting as it did off the whitewashed walls. Turning, he noted the level-with-the-floor stage area, where he had placed two chairs and a tall plant stand on which a potted red geranium was displayed, needed attention. He moved the chairs and plant stand more to the right.

"Quite right," muttered Mr. Brown.

He entered the furnace room just off stage left, which would serve nicely with its one arm chair and two straight chairs for the performers to rest. He adjusted the furnace to provide some heat as it was late fall, but it must not be too warm.

Returning to the main salon, he glanced around to be sure the pictures on the walls were hanging straight and slightly adjusted the ones of Ted Shawn and Ruth St. Denis, side by side, in elongated frames. Shuffling through a row of chairs to the opposite wall, he straightened the photograph of Maurice Evans costumed for his role as Hamlet. He opened the upright piano, which was against that wall.

Hearing the voices of Miss Senecal and Mrs. Allenby coming from the room off stage right, he hurriedly put on his suit coat before appearing in their presence. The room had been a coal cellar, but Mr. Brown had it refurbished as a fully-applianced kitchen.

"Ladies, have you found everything you will need?"

"Oh yes, Mr. Brown," replied Miss Senecal, who was attempting to match cups with saucers and setting out spoons.

"Everything is fine," said Mrs. Allenby, beginning to carefully slice the loaves of Pound and Madeira cakes. She addressed her partner,

"Don't forget the napkins, Miss Senecal!"

"I won't, Mrs. Allenby, and don't you forget the tea!" Both ladies laughed at their private little jokes. Mr. Brown nodded approval and, returning to the Studio, sat down with his papers to prepare the evening program.

Mr. Brown was a bachelor with two passions: music and the drama. His given name was William, but few of his acquaintances dared call him Bill or Will. He was a draftsman for the Planning Division of the City Government and the sober attention necessary to every detail of his work carried over into his avocation. One would scarcely surmise from his demeanor and attire that he could remotely desire to be a member of the acting profession. Mr. Brown was of Scottish parentage and almost always was of an age when he could have played the role of Mr. Pickwick to perfection.

His greatest enjoyment was to plan evenings of music, poetry and play readings for his adherents and friends. Generally, there were older men and women, some married, some single, who looked forward to an evening out. It was a time when the elderly were unafraid to walk alone on Benefit Street at night. There was no reason to fear.

It was 7:30 p.m. by the kitchen clock when the guests began to arrive, the chairs to be occupied, and the hum of polite chatter to fill the room. Promptly, at 8 o'clock, Mr. Brown stepped to stage center and began his greetings.

"My friends, you are welcome to..." He was interrupted by a commotion at the entranceway and all activity ceased, to watch the arrival of the featured performer of the evening. Madame Yolanda Ambrosini, the famous Federal Hill diva, was a tall woman with a dark face, large and masculine. Her costume was a collection of costumes: skirt on top of skirt, blouse on top of blouse, numerous scarves of various colors around a thick neck. She wore a red velvet turban on the front of which was fastened a large ostrich plume.

A quantity of necklaces, rings and bracelets glistened and jangled as she moved.

Mr. Brown came forward, graciously extending his arms, and Madame, rummaging in her large carry-all bag, brought out several sheaves of music, and thrust them into his hands.

"My music!" she said and without invitation swept into the green-room, where a gentleman, who could not find a seat in the audience, was sitting. From her carry-all, Madame extracted a tall medicine bottle and noisily placed it on the table and plumped down into the armchair.

"I have a cold," she announced, looking through heavy-lidded eyes.

"I'm sorry," said the gentleman, "do you have a fever?"

Madame stood, ignoring the question and the ostrich plume brushed the ceiling.

"That's why I'm taking this. It's pineapple juice."

To the sound of clinking bracelets, she uncorked the bottle and drank from it as the sharp odor of bourbon permeated the room.

"There. I'll be able to go on now. It's good for the throat."

Mr. Brown called on three members from the audience to read poems by Robert Frost, Ralph Waldo Emerson, and Matthew Arnold. Each one was received politely. It was then time for Madame to perform and Mr. Brown made the introduction. The audience applauded quietly, the accompanist took his place at the piano and Madame Ambrosini sailed out of the furnace room prepared to enchant her audience with selections from the operas of *Puccini*, *Gluck* and *Bizet*.

Chester Clark, a tall, youthful-looking man with white hair, a late arrival, slipped into the furnace room to take the remaining empty chair which had been placed nearest the door.

Madame finished "poor little Mimi's aria" to polite applause and bowing continuously as she gradually stepped backward toward the stage exit. Chester, unfortunately, was not quick enough to withdraw his stretched out legs and with a great gasp, Madame tripped, fell backwards across his lap, the upper part of her body well into the furnace room, and her head butting the table.

The turban flew off as she screamed, "Save the bottle. Don't let it fall!"

Chester strove vainly to grab the bottle, lost his balance and the two rolled onto the floor. The gentleman had reached over in time to grab the sticky bottle.

"Oh dear, oh dear!" said Mr. Brown coming in to view the situation, but perplexed as to what to grab or how to assist man or woman. Hovering over them he kept saying "This is terrible! Terrible!"

He could not lift Madame alone and poor Chester could not move with her weight pinning him down. Two gentlemen from the audience had to be called upon to help.

"My hat. I want my hat," Madame Ambrosini shouted, trying to cover her wispy, uncombed, uncurled hair with her hands.

One of the men retrieved her turban, the feather surprisingly intact. Madame was now sitting on her chair and grabbing the hat, she thrust it on her head, vigorously pushing under wayward spikes of hair. When the turban was in place to her satisfaction and the bottle was once again upright on the table, she immediately went faint and began to moan.

"Oh, what happened? Where am I? What happened?"

"You had a little fall and in an effort to protect you, Chester and you both together fell to the floor," explained Mr. Brown.

"Oh," Madame looked at Chester and seductively smiled, murmured, "Gracias."

Mrs. Allenby and Miss Sencecal took advantage of the interruption to retire to the kitchen to prepare the tea and to laugh unobserved. The audience quieted down. Mr. Brown read a poem by Byron.

Meanwhile in the furnace room, Madame was comforting herself with sips from her bottle and offering it to Chester, who readily accepted.

After finishing reading, Mr. Brown called again on Madame Ambrosini, but only, he gently added, if she felt up to it. Indeed she did! And she came forth to sing her best, playing to the house, as she heard whispered phrases of "Gallant woman!" "What a trouper!" "Beautiful voice, too."

The applause Madame received was tumultuous for her singing, but also for her honoring the "show must go on" tradition. Her performance closed the program.

General chatter filled the room as Mrs Allenby came round with cups of hot tea, followed by Miss Senecal with sugar, cream, lemons and napkins.

"Thank you so much." "How nice!"

Then both ladies circulated with plates of sliced Madeira and Pound cake.

"What lovely cake!" "How generous of Mr. Brown to provide two kinds." "Oh, he is so good."

Madame Ambrosini was sufficiently recovered from her fall and triumph to be prevailed upon to have some tea.

"Oh, it will do you good. And some Madeira cake?"

"Madeira?" Madam's eyebrows rose in eagerness. The white plume trembled.

"Yes. Or maybe you would prefer the Pound cake? We have plenty of it."

"I'll have the Madeira," said Madame Ambrosini, reaching toward the cake plate.

Frances L. O'Donnell

Fran is the mother of five children, eleven grandchildren and one great grandchild. She enjoyed years of nursing and teaching and has a great love for piano and cello; her passion in writing led her to write stories at an early age. Teaching in the literacy program and English as a Second Language remains important to her. She is interested in libraries, architectural design in Providence, RI, and taking photos of trees and landscapes which also serve as an inspiration to her work. Being a member of *The Rhode Island Short Story Club*, embraces her dream to work more vigorously to publish her novel, memoir and children's stories. She has received *Blaisdell Awards* for several of her short stories. Fran is an enthusiastic member and the president of the *RISSC*, keeping the faith to maintain the Club's ongoing growth and spirit.

Short Stories
> The Writing House*
> Charles and Joanna
> The Christmas Tree

Essays
> What Would You Have Done
> My Escape Into The Cave
> The SS Montrachet

Poem
> Sisters

Blaisdell Award

THE WRITING HOUSE

It was late and Sara decided to leave in the morning. Her entire day was spent packing and saying goodbye to family and friends. Sara's eyes filled with tears as she thought of the surprise bon voyage party her children gave her. With them all grown and exploring their chances in the world, she now knew it was time to separate from the anchors of who she thought she should be as a mother and rediscover a part of her that might be buried.

While switching television stations, she heard the late show host laughing and was interested in what she heard.

"And I repeat," said the author of the book, *The Oid Stone Can't Be Squeezed Any More*. A former actress of the Mansion Series became even more successful after her new book was published. Sara sat up with eyebrows raised and felt that a torch had been lit under her feet. The author then flipped her hair back, leaving a few small red curls hugging her forehead, then said in a high pitched tone, "And another thing, women barely whisper their desires, because they are too busy meeting their many challenges and challengers."

Sara laughed out loud and thought that a brigade of angels had been sent to her. The host, appearing astonished said, "Now wait a minute Miss Lamoure, women get many breaks in life."

Miss Lamoure then stood up, adjusted her short red skirt, laughed then said, "Ah, yuh Mike, but we must admit that a woman's development is often delayed while raising a family."

The late show host gazed at Miss Lamoure not knowing what to say, then in a smug tone asked, "OK, WHY?"

"Ahem," she said, in a melodious tone, "Could it be while raising children and having many years of busy schedules, not to mention the taxi service, be one of the reasons?" Miss Lamoure appeared satisfied now!

The host then grinned, knowing she won the pitch for her book, and said "Well I hope your book helps that gang out there."

Miss Lamoure, very composed said, "Well you know Mike, all I've been saying is that for some of us gals, there is no more juice left in the stone, get it?"

The host turned then looked at the audience and smiled, then said, "I get it."

The audience took over, and the applause was as one would expect.

Sara felt some satisfaction in knowing that another woman understood the challenges of raising children. She smiled as she jotted down the name of the book, although she knew this was one title she would not forget.

Tomorrow would be a new challenge, a new beginning, and a new journey, one that would be unfamiliar to her. She would miss everyone. She would miss her children's un-faded smiles, but the journey was not forever and she would be in touch with her family often. The idea of taking care of just her felt somewhat friendless, yet she knew it was time to surrender to her desires and connect to new dreams and reconnect with old ones.

Sara felt that the love, time and patience she gave her children were her legacy, their inheritance, one that she was proud of. Sara had no regrets for her past journey of motherhood. But now, it was time for her to have new discoveries.

The morning came quickly. With her SUV all packed and ready, all she had to do was eat breakfast and leave. She no longer felt fear, only excitement. Sara's experiences of travel were few, yet her yearning and interest to explore was heightened. She closed the door behind her, and called to her dog Mutsy, her mascot, her lucky charm. She sat quietly while Sara tied a bright pink and green scarf around her neck. The drive would be long, clear cross country, but Mutsy would be her company, her mentor. The turn of the key, the motor on, brake off, Sara was off to her new world. She felt a tear fall on her cheek. It was a tear of hope, a tear of joy, a tear of affection toward herself for keeping her promise to take the journey. Leaving sunny California for the mountains and wooded landscapes would be a new challenge and experience for Sara. She was eager now and welcomed the thought of walking by the streams and brooks at sunset.

It was time for her to write her story and think about her fruitful past experiences. Sara began to think about the time she was nine years old and living with her grandmother. An excitement began to grow in her. It was catchy, because Mutsy wagged her tail at every new town they entered. Breakfast in each town was enlightened by the sight of vibrant colorful birds, singing their songs and living their lives. Sara smiled and felt the security in what she was doing.

Almost there, Sara stopped to check the street map; only one block away! The house was easy to find as the moving truck had already arrived. As she pulled up, she was astonished at what she saw. The house was surrounded by very large trees with a hint of autumn, while others had a glow of pure orange, red and gold. Closest to the house, an unusual scattering of lavender leaves hugged the graceful branches of one of the tallest trees that held a small child's swing. There was a blue mist coming from the stream just a few yards away from the house. The area was breathtaking; Sara stood amazed at the brilliant setting. To the right of the house, stood mountains embraced by many soft white snow caps. The sun was still high enough to reflect the trees and flowers. The yellow and red mums lay against the old cobble stone walk.

There were boxes everywhere awaiting Sara's direction. She began to gather her personal treasures one by one, and place them on the top landing of the old porch. She stood back and looked at her new dwelling and smiled with approval. Mutsy also approved as she wagged her tail and barked playfully.

Sara was surprised and grateful that this day finally happened. A whisper of wind gave a creaking sound as it moved the faded sign that hung crooked from the house; it was worn and had peeling paint with curled edges. The tired letters lay against the old wooden sign that read *The Writing House*. Sara would write amongst the largest and oldest trees and on two acres of land. She would now have a place to write and would fill the house with promises and keep them. This house would be there for those who needed a place to write even if for only an hour.

She continued to appraise what needed to be done. Sara knew that a few buckets of paint, using the colors of the birds that entertained her during her trip, would be compelling. A flower and vegetable garden would follow.

As the weeks passed, Sara's plans became a reality. The sign was painted a bright candy pink and a pickle green color. The house that once held many faded peels of paint now wore a sedate color of sage green with bright pink shutters; each color bouncing off the other. Sara found that she was smiling more often and feeling hopeful about her new adventure.

New traffic had developed since the bus now stopped at the towns' market, and Sara was curious about the new activity in town. Despite the wind and rain, she decided to go to the market and replenish her supplies for the week. As she was filling her basket, she overheard two women, each carrying a suitcase and duffle bag, ask the clerk about *The Writing House*. They had heard that *The Writing House* was taking applications for an in-service program. Sara, smiling with enthusiasm, introduced herself. After all introductions and sharing, she invited them to see the House. Although Sara had not intended to have overnighters, the idea peaked her interest. While entering the house, the women appeared elated that they were in the company of another writer and interested person. "It's never too late right?" Sadie asked.

Her friend Leila laughed and said, "I hope not, I didn't come all this way for nothing, and after all, we're not that old yet!"

Sara warmly smiled at the women and became more interested in how they learned about *The Writing House*. Sadie was pleased by Sara's interest and said that a few years ago there was an article in their local newspaper about a woman who advertised poetry readings and seminars in writing memoirs and fiction.

"Apparently," Sadie said, "the woman had a bed and breakfast type situation for writers."

Sara listened intently as she served the tea with her grandmother's light pink china, delicately designed with small pink flowers and soft jade green leaves. She became inspired and asked the women how long they would like to stay at *The Writing House*. Leila, sipping her tea, colorfully answered in a high pitched tone, "As long as necessary to get us started on our writing!" As soon as she blurted out the words, she looked embarrassed; her face became flushed, and a bead of sweat sat atop her brow. Sara felt compassion for Leila and tenderly said, "It's ok to dream, because without them, we may loose sight of the real meaning of our life, our substance and our spirit; not to mention our purpose! Who we are and what we want is important for re-developing ourselves."

Leila appreciated Sara's kind words and quietly said, "Thank you."

Sara smiled then said, "I allowed myself the privilege of dreaming and welcomed new ideas, because it gave me the determination to find a place to write and re-connect with myself. I accepted support during the transition as it made it easier for me to keep my dream alive."

Sadie, now more open, discussed the loss of their husbands and their lives up to this point. After their long discussions, Sara understood their urgency to write and wanted to help them attain their goal as well as her own. They discussed their commitment to themselves and were willing to do what was necessary to write their stories. Sara showed the women all six bedrooms; each painted a vibrant or sedate color. Leila selected the watermelon pink and Sadie chose the aqua blue room. The three sunrooms that wrapped around the house had panoramic views of the many snow-capped mountains and unending landscapes of tall pine trees.

Sara awakened very early the next morning, excited that she was now the new proprietor of *The Writing House*. Sadie and Leila also awakened eager to get started, each one offering one idea after the other. The momentum of writing had begun. They sat by the fire each night, sharing ideas about their writing of the day. After three months, there were twelve women now writing with one another.

The weeks that followed were vigorous and productive. A union had emerged amongst the women; each one developing sensitivity toward each others' goals. Chopin, Bach and Vivaldi's music were among the greats to inspire, relax and generate new thoughts during their process of writing.

One evening, Sara began to talk about her children and how she missed them. She became a bit philosophical and said, *The Place That Once Housed My Babies Is Quiet Now!* It was so quiet you could hear a pin drop. The ladies shed their tears and talked about new challenges they were looking forward to. The women were passionate about their work and supported each other's talent.

It was TV night. Sara was surprised that Miss Lamoure, her new favorite author, was on the late show. Miss Lamoure, looking her usual vivacious and animated self, pleasantly stated, "Ladies, claim your inheritance, reach for the string of pearls!" Mike began to laugh, and said, "ok Miss Lamoure, what are you up to now?"

Miss Lamoure got up, adjusted her skirt, swung her hair back with a precise rhythm, smiled as she looked at the audience, and with a smirk on her face said, "ok Mike, here goes, Ladies, consider your-self the pearl being supported by the knot. Now, think of the knot as the work of faith, bringing you to another plateau. So then, one might say that the knots are faith supporting each pearl, which could be the gifts of grace." Drawing in a deep breath, she then continued, "The magic of pearls bring love and trust with supportive ideas that will cradle you. So ladies, be the pearl and claim your inheritance now!"

Shaking his head, Mike said, "I don't get it."

Miss Lamoure placed her hand in Mike's hand then said, "Listen, despite the support of the knot, the pearl is able to move freely in rotation. When one is consistent of knowing the truth and learning, one sits like the beautiful pearl being supported by the knot."

"So, what are you saying?" Mike asked.

"Well, I am trying to convey an important message to women, to love themselves more and be loved; like when the knot cradles the pearl." Mike smiled pleasingly.

Sara began to cry, and reminisced about the time she was nine years old and living with her grandmother. The women urged Sara to tell her story. "Well," Sara said, as she sniffled, "It was fall and a difficult time for my mother as she was getting a divorce. My Aunt Helen and Uncle Rene lived upstairs from my grandmother. My Aunt was very helpful in preparing me for school. She gave me a perm and bought me a beautiful new pink flowered dress. It was my first day in a new school in a new neighborhood. As I was about to leave the door my aunt Helen placed a pearl necklace around my neck, insuring that the clasp was secure. They were beautiful and I felt special wearing my aunt's pearls. I touched them throughout the day, making sure they were still there.

Upon my return from school, a student from my class, grabbed at my neck and broke my string of pearls. Shocked at what had happened, I quickly picked up each pearl and ran home, holding my fist tightly so that I wouldn't lose any pearls. My aunt, awaiting my arrival, saw that my necklace was broken. She hugged me as I sobbed and assured me that everything would be alright, because I was ok. She also promised to fix the pearl necklace, and she did. I will always treasure my aunt's lessons in love.

"It took me a while to forgive that classmate, as they were my first string of pearls, but my mother helped me to realize that it was freeing to forgive. She would often say that 'forgiveness is likened to the waves of the sea caressing the sand.' That idea has helped me in many situations."

Everyone hugged Sara and thanked her for sharing.

Newspaper articles of *The Writing House* were appearing everywhere, and the women's stories were being published. A new magical club was upon itself. Even the university had a special ceremony for their accomplishments, and issued each member a blue and gold cap that held a tassel at each corner. The ceremony was thought of as British, because the person receiving the accolades must wear their tasseled hat and hold their arms behind them as they walk zigzag up the isle of the auditorium; the British call it *The Dance* because of the characteristic and graceful way of walking. They are allowed one chant before receiving their award. It was said that Sara's chant was, *My Children!*

Sara sat on the porch step and thought about the many women she had greeted and housed and felt honored to have had the opportunity to be part of the gift of writing and caring about others. She was also grateful to the many famous authors who volunteered their time giving workshops to the many inspired women.

Sara is still amazed at the number of women who continue to arrive at the corner market, looking for *The Writing House.*

There is a colorful sign at the bus stop that now says; *If You Love To Write, Visit The Writing House.*

The Pearl section: January, 1985
The Trip section: February, 12th, 2007
Journal ideas from my writing group March, 1985

CHARLES AND JO-ANNA

It was that time of year again, when visitors from all over make their way up the mountains to the infamous lodge, *The Inn*. Charles had awakened to the brightest of sunrises, and began to shake as the air was getting increasingly crisp.

At the lodge, all preparations were being made for the many visitors who would come to admire, embrace and celebrate the most colorful time of year, the fall foliage. The old wooden barn is nestled amongst the tallest trees and the most beautiful foliage; colors ranging from a deep red to a sparkling orange and pure butter cream yellow. The trees are slouched enough to hug the side of the old entrance to the barn where the hot cider and cookies are served. Small white lights are everywhere bringing star-like effects throughout the lodge, creating an atmosphere of coziness and magic. Many toys, hand made rag dolls and souvenirs are sold on the first level of the lodge. On the second landing, there is a small restaurant that serves breakfast until closing at five pm daily. The dining room is filled with guests throughout the day, enjoying the cooks' specialty of pancakes and waffles, topped with real maple syrup.

Most guests arrive bundled in warm clothing and furry hats. The children's high pitched voices squeak happily as they explore their chances for a ride on the swings, while their families take pictures of the festive occasion of fall. Mothers are heard calling to their children, 'slow down' and 'come here dear,' as the park gets fuller and the morning grows older.

Once again, having to accept the changes of the season, Charles, the largest of the trees, felt his changes taking place; he began to hold on to any softness that might be left to embrace his body. The spring of his life was leaving faster with each passing day. Near closing time, Charles called to Jo-Anna, his love, his life, "I'm worn out, plain ole' worn out!" he shouted. Jo-Anna began to laugh with her special giggle, and said "Time for bed Charles;" her voice was soft and reassuring. "Tomorrow is another day dear. There will be many more visitors, many children, and barking dogs."

"Yuh, I know, not to mention what the dogs did to my feet today!" he yelled.

In a gentle tone, Jo-Anna said, "You're just tired Charles, after all, it isn't everyday that thousands of people adore you, take your picture and make endearing remarks about how beautiful and special your colors are." Jo-Anna then lowered her head and said, "Rest now dear, listen to the music." Romantic violin music was being played in the lodge, which could be heard from the outdoor speakers. Charles knew he had to accept the many changes that were taking place, but he resisted each year. With Jo-Anna lovingly by his side, and the violin music playing in the background, he finally gave in and fell asleep.

Charles would often comment to his friends that Jo-Anna was the most beautiful of all trees and that in the spring; she was the first to bud and bring soft pink flowers with her branches falling gracefully to the bottom of the old cobblestone walk. Of course, knowing of his love for Jo-Anna, his friends would nod with approval and agree that she was the most graceful and colorful of all trees.

Charles had awakened to loud whipping wind sounds. He looked about and called to Jo-Anna. There were leaves blowing everywhere. He began to tremble and noticed that his friends looked different. There was no color in sight and no visitors taking pictures.

Jo-Anna then called "Charles, Charles, where are you dear?"

"I'm here, right here, next to you darling." he said. "Jo-Anna, what's happened to you my sweet love?" he shouted, still shivering. He looked at her again and tried to make some sense out of what had happened to them; he had forgotten what the changes look like. In a saddened tone, Charles then said, "Jo-Anna, my darling, our leaves, they're all gone."

"I know dear," she said in a caring tone, "try to accept the changes my love and the transition won't be so hard for you." Jo-Anna smiled at Charles endearingly and said, "It's just another season Charles, and you know, we will feel warm again soon."

He looked away, embarrassed, and asked in a brooding tone, "When will we be warm again Jo-Anna, when?"

She looked at Charles adoringly and said, "Well, another holiday will be here soon. We'll be decorated with small white lights and many frills. It's called the holiday of Christmas."

Charles' face lit up and in a more gentle and hopeful tone said, "Oh, that's right, I remember now."

Jo-Anna smiled then said, "And before you know it, spring will be here, and we will dance again in the sunlight and smell the beautiful flowers and buds."

Charles looked at Jo-Anna tenderly and said, "Jo-Anna, will you marry me?" She lovingly answered, "We are married Charles!"

January, 2005

THE CHRISTMAS TREE

It was a cold winter night with snow falling quickly. As large white flakes accumulated, the ground became thickened with snow. There were blustering winds creating high drifts that lay against store-front doorways, fences and many barriers. With blizzard warnings in effect, the village stores would close early this evening. I hurried to the market place to buy my tree. It was Christmas time, my favorite holiday. As I parked my car I noticed a small girl holding her mother's hand. She had her nose pressed against the toy store window. Her little nose and hands were reddened from the cold.

The store-front was filled with dolls, trucks and colorful toys, all displayed in a compelling fashion. It was a fantasy-filled-store for any child's desires. While watching the little girl, I was reminded of the time I was her age. My favorite trip to the village was to stop at the toy store and look inside the window to see if the special rag doll was still there. I would look at Mother, somewhat eager, but never asked her for the doll. Mother always found a way to give us a special Christmas, but she never knew of my desire for the special rag doll. Each Christmas brought back the many memories of my past.

Today was a big day for me; today I would get my tree. As I arrived at the market place, "I'm dreaming of a white Christmas" could be heard from the loud speakers. The spirit of the holiday season was obvious as people were humming Christmas tunes and looking joyful as they shopped for their tree. The rush was on as the snow storm was picking up and the streets were getting more heavily covered with snow. The attendant shivered as he held up many trees awaiting my approval. When I finally nodded yes, he smiled with relief and placed it in the trunk of my car. This was a happy time for me; shopping for my first tree had become an achievement. As I dragged it into my cozy apartment, I began to think about my childhood again and the many times we wanted all the trimmings that went with Christmas; Father thought of buying a tree, decorations or a toy as frivolous spending. I knew that one day I would change the circumstances of my holiday.

And I did! There it was, my tree, beautifully shaped, standing in the holder, tall and straight. I placed my special star on first. It was as I remembered, likened to my friend Anna's. A small sparkling angel lay at each corner with a light attached to each one. I stood for quite a while and stared at the beautiful star. The angels lit up the entire room. I placed each ornament carefully on the branches. Each one, precious with colorful jewel-like gems, was sparkling and bright. Most of the ornaments were gifts from my brother and some I collected from specialty shops. I loved their uniqueness.

I caught a glimpse of the snow that was piled against the windows. It was snowing harder now, each flake becoming thicker than the last one. The windows were frosted from the cold, and the whipping wind brought loud screeching sounds. I could barely see out of the windows, but I heard the old man Mr. Carlson calling, "Fruits, vegetables, get your fruits and vegetables!" I could not imagine what he was doing out on such a night, but each night Mr. Carlson pushed his cart to sell the fruits and vegetables that he bought from the farmer's market earlier in the day. He pushed the cart each night to contain his memories. He no longer needed to work, but he needed his memories. I wondered how the old man could endure the cold, the wind and the snow. He lived alone in a small house near the bay. Since the death of his wife, his children had encouraged him to move in with them, but he could not leave his wife's gardens or her memories that lay vivid amongst the small rooms. Some walls were covered with his children's paintings from their childhood and other walls were filled with his talented wife's paintings. He had to hold on to the memories of his love, his late wife Victoria. He was Anna's Father, her treasure. Each Christmas, Mr. Carlson gave Anna the pleasure of selecting the family tree. She was my best friend since childhood; I learned all about trees from Anna.

As I held the last sparkling ornament tightly in my hand, I recalled the day my brother gave it to me. It was my eighth birthday. He tenderly told me to hold on to the ornament, 'because,' he said lovingly, 'one day you will place it on your tree, and it will be as beautiful as Anna's.' As the years passed, memories of my brother's love became more endearing.

Thinking back, I recall mother's pleading words, 'please let her have a tree this year;' her voice sounded like a wounded bird. Despite her efforts, Father's answer was the same. On that same day, Anna visited our home, eager to see our decorated tree; Mother looked at me sadly and shook her head, no! I knew only too well what that meant and was too embarrassed to tell Anna. We were both nine-years-old and so taken with the holiday as any child would be at that tender age.

My friend Anna's tree went up that year like all the other times. I so wanted a tree. I decided to wait until early morning to see Anna's decorations. Father wouldn't notice as he left the house before day-light each morning. The sun was about to rise soon but it was still somewhat dark. I jumped the wall and got caught between the rope and the wire that hung from the fence. I scraped my leg and bumped my knee, but persisted with my goal. "NO ADMITTANCE" was the large sign posted on the ten-foot-steel gate. My jacket was still caught on the wire, but I tugged and turned and somehow wiggled myself loose. I was frightened that I would be noticed as a large spotlight beamed across the sand. My eyes began to tear from the cold as I sat on the rock near the wall, waiting for the tree lights to be turned on. I recall trying to regain my composure, as my legs were cold and now bruised from the wire. I wished that I had dressed for the cold morning; I could barely feel my fingers. I wondered what mother would feel knowing I was out this early in the morning. I hoped that she hadn't missed me yet; I had to see the tree.

Anna's small cottage sat in front of the water. The sound of the surf broke with rhythm. Crusty sounds from the ice could be heard as the water crashed at the bay's edge. The momentum quickened as the tide came in. I slipped and fell again as there were many icy spots. Despite my scraped knees, I crawled and climbed back to the wall, wanting to get one look at Anna's tree.

I was on the outside looking in. I wanted to be on the inside with my tree, my presents and my family. The wind got stronger and I felt a blistering chill, but I persisted. Finally, there it was Anna's tree.

All the lights were lit. I will never forget the elation I felt as my heart pounded with excitement. The room was totally lit from the lights that lay on the branches. There were soft white angels attached to each end of the star. The angels' lights sparkled throughout the room, creating a rainbow of colors against the window-panes. A rag doll lay amongst the gifts that were neatly wrapped under the tree. When I saw it, I began to cry. I knew that a doll would not be my Christmas gift. I cried, "I want a tree. I want the angels. I should have a tree like Anna's." As I was leaving, I saw tree branches piled near the edge of Anna's house. I picked up as many as I could and ran home. I recall the excitement I felt and became euphoric when I thought that I too would have a tree, and I too would have a star. I felt a glimmer of hope as I quietly brought the branches home.

Mother was in the kitchen making breakfast, always making certain that I ate well. As I placed the branches into the empty milk bottle I heard Mother whistling her favorite Christmas tunes. I wondered why she was so happy; we couldn't buy a tree and we wore old shoes. Using Mother's strong green string, as we called it, I tied the small candles onto the branches. The milk bottle now sat proudly on the window-sill. I used mother's bright colored buttons and steel safety pins to make my angel star; and tied my bright red hair ribbon at the top of the branch. My star was surely not like Anna's, but the intention was there, and it was my star. I found a bag of nuts that Mother had bought for the holiday and placed them next to the milk bottle that now housed my branches. Using my special pink and green flowered handkerchief, I made a small rag doll and also placed it next to the bag of nuts. I was happy now because I knew that Christmas would come and Santa Claus would too! I stood back and viewed my tree. I was excited! I recall thinking, when Father sees this tree, he will change his mind. He will want a real Christmas tree with a special star.

I decided to light the candles that I so carefully placed on the branches. I wanted to surprise Mother with lights as I had seen at Anna's. The branches looked glorious for a minute or two. By the time Mother appeared, the curtains were in flames. I was shocked, never expecting a fire. Mother seemed worried but she kept her composure; we worked as a team, carrying buckets of water from the kitchen to the living room. Despite being upset, she was quick to put the fire out; fortunately the house didn't burn down. During the chaos, I somehow managed to salvage the bag of nuts and my handmade rag doll.

Father's return was memorable. Mother attempted to give him an explanation, but all he saw was the blackened wall and shredded curtains. I can still recall her lovingly defending me. There was never any talk about getting a tree in our home after that day!

Not long after that holiday, I packed my pink flowered pillowcase with a few clothes, but had difficulty putting my blanket in, because it meant that I was really leaving; and that thought really upset me. Looking back, leaving home would have been a laborious task for a little girl, at such a tender age. As time passed, any thought of leaving home lessened and drew me closer to forgiving father for his lack of sensitivity and generosity.

The following Christmas, I drew many colorful sparkling trees on thick brown paper that Mother brought me from the market. I mixed sugar, water and paints to create sparkling effects on the drawings. Mother smiled endearingly as I placed my creations in each room of our house. There was a contest at my school that year and Mother encouraged me to enter the drawings; she had heard there would be many prizes. Mother was optimistic about my paintings and thought I had talent. With her being so enthusiastic, I decided to enter the contest. I selected the brightest drawing, which had many colorful sugar drippings that created many sparkles and glitter. One week before Christmas, I was elated and surprised to learn that I was a first place winner for the most artistic and sparkling tree. My prize was a beautiful rag doll that I named *Precious*. I will always remember receiving such a thoughtful gift; my life transformed that day. I developed strength and became acquainted with self-reliance and learned that I could make wonderful things happen in my life.

I now placed the last ornament on the tree. It sparkled like no other. It was my brother's gift to me many years past. The kettle began to whistle. I would have my tea now and proudly view my long awaited tree, dressed in jewels! The living room was lit with the same rainbow effects that I once viewed at Anna's house. I felt joy in a promise kept, that one day I would have my tree.

The window was now covered with snow; I could no longer see out of it. The door bell rang; it was Mother, standing in the doorway with special food she prepared, and my brother, holding many presents. Despite the storm, we would celebrate my first tree and holiday together! Our festivity would include eating pork pies and raisin squares for dessert. Mother made them the best. We sat for hours talking about past events and sparse beginnings.

After Father died, Mother had her first tree. My brother bought the largest one he could find. The top was so tall he had to cut off at least two feet. We were young adults now, and found pleasure in watching Mother prepare for the Christmas holiday. We all had trees. We all had angel stars and many presents under our trees.

It is difficult for me to understand why Father chose not to celebrate a most wonderful holiday. He missed out on so much. The memories of those days will always tug at my heart. As a reminder that nothing is impossible, each year, I place my rag doll *Precious* under my Christmas tree.

February, 2001-2002

Frances L. O'Donnell

WHAT WOULD YOU HAVE DONE

Hello, my name is Floppy. Sometimes, I'm called Bobby for short, but that is a whole other story. I am a pointer and known for being a good hunter, and have often been told that my brown and white markings are quite handsome. I want to share my experience with you, about my one and only love, Gertrude. She is a petite, silky gray poodle, who is quite lively and high spirited. She is known for wearing the most colorful ribbons. I met Gertrude during one of my walks.

At five-o'clock each day, my master and I take a walk to the beach. We look forward to our time together. One afternoon, during one of our walks, a gray bushy tailed poodle, wearing a bright pink bow, began to bark at me. She was a real cutie, beautiful and vivacious. I knew right away she was flirting with me and wanted my attention. There was a fence surrounding the yard, just low enough for me to climb over. My master told me to heel and I did, but the poodle kept flirting with me and calling to me to jump the fence. All she wanted was to play; so she yapped, and I went for it!

There I was in the middle of what seemed like a world war. The owner came running out of the house, yelling profanities at me and my master. I recall him shouting, 'Get that dog out of my blank-blank yard.' I think the whole neighborhood heard him. The poodle looked at me through her big brown eyes, with what I thought was a pleading "come back and visit me" look. So there I was, trying to escape, jumping over the fence, while being yelled at and having stones thrown at me. I wasn't sure if I would, or should, re-visit that pretty little flirt, as I found this treatment quite deleterious to my health. It was definitely something that I did not want to experience again. Well, that is, unless Gertrude wanted to see me once more.

Well anyway, I found myself thinking of that sweet thing, and my possibilities of having a family with her. She really peaked my interest.

I hadn't met anyone like her since I was a young lad. She was full of vitality and charm, and so very playful. Each time I thought about visiting her, I also thought about her master's reaction to me and knew I must be nuts to return to that empire of madness. But, I couldn't get her out of my mind; so I made another attempt to see her. What a catastrophe I created. This is what happened.

It had been a while since my master and I walked in Gertrude's neighborhood, but today, we were going in that direction. As we began our walk, I knew I had to be exceptionally obedient, as Gertrude's house was on our route, and I had high hopes of seeing her. So I kept very quiet and obeyed all commands so that I might get a peak at my future love. There she was, sitting on the step of the front landing.

I took one look at her and began to prance like a proud horse ready for show; and when she looked at me she began to yelp and turn around in circles; she was definitely thrilled to see me. We were unmistakably on cloud nine. I realized at that moment, it was love at first sight. I pulled away from my master and got loose from the leash. I jumped the fence and did what any dog in love would do! We were together, me and Gertrude, showing our affection to each other. But, behold, her master came out and caught us; we were stuck.

There was no doubt, that it was I who would be named the father of that litter; if there would be a litter. Everyone was screaming at one another. Gertrude's master began shouting and saying it was entirely our fault. My master became angry and said that Gertrude had been flirting with me for quite some time. There was trouble alright, and there was also sadness because Gertrude and I were in love, so in love. I felt that Gertrude's master was completely unreasonable and irrational about the whole incident.

After a laborious effort to separate Gertrude and me, my master and I started toward home. She looked at me with real compassion as she pet me, and while trying to cheer me, she smiled and said "Floppy, I had no idea you liked poodles."

I appreciated the ease in which she tried to comfort me. So there I was confined to the house, with the exception of doing what I had to do outdoors; being restricted didn't matter to me, because all I wanted was to see Gertrude, my love; but I knew it was over. I even lost my appetite. It took awhile, but after a month had passed, I did feel better. We now travel a new route on our walks to the beach; since we no longer go by Gertrude's house.

One Sunday morning, we were relaxing and reading the paper, when suddenly the doorbell began to ring non-stop. As soon as the door was opened, I heard a familiar voice shout, 'My sweet poodle is pregnant and I want a check for the doctor's visit and the abortion!' My master was so shaken by the commotion, that I jumped up and skinned his leg just enough so that he would leave; after all, what would you have done, he was going to abort Gertrude's and my litter.

It was chaotic as he ran out, threatening that we would be receiving a lawyer's letter. With a check in her hand for $125.00 my master chased him down the street and handed it to him. I guess in this case, money talked, as the issue seemed resolved and we never heard from him again.

I was saddened to learn that Gertrude would not have my litter of pups, but I will always treasure those moments we had together.

The following month, a new family moved in with a black female lab; she seemed quite perky. Her name was Josephine, but they called her Josie for short. During one of our walks, we saw Josie sitting on the bottom step of her porch; as we passed her house, my master stopped and gave me a very long look, then rolled her eyes, and believe me I thought twice about all costs.

March 20, 2007

My Escape Into The Cave

It was early, the night fading into daylight. The air was crisp and the morning upon me. Large frozen snowflakes, like the crystals that hang from the dining room chandelier, begin to drop. Dawn is here and all the leaves have fallen. Despite the morning appearing brighter than yesterday, I feel the dullness of winter which is here to stay for a while. I decide that this winter will be like no other and will retreat into the cave as I did when I was a child, filled with wonder and hope. I sit in my favorite chair near the fireplace and wrap my soft green blanket around me. The room is warm and the fire is crackling. It is time to escape into the cave and enter the sacred place of determination and grace. Bach's *Italian Concerto* plays softly, and I am now ready to explore.

I imagine that I slowly enter the cave and carefully step into the center of quiet darkness to create a light and illuminate what needs to be healed. To the right of the cave, a large boulder reflects shimmering lights creating a rainbow effect. The sparkle is so bright that I slightly close my eyes. To the left, water is trickling down into a small pond.

Fireflies and dragonflies, appearing friendly, sit at the edge of the water, where a constant stream of mist radiates many soft florescent colors. As I look closer into the pond, I see the swishing movements of two frogs sitting on odd looking leaves, each leaf outlined with green, pink and crystal-like edges. The centers are shaded a deep purple that holds a green gem-like stone. Glitter is everywhere, like the sparkles of many diamonds. I wonder what kind of reality will become my magic this cold dark winter, and will I think about my magic-like dreams.

A childless swing lies in the far corner of the room which eluded me earlier. There is no laughter or child-like humming. Next to the swing, sits a soft pink candle with drippings melted down the sides. I move toward the back of the cave and see a large trunk covered with cob webs. It looks like a treasure chest, and I notice an exquisite emerald green stone attached to the clasp that opens it. There is more glitter covering the entire floor of the cave.

Suddenly, I feel the light in the darkness and am surrounded by many prisms lighting up the entire cave. I am grateful for this quiet time, and can now hear the humming sounds of children playing on the swings; I will continue to escape into the cave and trust the rainbows of hope and light.

I am not ready to leave the cave yet, but am abruptly awakened by the sounds of a squeaking milk truck and reminded once again of the anchors of winter. When visiting the cave, I am able to remember the gift of faith and the promise of life. I now think of my summers spent at the water's edge as my utopia, and embrace the memory of family gatherings and the sounds of children's laughter playing near the sea shore.

In appreciating the beauty of solitude, I learn that the cave is a sacred place for me to meditate. Winter will become a special time to savor the passion of writing all that is important to me.

For the first time in years, I found a space and the freedom to indulge myself in the quiet of winter by appreciating the light in the darkness; that I discovered in my cave.

February, 2006

THE SS MONTRACHET

There she goes, slipping away as quietly as she arrived, not disturbing a soul.
She makes her turn, her lights shimmering against the lights of the city,

Her reflection sitting atop the water's edge.
The tug on ship's stern,
White over red, pilot ahead,
Starboard running light giving attention to ship's starboard side.
The men scurry to their stations, making ship ready for sea,
First mate, second mate, Ready!
The red flag lowered, oil delivery completed!
Captain on bridge! Captain on bridge! In position!
Pilot in pilot house, standing by to get under way and answer all
ships bells.
There are no bands today—no cameras—no publicity!
Just the men who man their ship, enlightened by the many tasks
needed to perform, to pilot, and to service the reservoir of tanks
that wait on land.
The men, some young, some older, working tediously, beads of
sweat dripping atop their brow.
Their shirts, waved by the wind, stand like a flag at attention.
The merchant marines of *The SS Montrachet* spend many sleepless
hours charting their courses, repairing the hoses and insuring delivery
of our oil.
She is a proud large super tanker who makes her way up the many
channels, to familiar and new destinations.
We thank you *SS Montrachet* for the many deliveries performed and
wish you a safe return.
Where to next? Will anyone await their arrival?
The toot of the ship's whistle, the lines singled up, with the radar
humming its tune, rhythmical and synchronized with one another.
As my Son, the Captain waved, I waved back and realized that I
stood alone on a large dock amongst the quiet of the night.

January, 1991

Frances L. O'Donnell

Sisters

Yea, look at the sisters
There they go!
Yea, they dance together
And they have wept
But, oh, they laugh
And they grow together
Look at the sisters
Yea, they know love
For they are separate
Yet they are one
For they know love
Yea, there they go
Look at the sisters.

1985

EDNA PANAGGIO

Edna (Falciglia) Panaggio is naturally gifted with many talents. In 1999, at the International Society of Poets, she received a monetary award for one of her poems at their National Convention in Washington, DC. She has a Chap Book *Into the Spirit, a Poetic Witness,* published by Cader Publishing Company. As an actress, after appearing 55 years on stage, she graduated into commercials and films. She is a member of SAG/AFTRA UNIONS. Her knowledge of modeling for runway and print, together with her acting skills, she still instructs and coaches young students to pursue their dreams. She assisted the composer, lyricist, playwright in the casting of *Rage of the Heart,* a World Premiere performance in April 1997, in Rhode Island, which is presently working its way to Broadway NY, in 2008. She enjoys sharing her talents as a pianist and singer voluntarily with those who enjoy them as much as she does.

SHORT STORIES
    The Musical Born in Divine Providence
    Secrets From The Spirit
    65 Ledge Street

ESSAY
    Dear Caleb:

POEMS
    Spirits' Lament
    What Is Love
    Carol's Blessing to Behold

The Musical Born in Divine Providence

I received a phone call asking whether or not he was good enough to take my course. I was teaching television acting at a newly restored conservatory in East Greenwich connected with the old resurrected theater that had been vacant and not working for many years. I, of course, confirmed to Frank that, of course he was good enough, and I was sure he would be a wonderful addition to the group that had now registered. Frank proved to be an interesting student, who himself had a master's degree in teaching and had been employed by private and public schools as a substitute in his retirement. Little did I know at that time what an addition to my life the relationship of Frank and his family would mean to me.

I learned that he, like me, was a member of *Screen Actor's Guild* actively working in the New England area. We enjoyed going to monthly meetings in Boston, auditions and actual "shoots" together. He continued in my advanced private workshops with students I had gathered from other sources like the Learning Connection, a national modeling school, and college students that were hungry for diversified education from experiences I had learned in my past 20 years in the business. He was a very quiet man with a lot of compassion and humor who didn't speak much unless he had something positive to contribute to the conversation. His humor was dry. I was fortunate one day, while filming a group, to get a small line that he had thrown in while playing the role of an addition to a Talk Show performance, that registered a great deal of heavy laughter among the cast of actors.

Frank shared with me the gifts of his family. He had a brother who was a composer, lyricist and playwright. His brother was preparing a workshop performance of one of his musicals that would be in a church in Little Compton. It was the very musical I would be listening to with hope that I could be instrumental in a future World Premiere production of it in Rhode Island. He suggested I meet him. He felt that with my background and energy, I might be able to help him achieve that goal.

Frank and I met at his home where I got a preview of his brother's talents. The storyline and music I was hearing was overwhelming. The style portrayed a very gifted musical genius. The music had been recorded in England with well known English arrangers, and symphony. The vocalists on the recording had auditioned and because of their selection by the composer, they were discovered and became well known artists in England. The story was briefly explained to me along with bringing attention to the names of world known musical arrangers and producers that were closely related to the composer during his time in the West End. I was extremely impressed and was looking forward to meeting Frank's brother.

Off the main highway, down a winding country road toward the beach, on a hill of much selected property, we approached a gracious palatial dwelling. The composer lived with his mother, a very sweet lady who greeted me warmly. Both she and her sons appeared angelic with an air of righteousness, purity, love and serenity. My tour of the home showed exquisite taste with many levels finalizing a trip to the tower through a winding staircase. Looking out from that room showed an astounding view of Block Island Sound with the Island in the distance.

While sipping tea and enjoying home made biscuits that his mother had prepared, I learned of his childhood; how he had played the organ at The Cathedral in Providence at the age of 13 as a child protégé. He happily told us of his experiences in the West End of England; his production of one of his musicals to rave reviews off Broadway in New York; his numerous recordings of his music throughout Europe. The musical production in Germany in honor of the miraculous fall of the wall; his attempts to produce his World Premiere of the musical we were to discuss at this meeting and the fatal ends interrupting that dream. Then, we came to the actual time that I would be hearing his music as he presented a few of his compositions on his piano, which I learned was moisturized by equipment that kept it in prefect condition. I eagerly listened to his description of the apparatus. His gentle touch and expression in his presentation was indescribable. His aura of humility was new to me; so humble of his gifts. He began to play the already produced musical discs from *Rage of the Heart* and *Michelangelo* which was some of the most unique style of composing that I had ever heard. My spirit was touched; I had a lump in my throat and tears began to flow. I asked him to please turn it off because I felt compelled to take time out to pray. In my prayer I asked God that if he wanted the World to hear this music, to use us, if needed. We would comply and give credit to His Glory. It was no accident that we were together. It was obvious to all that we were a Spiritual Group that had gathered in this room.

After spending much time together, Frank and I hardly spoke on the way home. I was in awe of having been in the presence of this man I had the opportunity to meet. My mind was running wild as to how I could be partner to anything as big as this. What could I, this unknown woman, be in any way a step in this genius' request for help in his future? I knew that my life in the past 15 years had been very exciting in spiritual growth, but this was by far the most mind boggling.

Well, like all my actions, I began to immediately follow my quest. My mind turned to those I could trust and depend on to understand my vision and thoughts. The people I called had no idea of the magnitude of this wild appointment that we would be eventually entering into. The one person, Lou, took the ball with me. Frank stood by and worked with us and we began to run the gamut. The musical would be born. This was to be a World Premiere with union musicians and musical arrangers from England.

We had many meetings with the composer. Lou had found technical and business acquaintances that he had worked with in the past. Months went by; I was asked by the composer to assist him in the casting process. My work, then, as a Talent Scout, afforded me enough talent to choose from, and much time had to be spent in selecting the right person for the right roles. Most background roles were filled from these auditions, but the close supporting roles and the female actor needed to be exact in age, personality, and talent. The composer and I kept in close contact when one day he called to tell me that a friend in California had found our leading lady. He played her demo tape for me and showed me her picture. We both agreed she was perfect. She, her mother and step-dad came to Rhode Island for her audition and she proved to be the one we would choose. Of course, neither the composer nor I could realize that this young woman, who had been chosen for a role on Broadway, would refuse it to accept our offer.

Miracles began to happen. She accepted the challenge. They planned their move for a six month's stay in Rhode Island and the best was yet to come. Their request was for a nine room house that they would rent, choosing the East Side of Providence, and it needed to have stained glass windows and a piano available to the young woman since she composed music. I assisted them by perusing the *Sunday Journal*, and found the exact home they were looking for on the East Side. They rented it.

Our new eighteen-year-old female lead had confided in me that she had no male attachments at home since she and her family were very busy creating her career. I knew at that moment that she would meet a specific person who was being considered for the male lead and they would fall in love. They were both Christians, and when these two very handsome, talented and spiritual people met, it was love at first sight. He also was a musician. Because of his age, he was not cast in the lead. He was too young. He moved in with the family and became a great support to her. The house was large enough to lodge all sorts of family when they would arrive for the Premiere of *Rage of the Heart* which eventually opened on April 24, 1997 at the Veterans Memorial Auditorium. It turned out to be a tremendous artistic success.

The Orchestrator trained at the Royal Academy of Music. He was from the West End of England who had conducted shows including, *Annie, Divorce Me Darling, I Do I Do* and others. The Director came from the Boston Conservatory then in his 10th year as a faculty member. The leading lady and her handsome man were joined together in holy matrimony on September 9, 1999 at a beautiful wedding at her family's home. They presently live outside of Rhode Island very involved in Christian Music Ministry through their selected church.

At this writing *Rage of the Heart* is well on its way to Broadway, New York in 2008. The composer is opening his second World Premiere with his musical *Michelangelo* on April 27, 2007 using vocalists from Opera Providence at the Providence Performing Arts Center.

Frank, a devoted brother, Lou and I continue to support our composer whom we have grown to love dearly. We have gained a brother whom we are very proud of and so I write this short story to introduce Dr. Enrico Garzilli. He has chosen his residence and his music to be introduced to the world in Rhode Island because of his love for our great State. Bravo Enrico!

SECRETS FROM THE SPIRIT

After leaving a 30-year marriage, I rented a one bedroom apartment on the first floor of a rather nice complex in Lutherville, Maryland. My life began a drastic change. After I committed my life to the Holy Spirit in 1981, I was opened up into a service I would begin to exercise without question. Many friends to this day do not understand why I take on such tasks. I, also, am in awe of their outcome.

Soon after my separation, Trish, a thirty-year-old, daughter of a dear friend of mine became my friend. She attended a Bible study at my home on Tuesday nights. She had two children, a thirteen-year-old boy and a nine-year-old daughter.

During my marriage, Trish's father and mother were friends of my husband and me. We were into the magnetic life of heavy drinking. Her father was a gruff large man of Russian origin. He sold Cadillac's and made a lot of money. Trish and her brother were adopted. They lived in a very large rambling ranch house beautifully landscaped with a circular driveway. The long back porch looked over a picturesque yard with a beautiful in ground pool lined in marble; something you would find in Hollywood. I remember Trish in the pool many times with her little girl who, like her mother took to the water like a fish. Trish's mom was a very delicate Italian lady who never drank alcoholic beverages as we did. Her mother, who didn't speak the English language too well, lived with them.

Trish's adopted brother had a drinking problem. One day his mother called me to tell me he was missing. I would take it upon myself to find him in an effort to make some change in his life. After much investigating, I found him with a girlfriend. She was pregnant. He wasn't sure that he was the father of this unborn child, but he accepted the responsibility. He was in very bad physical condition. He had no job; he literally roamed the streets looking for ways to get liquor by stealing it from the stores, or found what he called friends to give him money to buy beer or anything in the line of liquor that he could get his hands on. I was drawn to Andy. He was pathetic. I would follow the path eventually getting him into a facility for help. The doctor I spoke with regarding his condition informed me that it wouldn't be long before he would die if he continued on his present course. I counseled him and eventually worked with his girlfriend to finally get him into a Teen Challenge home for people like himself. I found one in Virginia. I, personally, drove him there one cold day in December. I dropped him off and made him promise me he would follow their directions in leading him to salvation. The treatment proved to be very effective and to this day, he is married to the girl, has other children, is a good father, is no longer drinking, and is working in a responsible job.

Trish was divorced from her husband since they both had been heavily into drugs that destroyed their marriage. Their emotionally disturbed son, who also had a bad physical ailment, was living with his grandfather and grandmother while she and her daughter lived with a fifty-year-old man who adored her. He did not have a permanent job, had been married three times and had a daughter of his own that lived with him. I spent a lot of time with Trish and she expressed a strong desire to end this unhealthy relationship. We prayed toward that end.

A two and a half bedroom apartment became available in the complex where I lived, and I invited her with the children to move in with me. We would share the new apartment. Her son had a great deal to overcome since he had been verbally abused by living with his grandfather and turned out to be a real challenge. However, we knew with confidence that our arrangement would be beneficial to both the children. It was, and this interim would eventually lead to the plan that God ultimately had in store for them.

Since their father was close by and the children loved him dearly, I made sure that he joined us almost nightly for dinner and visits. I began to learn a little of his background. He had been a difficult child whose parents kept sending him away from them. When he became too much for his grandparents, he was sent to private boarding schools so no one would have to endure his behavior. He had his challenges, as we all do, but time, patience, endurance, prayer and faith in God led Trish, her husband and two children together again. They soon brought another child, son, into the world.

Shortly after she left, I had an extra bedroom. God had a hand in filling it up real fast. I was then attending a Born Again Christian Church where one of the members heard of my vacancy. I was approached and asked to meet a woman in her twenties. I met Cindy one afternoon, after services. She was grossly overweight, terribly fearful of everyone, and when I was introduced to her, she extended her shaking hand to make my acquaintance. I will never forget that first meeting. My son would be visiting me that day from Washington so I invited my new friend to join us at lunch. We went to a moderately priced restaurant with a usual menu of chicken, fish or beef, and she ordered chicken. She did not eat any of it, so I invited her to take it home. She was living with three other girls in an apartment and felt very unwanted. Within three weeks, she was living with me.

I learned much of her background. She came from a large family of brothers and one sister. She felt like an outcast in her own family and explained the abuse she had received as a child. She told me stories of how her mother would tie her hands behind her back at the dinner table and force her to eat. I didn't know too much of her mother except that she liked to sing and would frequent a local restaurant where she would entertain the clients singing the good old tunes. Her father, whom I eventually met, was a very quiet man. She loved her father but mentioned that he never interfered with any of the things going on within the family. When I met Cindy, her mother had passed on and her father was living with a lady who cared for him. Cindy abused herself with actions that could have been fatal. Thankfully, because of prayer, faith and trust in her Holy Spirit, she is healed from all of that now.

I would like to interject here that one day I was watching a talk show on television and a young woman being interviewed was afflicted with this same tendency. I went down on my knees and cried out to God that if there was anyone out there, that needed healing from this affliction, to use me as his instrument to reach her. Two months later, Cindy was living with me.

Cindy had been through counseling and had been a counselor herself at Weight Watchers. Her eating habits were very unattractive. She would toy with her food like she didn't trust it. In our early days together, I would have to discipline her gently as I would a child. I was firm but careful not to hurt her feelings in any way. I had grown to love the child in her.

We lived together in Baltimore for six months when my divorce became final and I made a decision to move back to my original home in Rhode Island. My daughter would soon be giving birth to her third child and I was hearing cries of despair from her. She needed her mother. Cindy insisted she come with me. I was apprehensive, since I realized she was becoming too attached to me. I didn't like that. However, in my quiet reasoning I found advantages to the arrangement. We talked it over and I made it quite clear that she would have to make friends and make a new life for herself in a new State and we would soon have to separate.

Her skills as a computer operator in third party billing made it easy for me to find employment for her. I went into the yellow pages and worked as her agent which placed her where she finally worked for seven years. She described that she was let go because they didn't think her appearance was right for their office atmosphere. Although we both thought she had a case against the employer, she had very little self-confidence and really did not want to pursue a confrontation. She gracefully left. After long counseling and going off to a Christian rehabilitation center in Chicago for duration of time, she returned and was diagnosed by a psychiatrist that she was disabled to function in a normal work environment and eventually was put on total disability. When Cindy returned from her hospitalization, plans were underway to find housing and support for her with government intervention.

By this time, the responsibility was beginning to be too much for me. I needed to make new arrangements. I explored senior housing to take a rest from all of this, and eventually took an apartment alone until senior housing became available.

I had a five-year intervention working as a Legal Secretary, for two years to pay for an apartment. Three years passed and a senior facility became available, all to the specifications that I asked for. When Cindy and I lived together, it was in a luxury apartment where we both shared the rent. I loved it. Without a room mate, it was mandatory for me at this time to find less expensive living. I said it with my mouth in the rental office, "I will be back here one day," never knowing how I would. I knew that senior housing would never give me such luxury but I asked for specifics from God in the place where I would be going. All specifications were there waiting for me. God gave me time to renew my Holy Spirit. Three years passed.

Rita and I had grown up together. Her mother was my mother's cousin. Rita was born in New Jersey and at the age of five, she and her mother returned to Rhode Island after her parent's divorce. They lived with us. We lived in a very modest four rooms in a six-tenement house. My mother and I shared a bedroom, and my dad and brother shared the other. Rita and her mother were welcome to sleep in the living room until they were able to find housing for themselves. They finally moved into an apartment where her mother would manage the apartment complex owned by her brother. Rita lived an over-protected life that never could make decisions. As young children, we were very close. Our parents were very close as cousins. We vacationed and spent most holidays together as the years passed. I married at age 24, moved away to Maryland and made residence there for 25 years returning home in 1987. During my years away, Rita had a job, lived with and was dependent upon her mother. She worked daily in a department store and her mother would drive her and pick her up every day.

One day, an oncoming robber snatched her mother's handbag. She immediately called the police. The policeman that answered the call became a very good friend to both of them. About that time, Rita's uncle was about to let go of all of the property he had and Rita and her mother would have to find a place to live. Their friend, the policeman, lived alone and asked the two of them to move in with him. He had never married, had recently lost his mother, and it seemed like a perfect arrangement. It was. Many years lapsed with good relationship among the three. The department store went out of business; Rita retired and never worked again. In 1986, Rita's mother died and Rita and her family friend, after many years as her brother, remained living together until his death in 1996.

Rita was then 71 years old. I wasn't too much younger. We really hadn't seen too much of each other since I had returned home. I went to the wake. Rita came to me that evening and said she would like to ask me something. The following day, in my morning devotional prayer, I had a spiritual wave telling me that Rita would be asking me to live with her. I always challenge what I hear to be sure that it is from the Holy Spirit. "Lord, she's never been married; I have two children, three grandchildren, a son-in-law, daughter-in-law, and my own two children whom she hardly knows. I'm divorced. No, it won't work out. Okay, if she asks me, I will know it came from you." I really didn't think she would come out and ask me. She asked, and in my obedience to God's service, after 6 months of clearing her out of the home left to her by their friend, funds from her mother and what she had saved, gracefully put us back into luxury living where I was 5 years previous. God honors obedience.

We have learned compatibility in spite of our different personalities. She is very retiring where I am creative. I still enjoy my career as an actress/model and enjoy a very full life. I include my cousin in many of the exciting modeling and acting showcases I direct. She is learning of life and is growing fast. Although she comments that her mother controlled her life, she allowed it and has a submissive nature because of it. Her beauty shines through all of this and is truly loved by all who meet her. In return for my obedience we are appreciating the many blessings we enjoy together. We have accepted His Holy Spirit, and He is proving the scripture that He is "the truth, the life, and the way." The Holy Spirit does not keep secrets. The Holy Spirit is real and shares with us the quality of life that God ultimately wants for all of us.

65 LEDGE STREET

Grandmother and grandfather came from Italy with their family with I don't know how many children. I only knew Aunts Mary and Rose, Uncles Pat, Jim and my dad. Another daughter, Amelia, I'd hear mentioned in conversation had been left in Italy. I believe she had married already. I did hear that a son died on board ship coming to America and was buried at sea. A side story was that my dad saw an angel follow them across the seas. He was seven-years-old. When they arrived, grandfather built or had this house built on 65 Ledge Street in Providence, RI. It was made with 6 tenements, housing 2 other families and a grocery store. When I was old enough to remember, grandfather had died and grandmother lived on the first floor, to the right of the stairway (as you faced the house) with Aunt Mary and Uncle Pat. To the left, was a grocery store rented by a family friend. Dead center was what some people would call a "water closet;" we called it a "toilet." The second and third floors could be seen to the right and the left, while climbing up the stairs. We lived on the second floor to the right and Uncle Jim and his family of seven children lived to the left. Two other Italian families lived on the third floor. We got to know them well and played with their children. All in all, we were very happy. The tenements had two bedrooms, a kitchen we ate in, a pantry, where the cooking was done, and a living room. Our "toilets" were also in the hallway, at the top of the stairs. My 7 cousins, their mom and dad, and we four shared the one "toilet." Now that was a picture, especially when the oldest son used to bring reading material with him as he occupied it.

Well, it was corrected later on as the years passed. Uncle Jim, who had deed to this house, had toilets with bathtubs added to the back of the "pantry" in all tenements. Now we had a bathroom! Before that, we bathed in copper tubs that we filled with water heated on the stove. I assume hot water tanks were installed to the new added feature. Yippee, now we had a bathtub, right under the window in the "bathroom" at the end of the pantry. We took our baths right next to the window on the chilled wall. Neither windows nor walls were insulated to keep out the cold. Winters in RI are bitter, you know.

Grandmother was both blind and deaf. Rumor in the family has it that she lost her eyesight due to an accident. Others said it happened by an operation that was performed to improve her sight. Possibly, cataract surgery was the most likely to be performed by surgeons in those days. Her loss of hearing seems to be genetic since a number of the cousins in our family have become deaf and need hearing aids. Not me, thank God. Uncle Pat lost his hearing. He lived downstairs with grandma and worked as a stonecutter with the company down the street that engraved tombstones.

Poor Pat, as I remember him, on weekends he would hit the bottle and become silent or sometimes quite a problem. Aunt Mary was very religious, astute in taking care of her mother, attended church daily, and when her brother would get into these stupors would bring home the holy water and practically showers him with it. Those stories were very amusing when told to us by my Aunt Mary, who finally became a nun. I was 11 months old when she left for the convent since she had been told that after the age of 33, it would be too late. Of course, her brothers, my dad and Uncle Jim with their wives agreed to care for grandmother for the rest of her life. Uncle Pat died many years after his sister left, but he was in no shape to care for a mother in her condition. She needed a woman's touch. He died of Tuberculosis. I'm sure lots of the dust settling in his lungs from the stone cuttings contributed to his death.

Aunt Mary, the nun, was lovely. I met her when I was in my teens, I think. She was in the convent for many years before she was allowed to come home for visits. We would sit at her feet by her long black gown. She was a Sister of Mercy, I remember. They named her Sister Angela.

Ledge Street, we all call it today, was our museum. Grandmother was unique in that she always had rosary beads handy to begin praying. In her darkened state of existence, she was at home with the light of God within her. She was able to sew her clothing if she felt a tear here or there. She pinned a needle with thread on her garment ready to perform that task. She actually could thread a needle by "feel." She would touch us and knew exactly who we were by feeling our height. As the years passed, Uncle Jim's boys decided to tear down wallpaper to prepare to utilize the empty bedrooms, in grandma's tenement, for sleeping space. Beautiful pictures were found painted on the walls under the wallpaper. It was assumed that possibly grandfather or Uncle Pat had painted them.

Daily, my mom or my aunt would tend to grandmother and get her ready for the day. She always dressed in a long dress, as from the old country, with a shawl over her head, no matter what the weather. I remember brown as the color, beige, or muted shades, maroon. Mom and auntie would wash her clothes and in those days, there were no washing machines. They both loved serving grandmother. When ready, she would ascend the stairs and spend the rest of the day in either our tenement or aunties. There was a special chair placed just inside the door of both tenements where she would sit.

When we arrived from school we would greet her with a hug and a kiss. We loved her. She was our angel. We would, as a group, get together and sing and dance in front of her. Of course, she could never see us, but with four or five of us in front of her the vibration would help her to feel the beat as the "house shook."

My father traveled as an entertainer with the Keith Circuit before he married mom. He just loved watching all nine of us using our talents to entertain each other. We had fun growing up. Someone would play either our piano or auntie's and we'd sing. My brother played trombone he started in high school, one cousin played oboe. Another graduated from New England Conservatory of Music, and still another taught music in RI and DC schools. I learned piano from my cousins who had students coming in and out constantly. We all had talent as actors and participated in plays with the Neighborhood Center Players, a theater group directed by a Miss Basso at Esek Hopkins Jr. High School. We all became actors, musicians and singers with the very best training and experience anyone could want right here in our own museum. One of the plays I remember was, *You Can't Take It With You*, which I always felt was our family story. I think entertaining in front of grandma gave us our beginning.

Grandmother got old, and eventually was confined to her bed on the first floor and mom and auntie had to care for her constantly. She had gangrene, which we know comes from a diabetic condition. She was 82 when she died, and I remember distinctly, at the age of 13, upstairs in my tenement kneeling down on a stuffed chair by the window. My grandmother was crying out in agonizing screams from the pain. The church bells were ringing. They always rang at the same time every day. "God, please take my grandmother out of her misery, please take her home." Before the ending of the chimes, there was a sudden silence. She was with God. My prayer was answered immediately at 12:00 noon.

In my other family, the oldest son, Ed, graduated Brown University and worked for Procter & Gamble. Rosalie, the eldest daughter, graduated RI College of Education, met and married Henley Hill and moved to Washington, DC. He was with the U.S. Government as interpreter between President Truman and the President of the Brazilian Government. She raised his two children and soon worked as a music teacher in the DC school system. Helen, went to normal school (that was the name for a secretarial school) where she learned shorthand and typing. She found work in DC, where she lived until retirement, with the U.S. Publication Department. She married when she was 40. In those years she received many citations from the U.S. Government for many systems that were implemented at her suggestions. Ernest, graduated from New England Conservatory of Music, became a private instructor for many young people who studied with him, and held a very important job with RI public schools as a music administrator. He held office with the RI Philharmonic Orchestra, and with his wife worked very hard on many other artistic community action programs supporting the arts. At this writing, they have all passed on, with the exception of Ernest's wife.

Elsie joined her sisters in DC and worked with the French Embassy. She was a very good actress with Catholic University's auspicious theater. She was offered to go on the road with traveling companies and Hollywood producers, which she gracefully turned down. Lil became a teaching nurse at the RI Hospital operating room. She implemented new systems that were highly acclaimed by surgeons and officers of the hospital. She attained her Masters in education so she could teach Operating Room Technique by traveling back and forth to Boston, Mass., after giving birth to two children. Jimmy, the youngest of that family, graduated URI after serving with U.S. forces in World War II and worked in executive positions for different companies for many years. My brother, Tom, graduated URI, became their Fund Raising Executive until his retirement. That wasn't enough for him. He continued to work for Roger Williams College on the faculty until that retirement. He always used his trombone as his hobby putting his own orchestras together, playing for weddings, and college functions with the big band sound.

And, here I am, the ninth child in this story. By the time they all got to me, it is a good thing I am who I am. I like what the Lord had in store for me. I just seemed to let the tide come in and out using stronger strokes in order to swim ashore and produce good things for the "now." I didn't get to college but I made sure I learned from everything put before me as a positive step to accomplishing a life for myself that would lead to completeness. I will never stop learning. After marriage and when the children were 5 and 9, my husband was transferred to Baltimore, MD.

In my 25 years as a resident of that fine city, I was able to perform with community theaters in several exciting character roles, became President of my own corporation, E&P Productions, producing cabaret entertainment for private elite clubs and organizations. In that capacity, I also produced trunk and fashion shows. My stage acting soared ahead and in obtaining an excellent Agent, auditions and bookings were successful affording me the opportunity to join the Screen Actors Guild and American Federation of Radio and TV Artists. As a result I am still working with many famous actors in movies, and have National and Regional TV Commercials to my credit.

When I returned to Rhode Island in 1987, my new life began to take hold by making new acquaintances. Twenty five years away gave me foresight to grasp on to life more abundantly than I ever thought life could be. And, more than ever, I love writing and sharing that abundance.

The walls of 65 Ledge Street hold many stories. Angelo's store existed in the front of the first floor for a long time until he grew old and retired. He lived to be 100. All the girls including those of the families on the third floor were married from this old 6 tenement house. Each was adorned in long white gowns with flowing trains on the arms of their proud dads. They descended the three old wooden steps, walked the concrete walk, and then got into the parked waiting limo which would take them beyond their past making ready to start a new life in their final step from the blessed 65 Ledge Street.

DEAR CALEB:

One day, six years ago, I saw your daddy and mom who needed one of my stars in my Heavenly Kingdom to come to earth so I could give those help and comfort. Your daddy had a very heavy sick heart and your mommy was very worried for your daddy. They came to me and prayed.

I looked through all my stars and chose the one I knew would bring new healing to daddy's sick heart. You were that star.

You went into this loving home of daddy and mommy bringing with you all my gifts from Heaven and you did what I expected my special stars to do. You shared them with mom, dad, and your brothers and sister. You did exactly what I taught you in Heaven. Your dad was able to feel the largest gift he could have been given in the earthly kingdom for the last six years of his life; you, my messenger.

Your daddy was one of those angel stars in my Kingdom of Heaven one day. I sent him to his mommy and daddy 54 years ago.

Now was the time for him to return to my Heavenly Kingdom. He was driving his car when it happened and as my heavenly angel, you were with him. You were there because of me, Caleb. You were with your daddy right up to the time I called him.

Today your dad has become one of my stars again to be chosen out of my Kingdom. When you grow up to be a loving father that I have chosen you to be in the earthly kingdom, I will send you one of my special stars, which will be your daddy.

Caleb, you will see him again, I promise.

In the meantime, continue to do my work as my special star. Spread my special gifts that are in you; love, joy, peace, patience, goodness, kindness and self control to your mom and family. Your mom knows best and be good to her. I chose her and your dad as your parents. Be good to others; children, old people, and sick people. Your daddy will be helping you from Heaven. He was good on earth.

These gifts will never leave you, Caleb. I promise. You are now my son, and brother to Jesus, the next step on earth. Go to Jesus daily and ask for his help. The earthly kingdom needs my stars to keep shining. You will help to make earth a better place to live. I sent you there for that. Your dad is safely with me.

Thank you, Caleb, for carrying the bright star into the home where your mommy will continue to do my work. Call upon me daily through my son, Jesus. He died on the cross for you. He planted his Holy

Spirit in you to help you. His mother Mary loves you and will help your mother along with all of us in heaven to guide you and watch over all of you, always.

Your loving Father, God, and my Son Jesus.

The night before my son-in-law's wake, I went to God on my knees and asked him to prepare a letter for me to give to my six-year-old grandson. Caleb was with his father when he was stricken with a massive heart attack while they both were driving about shopping for mom's birthday gift on July 8th, 2005.

I fell into bed with extreme exhaustion and immediately fell off into a deep sleep. The next day, when I opened my eyes, I was awakened with bright sunshine at 7:45 a.m. which prompted me to jump from my bed and start the computer. My fingers ran away with the above message. I had it laminated and displayed it in the funeral parlor during visiting hours. When the time ended, I retrieved the letter. That night, Caleb was emotionally disturbed with a persistent rash. My daughter was beside herself. He was crying and she, in her tired and stressful state, was ready to collapse while she bathed him in a tub of cool water to ease his itch. In my spiritual calmness, I urged her to go to bed and I would take over the duty of working calmly with my tired, stressed out six-year-old grandson. Back into his mommy's bed, and tucked in comfortably with cool packs, I began to pray over him, calling upon all the angels in Heaven, God and His Son. I was persistent in my call for help. Within the first hour I saw a calm come over Caleb and within the next hour, he was into a deep sleep; comfortably warm and relaxed.

He slept without a wince until 10a.m. the next morning when his dad would be buried. His mother and the rest of the family, 2 adult brothers and sister, had already left for church. Either Caleb or I heard them leave. He woke up, immediately started to dress himself, refused breakfast and wanted to leave for church.

We boarded a very hot vehicle this sweltering, hot day, and as I cooled the car off, he in the back seat and I at the driver's seat, I asked if he would like to hear the letter God wrote to him. He immediately leaned forward thrusting his body and head between the two front seats and said, "Yes;" almost like he expected it. He listened intently through the whole letter. There was a deep pause and silence at the end of it. "Did God really write that, Grandma? How did He write it?" I explained my prayer and request and answer. That God answers all prayers in His own way and I said, "What do you think, Caleb?" He thought for a moment and as he turned his eyes upward, with a left cock of his little head, he said, "Wow, God is something, isn't He? But it was a little long." With that, he fastened his seat belt and I started the car. We arrived just in time for the service. He found his place next to his mother in church and did very well.

At the grave site, the service was touching him and not a tear was shed until the bagpiper began "Amazing Grace." With deep sighs and tears rolling down his cheeks, taking deep breaths releasing all tension from within, Caleb in his own way was displaying God's miracle.

These past two years have displayed great faith in this family. What was once a family going in different directions, they have all come together to live in a beautiful home God has prepared for them. Their faith is carrying them through.

SPIRITS' LAMENT
Message from Spirits called by God September 11, 2001

I thought it was a dream, so bad, I couldn't scream,
Cruel faces acting crimes, shed blood using special knives.
The sun, a blinding light, twin towers, were in sight

When, suddenly we hit hijackers in the cockpit.
We all became a maze; God saved us in a daze.
All spirits came alive, to live this fearful drive.
Oh, dear ones, how you grieve, and the sights you can't believe.
Our bodies you can't find transformed a different kind.
We're working now from here. Those culprits that you fear
cannot survive the groans, that come from our God's throne.
Their deaths will be satire; they'll end in burning fire.
Your work on earth's begun, dear mortals, God's love,
Unite as One.
If you don't go God's way, you're just as bad as they.
The world will never be; the world God wants to see.
Destruction then will come; will be the end for some.
Don't know what God will do, God Bless, we'll pray for you.

WHAT IS LOVE?

Time is nothing; if it's spent to sit and watch,
it came and went.
And in this time of nothing more,
it doesn't have to be a bore.
If only one would think in time;
their heart is ticking ocean brine.
It can be used to one in need,
abundant growth from just a seed.
Take in the man who passes by;
who needs your heart to soothe his cry.
Who's very cold; needs you to hold.
Who needs a coat; he's named "the goat."
The one you see, who all despise;

the outside shows the wrong disguise.
He too, has love within his heart.
Created all the same; our part.
Its love created from within.
To leave it die could be a sin.

Carol's Blessing to Behold

It was Sunday; it had been a very stressful week.
Carol and others marched into the Atrium from Safe Haven,
the newly built Dementia Unit at the nursing home.
Like children, with hands tied to aids, each was led to their chairs.
The lights from the chandelier reflected in her eyeglasses,
The tip of her nose was red.
She was dressed in red slacks, a red and white striped shirt,
and white sneakers.
The entertainer played piano and sang joyfully.
I sat next to my mother's wheelchair; the room was filled with them.
Carol rose from her seat and began dancing, alone, perfectly
   to the beat.
My eyes caught hers as she brightly danced toward me.
Her smile was genuine and steady.
A power within me forced my arms outward.
We touched, and as she held my hands firmly turning
   palms downward,
She kissed the backs of them.
Her smile and gentle voice said, "thank you."
Carol blessed me with transcendental peace and fulfillment,
My day was complete and I was healed.

Earl F. Pasbach

Earl is a lawyer by profession, who has been writing poetry for many years and has given several recitations. He has published two books of poetry, *Perspectives* and *On Planted Feet of Whimsy*. A past president of the club and long time member, he has given much toward the integrity of *The Rhode Island Short Story Club*.

Poems
> Hayride
> At Sunrise
> Times of Twilight
> Siege
> Island in the Sun
> Oh Eleana
> At the Circus
> Rainy Daze

HAYRIDE

Saturday gold fall afternoon
while shadows slowly stretch,
as fingers point the coming dusk
and chilled fresh breezes fetch.
Young spooners wait the rising moon
shiny silver 'midst the elms,
anticipate with anxious heart
with thoughts of cupid's realms.
Appearance of the boulderous mare
with her hay-filled orange cart,
at seven sharp, with hearty snort
the hayride is to start;
off to who knows where?
Without a clue, without a care,
all bundled 'neath the starry night
fingers twined in soft delight.
Eyes suffused at heaven's bower
time moves in a cosmic flight,
as the gods of cold October
play the borealis white.
Songs steam forth into the ether
laughter skits along the way,
riddles, mime and eerie stories
trail behind the plodding grey.
A Hayride to remember
many words of love are passed,
some will vanish with the moonlight
others etch a spark to last.
Souls bewitched in warmth together

cuddled 'neath a Harvest Moon,
memories of a far tomorrow
of a night that fled too soon.

At Sunrise

As a ball eking red o'er the far away rim
fine streaks of the dawn in fiery fawn
enreddens the mauve placid waking lagoon,
a glimpse of the sea at the dawning.

The breezes are freshly drawn over the shore
bringing the magic of seaweeded tides,
joined with the tars of the whispering-pines
the smell of the sea at the dawning.

A lone gull is wafting high on the mist
beaking the joy of the free,
joined with the horn far out by the reef
the sounds of the sea at the dawning.

Salt born by the sea encaptures the eye
streaking the face with its sticky moist brush,
awakens the mind to another day's birth
the feel of the sea at the dawning

And to drink in the mist as rolls past the shore
with the mix from the world of the ocean's dark floor,
ennourishing body, spirit, and mind
the full taste of the sea at the dawning.

Where heaven may be is a query that we
wonder of and about times aborning, but
when streaks of the sun join rays of the moon
heaven's here in the sense of the dawning.

TIMES OF TWILIGHT

Subtle shades of a summer twilight
as the heat warms a cooling night,
the firefly lights to his lady fair
and cicadas' sing-song haunts the purple air.
The cares of the day ease and whisper
from their height at the shout of the noon,
and the mountains they seem to envision
fade with dusk to the size of the dune.
It is then when we gaze in the night light
as the shadowy shades grow so steep,
that our thoughts move to dwell on the phantoms
lying deep in our bones fast asleep.
Oh the twilight bestirs them from slumber
they arise and bedrift 'round mind's eyes,
with ached memories so full and nostalgic
the heart's laughter melds strange with its sighs.
Days of love with their joys pass at twilight
olden times that seem part of a dream,
when we joined soul to soul in the moonlight
rhythmed pulse, smiling eyes, with their beam.
How we knew they would last near forever
too naïve to behold curves ahead,
that a straight path is of but vain wishes

on a route marked from alpha to zed.
But no matter the gist of the daylight
when relentless, routine and forlorn,
the phantoms of yore in the twilight
sing again the soul's joyous love song.

SIEGE

Notice first the maple's limb
Aquiver o'er the buckets
collecting sap unto the brim
in a measured cryptic beat
with message to the crocus
lurking silent 'neath my feet.
Soon a burst of gold forsythia
scents the nascent zephyred breeze
attar of sweet petaled-cordite
winter time is under siege.
Now the swallows in formation,
motors chirping overhead,
shield a troop of budding daffodils
popping safe within their beds.
Icy winter in retreat
firing back its chilly sleet
plans its battle of resistance
on each winter-blasted street.
Waking forth the grouchy grizzly
from his dark and cozy lair
to trod on melting streamlets
frothing down a rocky stair.

The invasion has begun
in a floral March-time siege,
the winter gasps its last
falling to its chilly knees.
Hail the Army of the springtime
dressed in varied shades of green,
marching forward and triumphant
changing nature's fluid scene.
The winter-mute azaleas
salvo forth in colors rare,
the landscape comes alive again
in a multi colored flare

ISLAND IN THE SUN

In a balmy deep-blue tropic sea
a small green island calls to me
where palm trees lean with open arms
a welcome home to mystic charms.

An island where the morning sun
begleams dewed mountains one by one,
up from a valley lush and green
where rising mist is barely seen.

And flying far above my head
a host of bright-hued winged friends,
sing matins of the early morn
before the daytime tasks are borne.

And on a languid scented breeze
with bougainvillea to my knees,
a mind awakes to paradise
of gentle hearts and wafting spice.

Inspired by sea of blue surrounding
of dreams and joys not few abounding,
a flamingo silhouetted moon
sails high above the purple dune.

In hammock tied twixt royal palms
to sense the breeze unto my arms,
and dwell upon a silver dell
of sparkling jade on golden shell.

A rich and fortressed warm oasis
of azured wave with foaming faces,
my island in the sun, somewhere,
where tropic waters, northward run.

OH ELEANA

We will meet once again oh Eleana
when a tropical breeze gains a shore
as the zephyrs of spring's shy emergence
subtle knocks on a cold winter's door.

We will meet through the flickering sparkle
of an eye gleaming moist as the dew
in the morn as the dawn's golden fingers
turn the dark of the east to the blue.

We will meet once again in sonata
music shared when the days were so young
melodies of a soared inspiration
picnic days, voices blend, though as one.

We will meet once again in a passing
with a quick glance of stunning surprise
in the eye of an old recognition
though arrayed in a foreign disguise.

For the spirit is of things immortal
reigning over dark boulder and bone
joins another in long absence waiting
in a mellowed-felt feeling of home.

AT THE CIRCUS

There is nothing like a circus,
An elephantine circus,
A monkey screaming with a fez
The barker who steps up and says
With megaphone up to his nose
That when you see fat tattooed Rose
Dancing, prancing on her toes
In pink and purple hose,
That ticket bearers will repose
In wonderment's rare clothes.
And what a fearful sight!
Of tigers, nervous, tight
Ready quick to snap

at whistling whip's snap crack,
Adventurer's delight.
The elephants in line
In swaying jury file
Tails to trunks entwined adjunct—
A mighty army grey
Marching with calliope
The Big Tent rising to the sky
With bold star-spangled aerialists
About to do or die; and as to earth they fall
are caught upon the wing
By clutching hands outstretched in flight.
What aerobic plight on this candy-appled night!
The tense high-wire keeps all on edge
As on a ledge, a sudden miss will
Spill us flailing off—keep steady Eddy—at the circus every year.

Move along and watch your balanced weight
And keep your foot out straight—
he's home—relief and true elate.
But wait:
The clowns are at the gate.
Those crazy clowns in funny gowns
Tooting, hooting-silly sounds, hilarity abounds;
Water spouting, noses flashing, sirens everywhere
Ladders leaning, hoses streaming, no fires anywhere!
Laughter, wonder, feral thunder, silliness and fear
How they work us, poke us, perk us, hocus pocus
Completely over-awe us, emotion's wrap is porous

Rainy Daze

Rainy Days, Rainy Daze looking through a watered haze
of splashing bombs against the pane; and on the lane
gleaming streaming running streets with rivers running on
by curbings face to empty in a grated waterfall in falling
race to reach the sea through ziggered zaggard underground
morass. The pitterpat and patterpat of raindrops fat
that skit and scat and split and splat upon stretched
umbrellas' mats to dribble off bright spiny tips upon quick
hips and cause cold lips to purse and even worse to cough
and curse when running tires splashing fires of silvered
sheets from puddle pools to lash and search for legs that
move with sodden shoes that finally find a sanctuary warm
and dry where with half defiant eyes to look up into
falling sky of grey and silver sheet still coming, humming
til the darkened splashing day encroaches night—a
gloomy sight—to take a breath and set out into watered
night without much sight except the light catching every
raindrop in meteored attack without relent while home
returning feet squishing left and right hurry in the
darkened wet and fret and fret with more rain met until a
safe turned latch does snatch shelter from the addled
helter skelter of the constant pelter pelter in a thousand
different ways—Rainy Daze.

LISA A. PROCTER

Lisa A. Procter is the author of the novel *Stained Glass Windows,* published November 2006. She has been published in the *Catholic Visitor*, *Providence Journal*, *Rhode Island College Anchor*, *Famous Poet's Society* Edition 2002, and in the *International Library of Poetry* Edition 2000. She holds a Master of Arts Degree in Holistic Counseling from Salve Regina University, Newport, Rhode Island. She is an artist and avid gardener.

SHORT STORIES
Something for Nothing
Snowman

POEMS
Insanity of Solar Suicide
Insanity of Time
Familiar Changes
My Dusty Face
My Master Puppeteer
Blessed Sacrament I
Sacred Stone Walls
Insane Metamorphosis of Violence

SOMETHING FOR NOTHING

Peter did not know what he should do when after trying on the old suit; he reached into the pocket and found $500.00. Peter decided to go back to the Salvation Army to see if he could find the owner of the suit. The old woman at the Salvation Army knew Johnny, the man that dropped off the old suits. He had lived in Providence his whole life. As Peter knocked on the door he wasn't sure of what he would say, "I see you found the money," said Johnny as he opened the door. Peter's mouth dropped open because he couldn't figure out how this old man knew who he was or why he was there. "Come in, come in I was expecting you. After Peter settled in, Johnny came out of the kitchen with a pot of tea and a homemade blueberry pie. Peter was still taken back as Lucy rubbed up against his leg and purred. "This is a good sign Lucy likes you," said the old man. "I have come to return something. "Oh, you can keep the old suit, but if you return the money. Then I will expect something else from you," said the old man. "And what is that sir?" Peter asked as he looked around the sparsely furnished apartment." Well, to come once a month for tea and be a companion to walk into the mountains or down by the lake to fish," said the old man. "Oh," said Peter as he thought of his already busy schedule. "The masses claim money can not buy love, but I've found a way to do it. Not having my money will tie you into learning to have me an old man to spend your time with. So, what is it me or my money?" asked the old man. "I'll take the money sir, but I will also meet you next week to go fishing, because I miss fishing with my Dad. I didn't do enough of it sir, before he died," said Peter sadly. "Let me ask you; questioned the old man why did you buy the suit?" "Oh, the suit looked like one my Dad wore," said Peter with a smile.

SNOWMAN

Sometimes it starts with darkness and bitter cold winds that swirl and whip about the yard. Maybe it is thoughts of years past, memories that one wishes they could relive or memories one wants to forget. It is hail and rain that pelt at your windows and rattle them. It is a seasonal essence that causes a chill to shake ones bones and rattle one's mortality. When it arrives it forces a person to lay low, like under the afghan on the couch, quiet curled up in the chair by a fire, or retreating in a hot bath. One is forced to slow down, like with a drum roll that slows. Nature's tempo slows with a blanket of white and animal's hearts beating slowly. A drum roll, the doldrums? You carry within you the essence from which you were made, a Creators Spirit. A creative spirit! It is not the doldrums, but a resting to rejuvenate. "I" am created by the essence of creativity that lies within each one of us, since we were born, a seasonal essence, manifested under the writers pen, at the end of the glassblowers pipe, in the wood of the carpenters hand, in the hues of the artists brush, sandcastles from the child's pail in the sun at the ocean. And today I swirl and twirl and whip about your yard, and in your mind, manifest of wondrous snowflakes until the children create me. I am your snowman, and I carry within me the essence from which I am made, creativity.

January 4, 2006

INSANITY OF SOLAR SUICIDE

There are some I know,
Private, personal, not wanting to show,
They all pull their shades, prefer the dark!
A plague of seasonal depression their mark,
Shades and heavy window drapes,
Adorn every glass opening,
From light they escape!
Some people believe that the sun causes dust,
I smile and turn to know,
It is in God's presence I trust!
And in the closure of their blinds,
They can be at peace from the world, sublime.
We all need to hide from the violence and fights,
The rat race, tension and pressure that we know!
Who are worse? Them or I?
Awake and pacing many nights,
Leaning on the sill in the moonlight glow,
All my windows barren, to worship stars and sky,
All winter, I sit and wait for daylight savings,
Fighting off beach and bikini cravings,
Out in my yard barely clad,
Raking, planting flowers, my heart glad,
No sunscreen, no block,
In my younger years when I was chicken,
When suicidal thoughts, ideation,
Plans and ways were slim pickens,
I'll live life on the roller coaster ride, Use no sun block,
And commit the slow solar suicide!

April, 2001

Lisa A. Procter

Insanity of Time

Too!
Intense,
Moments of,
Eternity!
For some, family and friends,
Late is not acceptable the means to the end!
Intense social pressure,
Engagements with dates and time,
Simple, yet, complex!
Business meetings, arrangements,
Yet, the whole universe, runs by a seasonal mix,
Winds and weather obey their time,
The heaven's present stars,
Eternal forces control the tides, new crescent moons,
A lover's lure,
Waters rise high on full moons,
Wolves sing natures tunes!
Everyone so very aware of the numbers on clocks,
Many don't live in the "now" and laugh when death calls,
But it is "death" that "mocks"
Time to all!

June 30, 1999

Lisa A. Procter

Familiar Changes

As snowflakes flurried in the air,
He sat quietly in a familiar chair,
And if he'd ever let me know, would I find,
That as he heard the familiar, clank, of the campus door,
It was a thought of me that crossed his mind?
Even before his eyes met mine, and our hearts sank,
All day long through the halls, the sound
The familiar clank of the door a busy mind does not hear,
All day long our hearts beat, to Gods time,
We live in this world thinking we're,
"True to thine selves" being quite frank,
No longer is our heartbeat familiar,
When we allow ourselves to feel the love that we have found,
As snowflakes flurried,
I walked in prayer, my soul laid bear,
No longer taking the familiar for granted in my mind,
Will he ever let me know why he opens, my hearts door?
As snowflakes flurried,
I left him quietly in his chair,
To go and love and serve others in a bind,
My ears, my eyes, hands and hearts waiting for the clank of
    God's door,
Praying that God's love will be ever present in my busy mind,
Did I ever really know love before Him?
No longer is my heartbeat familiar when I close the campus door!

January, 20 2003

Lisa A. Procter

My Dusty Face

I gently raised the picture from its place,
Glowing eyes and smiling pure,
I sprayed the cleaner,
And washed the glassed face,
An aged voice from the other side of the room whispered,
"You should have seen her,"
"She always looked good in lace!"
Many I've loved and are gone,
Who are left, are just a few,
"Look there the picture of my son, no cure!"
Their memories are framed now and sit in this place,
We live and we love, we die and are born,
We reap what we sow and pay the price when it is due,
I gently lowered her loved ones picture,
Turned and looked into the mirror,
I came from dust, and will return to dust,
Then others will dust my face!
As I join the communion of saints!

November 24, 2004

Lisa A. Procter

My Master Puppeteer

The world is a stage and we are all players,
But he...
He stands behind the stage,
The theater is black,
He's watched the world, and he, he has aged.
The stage has always been small and level,
His eyes have watched through crystal beveled,
He dresses in the black attire of silence,
His hands and fingers play the wires of distance,
Thoughts and emotions suspended and controlled,
Intricately timed to dance on the stage of life's uncertainty,
The ticket has been sold,
Gently he takes me from my case,
Mends and entangles life's strings,
Positions me on a firm base,
I respond not, to what I am told,
But to his silence and the wires of distance,
That he has kept as the backdrop of his world as he grows old,
His shyness makes me dance, alone!

July 14, 2002

Blessed Sacrament I

The veil tore in the Temple and it was done,
I see the marble white angels, the gilded gold,
The Holy One!

The brilliant colors of stained glass,
I see the grain in the wood carved pew,
Together, yet alone, at Mass with you,
It was for this very moment in time, the eternal now!
That He died for your sin and mine,
Our love passes thru the fabric of life,
The veil of knowledge that causes the strife,
Like the sun through the glass,
We are still able to "feel" and "see"
But held to the accountability of relinquishing transparency,
I finger the green shamrock beads,
And lament of not knowing his plan,
You stand tall behind others,
Hand resting on the wooden pew,
Waiting, hidden, forefinger rubbing your thumbnail,
As if to soothe yourself, but all along knowing it is true,
We are connected like the Holy Fibers woven in the altar cloth, veil.
It is our hearts that tear, knowing it is true,
And He won't forsake us!
It has been passed down in time, this love of ours,
Like the faith of our Church,
Soldered like the pewter that holds the colored glass,
A small piece of God's love and our love to each other,
A tile in a mosaic, the larger picture hidden behind others,
And He knows our hearts, our thoughts and intentions,
As we approach the altar, we are transparent!

April 30, 2005

SACRED STONE WALLS

And if she sits on hard stone walls,
Will she learn what hardens men's hearts?
And if she sits on hard stone walls,
Promising never to depart.
Will she learn the lessons of why our hearts call?
Sacred secret spaces for poison ivy, chipmunks and ants
A boundary to men, a refuge for plants, an altar to God!
The smooth and rough hard rocks,
Hold the separateness of animosity,
The boundary of hatred, that sacred stonewalls, mock.
The builders long since dead.
And if she sits on hard stone walls,
Will she learn what hardens men's hearts?

SACRED STONE WALLS II

You see them scattered in the field,
On the drive,
To clear the land,
They think it mattered to mark their boundary with a seal,
Is it the lesson of fear of being deprived?
The sacred stonewall marks their field, their place, their home,
You see them scattered on the drive,
They bound themselves in and others out,
Oh! Sacred stonewall,
I ask you why their hearts call,
Are they deprived?
Or are they just an architectural convenience,

To clear the land and plant the seed,
Who clears our hearts and fulfills our needs?
And if she sits on hard stone walls,
Will she learn the lessons of why our hearts call?
And what hardens men's hearts.

SACRED STONE WALLS III

I stare into the plate glass window,
Like I stare into the cold still lake,
Black and clear, reflecting back what is before it,
The stonewall and the trees,
Parked cars and clouds,
I cannot see in, I do not know how,
There are people and objects in the room, make no mistake,
Like staring into a cold still lake,
You shift your focus, the angle of your glance,
To see deep within is a knack,
It is not until a cloud or a shadow moves upon it,
That you can see the fishes and the weeds,
It is not until your heart has been broken do you feel other's needs,
The reflection, clouds doubts,
We cannot see in, we do not know how,
There are pains, fears, joys, and doubts in a heart, make no mistake!
You shift your focus the angle of your glance,
You think for a moment, life might give you a second chance!

Sacred Stone Walls IV

And if she sits on hard stonewalls will she hear your heart call?
And will she learn of stonyhearted men?
To write in my diary as I sit on the boundary,
Oh! Alass! What can she do?
And God has brought her here to the stonewall,
To the stonewalling that has gone on in her life,
He will hide her on the rock, in the cleft, Exodus 33
And he will not pass her by,
She will see His glory!
Men obstruct the debate of God's love, by stonewalling,
Drawing boundaries on their love.

Sacred Stone Walls V

And women go to the walls and wail,
Some walls are too high and hard,
They do not see God's glory,
Women cry out until their blood runs pale,
They lose their babies in the silent war on doctor's hands red and gory,
They lose their sons on foreign soil,
They lose their children to drugs and ale,
Yet, sacred stonewalls and headstones are silent,
They still go to the walls and tell their stories,
And if she sits on hard sacred stonewalls will she learn the lessons
 of what hardens men's hearts and makes them call

2004

Insane Metamorphosis of Violence

Are we the Host?
Or Hostess? to...
A violent society!
Do we look away?
When children, friends, parents, and...
Strangers need us the most?

Centuries of unempathetic genealogy!

Here I am,
In my chrysalis of death,
I am here it is mine,
When I was young, I crawled the line,
Who was there? Who loved me? Celebrated birth?
Could they validate feelings? Could they care?

Alone, I am here
In my chrysalis of death,
I want you to come in,
Can someone permeate the membrane?
Of hurt, rejection, prejudice, despair!
Developing wings,
This pervasive social isolation stings!

I am here in my chrysalis of death,
A sheath so thick, I was taught,
Not to care!
I fed upon a Host,
Of material gain, competitive worldly boast,
Meanness, poverty, jealousy, wealth covetously wrought!

Phoniness, selfishness,
Hybrids of intoxicated liars of anger and hurt,
An empty shell of metamorphosis!
Untouchable feeling ghost!
So let me take you with me beneath,
I do not want to be alone under the dirt,
Wings, red stain,
Tears not drying,
Killing you, killing me,
Capable of dying,
Unbearable psychological pain!

Metamorphosis of life and hope,
Social developing gone wrong!
No Christian resurrection song!

A slimy worm that could not cope,
No beautiful butterfly to spread joy.
Should we get on our knees?
Our hands on our face,
Look to that Nazarene boy?
Embrace the faith?
Unlock wounded people with ,
Self-sacrifice, forgiveness,
Empathizing keys?
Faith filled butterflies fluttering
Place to place!

August 14, 1999

Doris Riggs

Doris Riggs was born Doris Robinson in 1915, the only child of Oakley and Clara Robinson, in Clinton Corners, New York — a town too small to be on most maps, but which assumed continental proportions in her memory, shaping her thoughts and unshakable perceptions of life until she died 15 years ago. She attended Smith College, met and married Lorrin Riggs, who became internationally recognized for his research in vision, had two children, entertained Nobel laureates in her home, traveled the world...But through it all she remained essentially the same little girl, living above her father's general store in a village where everyone knew everyone else, a cozy and vastly more innocent world that figured in many of her stories. Doris was a member of *The Rhode Island Short Story Club* for many years and treasurer of the club in 1987.

SHORT STORY
    The Day We Lost Grandpa

The Day We Lost Grandpa

Among the townsfolk my father was considered a very forward-looking man. This didn't mean that he never looked anywhere except straight ahead. If he had not been looking straight ahead, however, on the day when we lost Grandpa, the situation would have been noticed sooner; but I'll leave that to explain itself later. All that I want to say now is that when Father decided to build the new general store in the center of our small mid-Hudson village he proceeded with the brand new idea of adding a separate four-stall garage. It was in the year 1911, and all the more astonishing because at that time he owned the only motor-car in our part of Duchess County. This was a regal,—an open-tonneaued affair, resplendent with tufted leather seats, bulbous horn, acetylene headlamps, and an abundance of brass strut work.

Father was quick to take advantage of the prestige of owning a machine like this. In it he promptly conducted a satisfactory courtship; then he married, settled into the large apartment above the store, and eventually I arrived on the scene. Several years later, one of Mr. Ford's early Model T Touring Cars also arrived and took its place beside the Regal, in stall number two of our ambitious garage.

My recollections of the old Regal days are not very clear; I was much too young. Mainly what I remember is a vast array of gleaming brass, and the taste of wet veiling. In those days long linen dusters were required dress for all adults, and in addition female heads were swathed in masses of gauzy veiling. No exception was made for female children, as far as the veiling went, and if they happened to be chatter-boxes, like me, the taste of wet veiling will be a memory that lingers.

Happily the new Model T was to dispense with such of this anti-dust paraphernalia. It had its own collapsible fabric roof, and roll-down side-curtains with little windows set in made of rippled-looking

Isinglas. So pleased was everyone with this new protection, in fact, that we seldom went anywhere without enjoying the novelty of having all of the side flaps down and buttoned into place.

It was a fine day in mid-May, and we were setting out for a visit at the farm of Great-Uncle Theodore's and his wife, Aunt Rhuemma. Grandmother stood on the concrete apron before the garage now, in her best brocaded black satin dress, waiting for Father to start up the engine and back out. A white lace collar, pinned close, set off the fresh color of her chubby cheeks, already aglow with the prospect of a pleasant gossip with her sister, Rhuemma.

Grandfather, store teeth in place and moustache neatly brushed, was standing beside her in his good black suit. No urging was necessary to get him to go along for a visit with his brother-in-law, Uncle Theo, I heard him say, was so full of vinegar that it was as good as a circus to hear him talk.

Although I had no conception of what vinegar meant, in this context, I certainly was aware that Great-Uncle Theo generally could be counted upon to scare the living daylights out of youngsters. Past experience had shown me that the best was to enjoy a visit at his place was to observe, without attracting attention, and early on I formed the habit of standing well back, and simply savoring what I could of the general hullabaloo.

Impatient, meanwhile, I started to dance about Grandmother on the toes of my new high-button shoes. Short and chunky in her ground-length skirt, Grandmother's figure always struck me as incredibly like an enormous, squat black fire-cracker,—except for the sheer depression below her bust which marked the waistline. Although Grandmother never wore an apron with her Sunday dress, I knew that this deep slot had been created expressly to hold apron-bands, for on every other day of the week they were snugged about her middle precisely within the confines of this indentation. My blue hair-bow bouncing up and down, I circled again to view the full circumference of it with awe. To me it was by all means the most remarkable feature of the grown-up female form, and I longed for the day to arrive when such a depression would begin to develop on me.

Sounds already were issuing from the interior of the garage. Cranking the Model T into action was always a tricky business. Generally my mother's presence was required to assist. She was expected to sit close to the driver's seat and to advance or retard that spark on command, and to adjust the throttle as needed. Since she had no grasp of mechanics whatsoever, failed frequently to distinguish the spark lever from that of the throttle, and never was able to remember what it was you were supposed to do when you retarded something, it was doubtful that her services were beneficial.

Once the motor caught, moreover, that agitation of the chassis, jouncing up and down on its own leaf-springs, added to the loud coughing noises of the engine itself, were circumstances that left Mother so drained of nervous energy that it took approximately the first half hour of every journey for her to recover.

Nonetheless, there was some justification for her exhaustion, for Henry Ford's concept of gears in the Model T allowed for no such thing as a neutral position. Once the engine had sputtered into life the entire vehicle commenced to fidget and shake in a palpitating effort to do something,—either back out of the garage of its own accord, or else, like a snarling animal insufficiently restrained on its leash, creep forward to pin the hapless soul on the crank handle to the nearest wall!

For successful getaways much depended on having the handbrake well set, and an individual of substantial size at the cranking end, who knew just how to lean his full weight against the radiator to halt each threat of encroachment and exactly when it was safe to let go and launch a wild dash around the front fender and into the driver's seat. Fortunately Father was a very heavy-set man and generally managed all of this arm and foot-work nicely. He was in the process of backing the car out of the garage now, and Mother appearing somewhat pale, was sitting beside him.

I hopped over the running board and was the first to climb into the back seat. Clutching his black hat and the inevitable Sunday cigar, Grandfather got behind the driver on my left, and Grandmother was on my right.

Long ago Grandmother had trained her husband well; there was to be no tobacco-chewing on any of our Sunday outings. He insisted rather stubbornly, therefore, on the cigar, although he was scarcely ever known to light it. Grandpa was not overly fond of cigars. My mother, however, was always enormously relieved to see him conform to Grandmother's rule, for Mother had been brought up in Brooklyn, which had done nothing to develop a tolerance in her for the country habit.

Little could be seen of the passing countryside through the Isinglas windows, from the level of a five-year-olds' eyes, but the sensations of riding were, alone, sufficiently novel to keep me happy. There were plenty of details, too, to attract my attention. Grandpa's shagreen watch–fob, for one. The complicated set of cross-pieces that held up the fabric roof; sunlight picking out the tortoise pattern from the comb at the back of my mother's hair; and closer still, there was always the mesmerizing satin perfection of Grandmother's stomach, rounding smoothly out below her apron-slot as she sat beside me.

Happily Great-aunt Rem, too, was constructed much like her sister. As we drew to a stop in their dooryard Aunt Rem stepped out onto the porch to greet us. As a farm wife, her Sunday outfit included a large calico apron. I was overjoyed to see its' bands clinched neatly into place in the proper depression.

"Come on in and set down!" It was Uncle Theo roaring from inside the house. He considered Sunday a day for rest and catching up on reading *The Country Gentleman*, and was never known to budge out of his easy-chair for anyone. He liked company, however,—providing it was men folk; women and children were expected to fend for themselves at his house and Uncle Theo preferred that they do this at a convenient distance from him.

Grandmother and her sister retreated, as usual, to the kitchen to discuss such affairs as baking, canning, and the probable output of their gardens. My mother had learned long ago to stay out of this kind if conversation for it was carried on in a language with which she was not familiar. After a few more years of living in the country she was to discover that *pieplant* meant rhubarb, *huckleberries* were the same as blueberries, *ersters* translated into oysters, but that *ersterplant* was—of all things!, ordinary purple eggplant. *Garden sass*, on the other hand, could refer to almost anything green that grew in the garden. The exchange of recipes was equally baffling for Mother's tutoring in cooking in the city of Brooklyn left her totally unprepared to measure ingredients either by the pinch or in the large walnut size.

Discreetly, then, she settled herself in a rocker in the far corner of the sitting-room, and I took up a position at her knee. Fastening my gaze on the wiry wisps of gray hair and beard that formed a sort of a halo around Uncle Theo's snapping black eyes and tiny Kewpie-doll crab-apple-red cheeks, I waited patiently, but not without trepidation, for the show I knew was about to begin.

Uncle Theo had clapped the pages of *The Country Gentlemen* together. Without a glance he flung it onto the floor now, hooked one thumb under the elastic of his suspenders, plucked it up, let it snap down on his shoulder with a thunk, and drawled, *Waaal*,—how long did it take you, in that there danged Ford?

Father consulted his pocket-watch and replied that it had been just forty-five minutes since we left our garage. Uncle Theo jerked upright. "Git out!" he thundered.

Father and Grandpa continued to sit right in front of him, grinning ear to ear, until I realized that I had been tricked again into fright by my great-uncle's ferocious manner of speech. Conversation with him could never be placid; outrage, in fact, seemed to be his stock-in-trade. The Model T now calling to mind the sore topic of road construction, Uncle Theo slammed one fist into his palm and proceeded to take out after the lazy incompetent Town Supervisor and then went on to lambaste the county's Road Commissioner. Father endeavored to put in a good word for the latter's performance, but Uncle Theo would have none of it; he jabbed a forefinger in Father's face and said that 'that ignorant so-and-so don't know the difference between a sink-hole and a syringe bush!" And he thwacked one booted foot on the floor for emphasis.

Grandpa loved it. "Ho! Ho!" he shouted, brandishing the cigar.

Uncle Theo went right on from there to tick off every one of his no-good sons-in-law, and dwell briefly on the short-comings of 'the whole danged passel' of his witless grandchildren. Finally he was compelled to attend to the cud of tobacco that he had been chewing on for some time. It caught while in the heat of argument, Uncle Theo was given to get rid of the cud in the same way that he disposed of *The Country Gentleman*, without looking. Aunt Rem, unlike her sister, had had no success in training her husband at all, and her only solution to this particular problem was to keep over-sized mats, each centered with a very large cuspidor, on both sides of Uncle Theo's easy-chair.

Prising an Apple Plug out of pocket of his faded denim shirt, Uncle The bit off a fresh chew now and settled back in his chair to start out on a new theme. My attention hadn't flagged in the slightest. There was no telling with Uncle Theo what might come next.

"Tim Oliver's got the next farm but one from here," he started out mildly enough. "Well, t'other forenoon his corncrib caught afire, and before it got done it took the hay barn with it. Tim had taken it into his head to go to the auction over to Clinton Holler that day, and he up and left his wife to mind the place. He leaned forward to poke a knowing finger into Grandpa's knee. "Now I want to tell you that Sarey-Ann ain't no better than she ought to be, and it seems that she and Ike,—he's that shiftless hooligan Tim's got working for him—was lallygaggin' around in the front parlor and didn't notice a thing until the smoke got in and damned near liked to choke the two of them."

With this, Mother leaned over and suggested that I might like to retire outside to play. But I shook my head. Luckily Aunt Rem entered just then with a tray full of last season's elderberry wine. Mother was aghast when she saw me reach for a glass.

"Leave'er be!" Uncle Theo rumbled. "T'ain't nothin' but elderberry juice and water. Go on the porch, Sis, and enjoy it."

Not knowing and elderberry from chokeberry, Mother was helpless to argue, but she quickly poured half of my glass into hers and let me depart with the remainder.

Before long the visit was over and we were on our way home. A short way from Uncle Theo's, the dirt road passed through a fine expanse of open woodland. Mother had brought a small basket and wanted to stop and search for arbutus. Father stopped the car and we all fanned out through the trees to poke around under leaves for the tiny fragrant flowers. When the basket was almost full, a sudden clap of thunder sent us flying back to pile into the automobile. Father cranked up hastily, but with no difficulty, and all eyes on the road ahead of us we started off.

Wanting once more to look at the woods, I edged over toward Grandfather's side and kneeled up to look out, but very slowly it began to percolate into my childish mind that something was wrong. I glanced over at Grandmother, who was also looking out of the window on her side, quite unaware apparently that anything was amiss. There was a wide expanse of empty seat between us. Suddenly I realized that it was much wider than it should have been! In a flash my feet were standing on the seat and I was peering through the window at the back. A long distance away Grandfather, his hat awry, was running down the center of the dusty track, waving both arms in the air.

'There's Grandpa," I said. But nobody paid attention. "He's waving his hands in the air."

At that Father's foot slammed down on the brake and all heads craned 'round to look back. There was a great silence as we waited for Grandfather to catch up. Puffing heavily, he finally reached the car and got in.

"I saw you, Grandpa. You were running!" The novelty of this seemed to astonish no one but myself.

"Where were you?" Grandmother demanded.

"How was I to know you'd be such a time pickin' posies? I took a little walk in the woods on the other side of the road."

"What took you so long?" my father wanted to know.

Grandpa snatched the tipsy hat off of his brow and slapped it hard onto one knee. "Dad gum it! I had a little errand to attend to. And besides,—I stopped to light a cigar."

Grandma leaned back in the seat again and folded her hands stop the small satin shelf of her stomach. "You'll be the death of me yet, John,—with that cigar."

After I had had my bath that evening I ran naked to my mother's bedroom to look into the big mirror, but there was no sign as yet on the smooth expanse of my tummy of any crease to hold apron-bands. I think it dawned on me then that growing up might be a tedious process.

MARIE C. RUSSIAN

Marie DeSpirito Russian was born shortly after the 1938 Hurricane. She was married to the late Bernard W. Russian for forty-three years. She has two daughters and five granddaughters. Marie has a love of poetry and has always shown an interest in writing since the age of eleven. She continues to write poetry and short stories and is presently writing her family history. Marie is a member of *The Holy Angels Women's Guild* in Barrington, RI. Her volunteer work includes The Barrington School System, The Barrington Public Library, St.Luke's School Library, School One Library, and many other civic organizations. Her latest project is volunteering in the *Literacy Program of East Bay*. Marie is a member of *The Rhode Island Short Story Club* to which she has been treasurer for many years.

SHORT STORY
    Staying At My Grandmother's

POEMS
    Traveling the Lonely Road
    Carol's Shaggy Dog
    The Bag We Drag Behind Us
    We Danced Well Together
    Cancer (In Memory Of Bernie)
    I Miss You
    Bernie (In Memoriam)
    Your Kisses
    First Anniversary – 6/3/06
    I Will Love You Forever
    George Jones' Song
    Sasha

STAYING AT MY GRANDMOTHER'S

Whenever I stayed over at my grandmother's, the first thing I did each morning was to look out from her kitchen window. Every season brought a new and beautiful scene. In summer I'd see my grandmother's vast garden filled with the richness of tomato plants, from which she made her very special tomato sauce. There were also rows of string beans, eggplant, squash, cucumbers, peppers, lettuce, broccoli and Swiss chard! I took delight in staying with her because she taught me how to preserve various vegetables. My favorite job was capping the bottles of tomato sauce.

Winter brought the snow with her dog Whitey prancing around in it as though he were a great snowball. It also brought across the field a little boy too cold to go to the outhouse, thus urinating from his front porch! At the time, my grandmother's house was one of the few with an indoor bathroom. Each time she cleaned it, the smells of Sulpha Naptha disinfectant cleaner wafted through my nostrils, causing me to catch my breath.

One winter, when I looked out in anticipation of seeing Whitey playing in the snow, all I saw was a patch of red in the street. I had heard screeching tires, but was unaware of Whitey's misfortune. My grandmother ordered me away from the window to protect me from the scene, but I knew it was not good news. Her tears had fallen on my cheek and I sensed that I had lost my good friend Whitey.

Summer was the best time for me there. My grandmother let me make mud pies and I made sandwiches with the mud and the large leaves from her hydrangea bush. This was a fun treat which my mother NEVER allowed me to do.

Being an only child at the time, I created my own playmates. I had a great time using my imagination.

Fall brought the apples on her tree, and I delighted in playing in the pile of raked leaves. I loved feeding the rabbits in their cages and watching their babies grow. To this day, I will not eat rabbit, though I reluctantly cook it for my husband.

Then came school and my world changed. I missed all those happy days with my grandmother, but I discovered a whole new world at school.

Traveling the Lonely Road

How I wish I could go to
Canada with you again
Seeing Niagara Falls from
The other side
Its swift waters flowing
With such intensity and beauty.
All those gourmet restaurants
We visited with friends.

Italy will never be the same
Without you,
Dancing in my family's courtyard,
An accordion playing sweet
Romantic songs
While we laughed and danced,
—ate and loved.
All those islands we visited
With our children
Learning other people's customs,
Making new friends.
I can only travel those places again

In my mind,
For without you
No vacation can compare
To the times we shared together.
In our travels you were the one
Who always took care of us.

You showed me the world
And now my world is empty
Without you.

Who will carry my suitcase
Now that you are gone?

Carol's Shaggy Dog

The child took scissors
Prim and proper
And nothing in this world
Could stop her.
A little snip here
A little snip there
Was how she cut
The puppy's hair.

The Shitzu looked
Like he ran afowl
The owner then
Began to scowl.
Who could have touched

Marie C. Russian

My puppy's hair?
It wasn't me
The child did declare.

But tucked behind
Her back, in hand
A scissors hidden
Like contraband.
It was an accident
She said,
I only tried
To see his head.

Now shaggy Gizzy
Sits perplexed
And wondered what
Was coming next.
Carol wanted to give
The child a wack.
But instead, she smiled,
It will grow back.

Poor Gizzy, on the couch,
He sat
And thought, in dog language,
Imagine that!

July 21, 2001

Marie C. Russian

The Bag We Drag Behind Us

FEAR—That's my bag
And it really is a drag
To haul that bag behind me.
I try to ignore it
Not give it a name
But it follows me anyway
And puts me to shame.

I shrug off its existence
And deny that it's there
It sits right beside me
Tho' I pretend not to care.
It rears its ugly head
When I try to speak.
It makes me feel uneasy
It makes me look weak.
I'm determined to hold
My head up high
I'll pretend that my fear
Is just a lie.

WE DANCED WELL TOGETHER

We danced well together
I followed closely your every move.
When you spun me
I knew just when to come back to you.

We'd glide across the floor
Cheek to cheek
And heart to heart,
Our hearts beating as one.
And rightfully so
Because we WERE ONE
When we danced together!

Sunday, September 12, 2004

Written for Bernie when he was feeling very depressed. We were listening to some romantic dance music and these words came to mind for him. I promised him that we WOULD dance together again someday.

~ ~ ~ ~ ~ ~ ~ ~ ~ ~ ~ ~

On the 2-month anniversary of his death August 3, 2005, I dreamed that he was looking for me as I walked with a friend and he took me in his arms and danced with me!

CANCER
In Memory of Bernie

The words came out like daggers,
Piercing my heart,
"Cancer," they said.
I could not think of being apart,
Of having my loved one dead.

"Where are You, God?" I cried,
"Why did You leave me empty inside?"
And at that point I just knelt,
Overcome with the grief that I felt,
And a part of me, too,—died.

Thursday, April 28, 2005

I MISS YOU

I miss your sunshine smile
Whenever you looked at me,
Your laughter at our grandchild's play
Your cupid lips which kissed me tenderly.
Without you there is no complete day.

I miss your presence when I see our friends,
They are sometimes afraid to speak your name.
I miss our holding hands together in the park.
I know nothing will ever be the same.

Our bed is empty of your frame
I cling close to the edge of my side.
I miss your body's warmth and tender love.
How will I, without you, abide?

My heart is buried now within your soul,
A lonely grave is all that's left of you.
The nights are dark for me, and cold.
There was no greater love for me than you.

July 8, 2005 – 1:10 a.m.

BERNIE
In Memoriam

I looked up from washing dishes
And noticed my window
Spattered with many butterflies.
I imagined they were angels
Coming to tell me you were okay.
As my tears mingled with soapsuds
I smiled and thought
What beautiful creations God made
With butterflies, angels
And you.

Wednesday, November 30, 2005 – 5:50 p.m.

Your Kisses

Every once in a while I close my eyes and
Imagine you kissing me tenderly, softly.
At that moment I could feel the tingling
In my body
How I miss your loving kisses—
The kisses I will no longer know or feel.
All I have left are beautiful memories.
I keep those close to my heart.

January 1, 2006 – 6:00 p.m.

First Anniversary – 6/3/06

Saturday was one year
For the anniversary of your passing.
I call it passing because
You have passed away
From me and my world.
I didn't cry at all that day.
At your Mass I was stoic, calm
But, while getting ready
For bed,
I thought I could not stand
One more night without you
In an empty bed.
I longed for the smell of you,
So I sprayed your cologne
Ever so gently on your pillow,

A sweet, light fragrance
Which made me desire you more.
After going through my routine
Of prayers, etc.
The tears began to flow.
I could hold them in
No longer,
So I turned off the light,
Laid my head next to your pillow
And devoured your fragrance
As I wept.
It didn't take me long
To calm down.

Drifting off to sleep
I began to dream
That you were holding me,
Comforting me with your arms
Which once were so strong.
I began to feel a peace
Within me,
Knowing that you were
In God's hands
And suffering no more.

Friday, June 9, 2006 – 12:20 a.m.

Marie C. Russian

I WILL LOVE YOU FOREVER

The day before my birthday
I asked for a sign
To tell me my husband
Was at peace,
And questioning whether he could
Still love me after death.
I went to bed as usual
Thinking of Bernie
Wishing he could be with me
For my birthday.

It seemed that suddenly I saw
Upon my marble table
A card which read:

GO WELL
FOR I WILL
LOVE YOU
FOREVER

Then I heard another person
Next to me, sleeping softly.
I could have sworn
It was Bernie.

Was it a dream
Or was it real?!

Sunday, September 24, 2006 – 5:42 a.m.

Marie C. Russian

GEORGE JONES' SONG

As I listened to the wail
Of George Jones' song,
"He Stopped Loving Her Today,"
I wondered if it is true.
Does the one who is gone
Stop loving the one who
Remains?
That would be a hard thing to accept
If, in death, you stopped loving me!

I have dreams that,
When it is my turn,
I will come to you
And you will love me
As before,
Only on a higher plane.
It is difficult enough
Not having your love with
Me now.
I don't want to think of
Losing you altogether in death.

SASHA

On a very rainy day
In June's oppressive heat
She entered the restaurant,
Silver sandals on her feet.
Flared skirt bouncing
And sunglasses askew,
She brought sunshine in her smile
Which was meant for me and you.

She was on top of the world
As she ordered, "Pancakes, please,"
She got busy drawing pictures
While the waitress she would tease.
She was far beyond her years
Like as actress she would be,
But you mustn't lose sight
Of the fact, she's only three.

She made friends with all the patrons
Spilled the creamer and then some.
She was getting even worse
Than the time when she was one.
All the patrons smiled at her
As she giggled with glee
She was naughty and funny
But then again, she's only three.

Monday, August 26, 2006 – 12:52 a.m.

June Smith

June Wilkins Smith won poetry prizes while a student at Hope High School and Wellesley College, but wrote few poems for many years afterwards. She received her Master's Degree at the University of Rochester, and, after a brief teaching career at Bradford Junior College, she met and married the Rev. Charles Smith. Moving to Connecticut, they raised five children. Later she taught part-time at Quinnipiac College and then at Fairfield University. She began writing again in 1990. She and her husband, now proud grandparents of five, have retired to Providence, where she participates in writing groups and poetry workshops.

SHORT STORIES
>   Downstairs to 1872*
>   Fragments of Failure

Essay
>   Memories of an Inspiring Teacher: Dorothy C. Allan

Poems
>   If Eve Had Known
>   Yellow Rooms*
>   Apostrophe to Opportunity*
>   Stellar Stove*

Blaisdell Award

DOWNSTAIRS TO 1872

June was tired. She had worked all evening entering data into her genealogy software program. Her granddaughter, Jackie, had e-mailed her from Connecticut: "Can you, would you, pleeeez, pleeez, send me all the names and dates of your ancestors and Grandpa's for a sciense projeck we have? And can you scan pictures of them and email them to me? Its dew on Monday. I'll do anything to thank you. Ill even use the spell checker on my email."

That last promise was a big concession; Jackie usually said she did not have time to learn to spell. As a grandma, June wanted to fulfill Jackie's request. Besides, this e-mail message was an incentive to get started on a task June had wanted to do anyway. She owned information—typed, handwritten, penciled from oral reminiscences; old pictures, old letters. She wanted to print out family trees. She wanted to assemble the old pictures in albums and eventually write brief biographies of those ancestors she knew anything about. She was especially touched by an old letter, written in 1872 by her great grandmother from Iowa to relatives in Pennsylvania. It described the children and apologized for her writing in pencil because the ink had frozen.

The project was going well. By midnight June had been able to print out charts of her pedigree and her husband's pedigree, four generations back.

As she sat at the computer, reading the printout, June knew she was drifting into sleep, for every name she saw on the genealogy chart seemed to turn into a stair she was standing on. The stairs were not solid but made of iron, like a fire escape, but the ironwork of each step was shaped like the letters and numbers of a person's name and dates. She looked anxiously at the step she was standing on, to see whether her death date was there. It was not, only her name and birth.

"Of course," she said aloud, nearly waking. "This staircase is only a printout of my own files."

As if to confirm this fact, as she stepped on her Grandpa Caldwell's stair, she saw the asterisk she herself had typed between his two middle names: Harry and Patten. She had wondered why he had two middle names. Her mother had explained that he was named Morand Patten after his own mother's beloved half-brother; but he disliked the name Patten, and substituted the name of his own younger brother, who had drowned while still young. She could understand then why he had liked the name "Harry." But why had he disliked "Patten?"

Of course, as a child, she had disliked her own name. Her playmates had teased her. They called her "Junie," as they called boys named Junior. Or they called her "June Bug." For a while, she asked everyone to call her by her middle name, but "Emma" turned out to be worse. "I Emma girl named Emma," was the mildest tease. The worst was, "Hello, Enema, see you in the bathroom, ha, ha, ha." When the teasing years ended, she had become reconciled to "June" but still hated her middle name. She knew, of course, Emma was her Grandma Caldwell's June's mother, Estelle, had gone to Boston to be with her mother when June was born, leaving Daddy, who had to work, in Providence with his parents until his wife and infant came back. Grandma Caldwell had helped care for mother and baby for several weeks. Dad admired Grandma Caldwell, too and had agreed that their baby would be called "June Emma," June herself had happy memories of this roly-poly woman's visits, who raised her knees under the sheet to make a hill for her granddaughter to slide down. But she died when June was six. It would be fine to be named after her, if only her name hadn't been so horrible. They could at least have called her June Frances, for Emma's middle name had been Frances. June seriously considered changing her own middle name to Frances.

Standing on Grandpa Caldwell's stair, June began to wonder again why he hated the name Patten. Was he teased about it? she wondered. Had playmates called out, "Morand Patten, is your mother going to use you for a pattern?" or "Morand Patten leather, is your sister going to wear you on her feet?"

June stepped down to the stair below and read Morand's mother's name, Similda Fisk. Similda's openwork step framed a view of the stairway below, which descended endlessly. Looking to the side to avoid dizziness, June noticed a landing and walked onto it. There was a door made of rough planks. She lifted the black iron latch and walked into a low room heated by a cheerful fireplace; but a cold wind blew in with her. Quickly she closed the door behind her. Children sat playing on a hooked rug before the hearth; a tall boy was tending the fire; and a young woman in a long dress jumped up to greet her.

"Come in out of the cold, my dear!" she cried. "My, you have no bonnet on and no coat. And walking in slippers. You are hardly dressed for an Iowa winter."

"Iowa!" June exclaimed.

She looked down at her shoes, her black suede flats. She noticed the woman's shoes buttoned high on her ankle. She wished she had some laced brown boots, such as her granddaughter sometimes wore with long skirts.

She said, "Iowa's where my grandfather..."

"Wait!" cried the woman, concerned. "Before you tell us your errand, let me rub your hands. Why, they don't seem cold. You can't have walked far. Did the stage bring you?"

"I came by the landing," said June.

The woman frowned, puzzled, and replied, "You must mean the railroad platform."

June muttered thoughtfully, "I shouldn't be surprised to be in Iowa;

after all, I came by Similda's step."

"Well, of course you came up my step. But how do you know my name? Most folks call me Minnie around here. Where are you from and what brings you to the farm?"

"I'm from New England and I'm...I'm looking for the Caldwells. I'm tracing the family tree."

"Aren't too many trees here," Similda said. "How'd you hear about us?"

"From my Mother; she's a Caldwell."

"I know Mr. Caldwell's folks are New England people. Are you from Ipswich, too? Pity Mr. Caldwell's not here. He's off teaching school. Comes home on the weekends. Who is your mother?"

"Her name's Estelle—Estelle Caldwell." June bit her tongue to keep from saying, "She's your granddaughter."

"I never heard of a Caldwell by that name."

"She isn't born yet," June thought but did not say.

"But I'm always glad to meet family." Minnie continued. "I miss my own folks a lot."

"Back in Ohio?" asked June.

"Well, you do know about us."

"Yes, from a wonderful letter my mother's Aunt Cora gave her."

The two little girls looked up quickly. June realized one of them had to be that same Aunt Cora.

"I wonder what letter that could be. I have owed my own family a letter for such a long time. But now that the railroads have come through, I hope some of them can come for a visit."

"Your mother, and your sister Emma Sue..."

June had remembered her Grandpa had an Aunt Emma Sue and a sister Emma, as well as a wife named Emma later on. People must have really liked that name in those days. She continued speaking to Similda. "and your brother Morand?"

A boy of about five raised his head from his play.

"Yes, we are talking about your dear uncle after whom you are named." Similda picked up the boy and hugged him. June's head felt dizzy as she realized the boy she was looking at would one day become her grandfather.

"Morand Patten," sang one of the girls, who looked to be about seven. "Patty, Patty, Patty."

"Stop teasing him, Emma," said another girl, a little taller. "You are jealous he has Uncle Rand's name."

Emma retorted, "I am not jealous. I have Aunt Emma Sue's name. Cora, you are an apple core." She turned her attention to the toddler. "Harry is hairy," she laughed. "He has hair all over him. And Walter is a Walnut."

The tall boy grinned and put another log on the fire. Minnie set little Morand Patten down on the rug.

"Cora," she said, "Help the children get ready for bed. We'll find a place for Cousin...What is your name?"

"June."

"Hmm. Sounds like a boy's name; short for Junior?"

"Oh, no. It's just June."

"I never heard of a relative of Mr. Caldwell's by that name. But the hour is late. We can talk tomorrow."

White snow was piling on the window panes. There was no clock. June did not want to peek at her quartz watch with its vinyl strap. If they saw it, they'd never understand. She didn't understand, either! She was glad she was wearing her stylish blue wool skirt that reached almost to her ankles, and her black Winter L'Eggs hose. That way she was not dressed too differently from Minnie.

"Where is your bag?" asked Minnie.

"I have no baggage with me."

"Did you leave it at the station? Never mind," said Minnie. "I'll lend you a nightgown. You can sleep with me. Mr. Caldwell is away, and you will be more comfortable than on the bench in here."

All the children came to give their cousin a good night hug.

Emma sang, "Cousin June is a calendar. April, May, June."

Little Morand Patten piped up, "Emma, Emma, Enema."

"Randy," scolded Similda, "don't say that. It's naughty!"

"Emma is my middle name," June told them. "June Emma."

She lifted the little girl and said, "Some day when you grow up you will come visit me and my mother and father in Rhode Island. And you will bring me a present, a beautiful gold pen. And I will always keep it and remember your visit. You will be seventy-five years old then, and I—I will be a little girl!"

Little Emma laughed, delighted at what she thought was make-believe.

June got down on the floor to say "Goodnight" to the toddler, Harry. Tears filled her eyes as she hugged the charming child, who, she knew, would die in a few years. Five-year-old Morand took Harry's hand and led him in a fatherly manner toward boys' bedroom.

Minnie showed June to an unheated bedroom. But June felt she could not bear to change into the nice flannel nightgown for fear of freezing in the process. Besides, she didn't want to cause Minnie astonishment over the twentieth-century underclothes June was of course wearing.

"I'll just put this gown over my day clothes," June said. "I will be warmer that way. And I'll sleep on the bench near the fireplace. I'll be leaving first thing in the morning."

"If you like," Minnie said. "But I'll give you a hot breakfast before you leave. I won't let you go hungry into the cold. Is the coach coming for you?"

"I'll just go back the way I came," June answered evasively.

When the house was dark and quiet except for the crackling of the dying fire, June slipped the nightgown off over her head and laid it on the bench. She tiptoed to the door, lifted its latch softly, and cautiously peered out. Instead of an Iowa winter night, she saw the landing she had come by. Closing the door quietly, June walked toward Similda's stair. She read the iron scroll work: Similda Fisk, 1839 to 1872. That very year Similda would die, and Mr. Caldwell, as she called her husband Daniel, would take the children back East to be near his family in Boston.

She mounted the next step and looked at the iron letters with the two alternate middle names separated by an asterisk. She felt she had come closer to understanding why her grandfather had taken the name Harry. She had sensed his love for his little brother and could appreciate his wish later to honor his memory. But didn't he also love his mother, and wouldn't he remember that she had loved her own baby brother so much she named her son after him? June found herself wishing that her Grandpa Caldwell had kept "Patten" for his middle name in memory of his dead mother. Who had given it to him. He could have just added "Harry" after it.

"Wait a minute," June said aloud. "There was no new knowledge of my grandfather's feelings in that farmhouse, only what came out of my own head—and heart. And what about me?" June surprised herself by exclaiming, "I have a mother, too. How heartless of me to want to discard the middle name she chose for me out of love for her own mother, the Grandma who loved me so much when I was a little girl! Of course I want to keep the name Emma to honor them both—and to honor my Great-aunt Emma, too, whom I have just met again!"

As she spoke, the iron stairs turned back into the black ink of the printout. She was still sitting at her desk, staring at the genealogy chart, over which she had fallen asleep. Her quartz watch said 1:00 a.m. Nearby in the display case lay the gold pen with a mother-of-pearl handle which Great-aunt Emma had given her on a visit to New England so long ago.

"She told me she thought she could never write anything beautiful enough to be worthy of that pen, but perhaps some day I would. And how I would love to! And perhaps Jackie will some day, too. And some day she may go down the iron stairway and visit Similda and little Emma and Morand, and stop by to visit me when I was a child. Oh, nonsense! I must be dreaming again. I'd better go to bed. I'll scan my charts into an e-mail attachment to send her in the morning. Then I'll start scanning the pictures. Too bad I don't have one of Minnie," June yawned. "She was nice."

FRAGMENTS OF FAILURE

Sylvia stared at her 1040 Form. Although her desk lamp was lighted, and sunlight streamed in, the numbers she had penciled looked blurred. The magnifying glass made them larger but no clearer, and allowed only a few digits to be seen at a time. Yet, deciphering the numbers alone would not enable her to compute her taxes. She had another problem, too: when she subtracted, she could not make the answer come out smaller than the number she had started with.

She did not want help. Ever since Old Ray, her husband, had died, she had filled out her tax forms herself. Whenever she had a difficulty, she tried harder. Why admit failure? Young Ray and his petite wife, Rita, were eager to help; every week they drove her to the supermarket. The trouble was, when people help you, they always think they know a better way.

Usually Sylvia did her thinking in bed when she couldn't sleep, or while resting. Now she pulled her afghan over her on the sofa, and began to think. Her first step was to state her goal. She had thought it was to compute her taxes; now she saw that as a means to the real goal, to file her tax return. Then why not ask for help? Because there was another goal, even more urgent—to keep her financial affairs hidden from anyone who might be tempted to meddle.

She had a device for thinking about problems: she pretended someone else had come to her for advice. She would take a protective interest in this imaginary person. In this case, she would warn her not to go to a private accountant, or to a relative. The person would need an objective company that specialized in taxes and would have many persons working with set rules and fees, so they would be less able to overcharge or butt into her business. She decided to take her own advice. She could ask Young Ray to drive her to H. & R. Block. That way he could help her without finding out too much. Pleased with her idea, she soon fell asleep.

She woke with a start, frightened to find herself on the sofa, surrounded by darkness. The clock, barely readable, showed it was not the middle of the night. It was only half past seven. The bell rang again.

A voice called, "Mom?"

It was Young Ray. She opened the door. Wasting no time, she asked him to drive her to H. & R. Block. Ray hesitated.

"Mom," he said at last, "I can drive you. But you don't need to pay anyone to do your taxes. I or Rita would be glad to help you. If you can't see the questions, we'll read them to you."

Oh dear, Sylvia thought. To delay answering, she invited him in for cookies and milk.

"Thank you for offering," she said carefully. "But this time I just need a ride at your convenience. Of course, I could take a taxi."

"You don't need to take a taxi. Just tell us when you want to go. It's too late tonight."

Her strategy had worked. He was so busy offering to drive that he had ceased offering to do her taxes.

Ray suggested they go on the following evening. He and Rita would come around five-thirty and they could all go to The Ground Round for supper (she could chew ground meat), and then they'd do her errand.

Both of them! If they drove her, they would also come inside with her. How much would they overhear? They assumed her problem was eyesight. That night she composed words to say to the tax consultant that would not give away her failings. The next afternoon Sylvia dressed early. When they came for her, Ray carried her brown envelope of tax materials, Rita carried her handbag, and Sylvia walked down the steps, one hand on the rail and the other on her cane.

At the restaurant Young Ray said many funny things. Rita giggled. Sylvia smiled. When they drove to their destination, Rita walked in with Sylvia. A plump woman took Sylvia's brown envelope. The woman looked everything over.

"Why, you've already done it," she exclaimed. Sylvia could glimpse Rita lifting her head at the rear of the room.

"I just wanted you to check the arithmetic," Sylvia explained quite loudly.

That was the sentence she had composed. It would sound as if she was just making sure of something she had already done. The woman took the papers over to a computer, spent a while peering into the computer screen and fingering the keyboard, finally went to another machine and picked up some papers.

"Here are your two returns, Federal and State," she said, not giving them to Sylvia. "We will mail them from here. And here are the copies for your files. That will be thirty-five dollars."

Sylvia murmured, "There should be four things."

The woman answered, "This is all you need."

"Are you satisfied with their work, Mom?" Ray asked when they were seated in her living room with cookies and tea.

"In some ways I am."

Sylvia explained about the four things.

Ray asked her whether she had shown Estimated Tax forms, state and federal, to the woman. Sylvia said no, she never had any.

"They must have come in the mail," insisted Ray. "Why don't you look?

"I'll help you look," offered Rita cheerfully.

Not if I can help it, thought Sylvia. But she only said,

"I'll look in the morning. But I am sure I never saw any."

Ray spoke quickly: "We can get you some blank forms from the tax office. I can walk there from my office tomorrow and get them. You don't need to search. That could be frustrating."

"Thank you, Ray," Sylvia said warmly. "And tomorrow is only the 14th. I will still have time."

The next evening Ray stopped by on his way home. He handed her the Estimated Tax forms. To her surprise, tears came to her eyes. Ray put his arm around her and said gently,

"Sit down, Mom. We'll get these started right now. Look, I'll fill in the blanks. First name and initial, last name, Social Security number. Do you have it memorized? The easiest place to find it is on your copy of your income tax. Where's that envelope?"

"Wait, it's here," she said, fumbling in her wallet for her Social Security card.

Ray wrote the number, and filled in her address.

"All you have to do is put the amount over here, on this big long dotted line after the dollar sign. How much are you going to pay each quarter?"

This was the question Sylvia dreaded.

"If you give the same as last year, you'll probably be all right. What did they say at H. & R. Block? Do you get a refund? Hey, wait! Did you apply your refund to your first quarter's Estimated Tax? That might be why they said you only needed two things."

Sylvia wished she knew.

"Well, let me see your copy of your tax return, Mom, and we'll find out."

"I will look at it in the morning," said Sylvia. "Thank you for giving me a head start."

Ray left. She was glad to go to bed at last because she needed to plan her morning's work. She would look at her copy of the tax return. If it did not say to apply the refund to her first estimated payment, she could write a check for what she had paid each quarter last year.

She slept well. The next morning she pulled the envelope from H. & R. Block out of the drawer, turned on the floor lamp, and looked at the 1040 Form with its typed answers. As she scanned the second page with her magnifying glass, she found the words in capital letters "REFUNDED TO YOU" and followed the dotted line all the way over to the column of figures. There was a money amount there. Further down she found a phrase "APPLIED TO YOUR 1999 ESTIMATED TAX." She moved the magnifying glass all around that area but could not find an amount written, nor even a box where it could be written. It was time to carry out the second part of her plan. She pulled her check book out of a drawer and ran the magnifying glass up and down the pages of the register until she found the entry for the January Estimated Payment to "IRS" for $1,000. So much! No wonder she was getting a refund. But she took the Voucher that Ray had filled out and wrote "$1,000." Then she wrote a check, squinting through her eyeglasses and running the magnifying glass over the check to find the proper lines. She addressed it, as always, to "Internal Revenue Service." She recorded the check in the register but did not try to subtract it from the balance. It was no use. She cut out the voucher and put it into the pre-addressed envelope with her check.

She prepared the check to the state in the same way.

When Ray phoned from his office, she tried to keep the triumph out of her voice.

"I have both checks ready to mail," she said.

Ray exclaimed, "Well, good, Mom! Let's celebrate. After work, Rita and I will drive you to get them mailed, and then we'll go somewhere to eat."

When they were riding in the car, Ray said, "Evidently your refund was not applied to the first Estimated Tax payment?"

"That's right," Sylvia answered. In reality, though, she wasn't sure.

"What did you think of the change in payee?" asked Ray.

Sylvia could make no sense of his question.

"The pay-ee?" she asked

"It sounds as if the government doesn't trust the IRS with its money any more, so it's having the checks written to the U.S. Treasury."

"The what?

"Mom, you did write your check to the United States Treasury, didn't you?

"No, no, to Internal Revenue Service. I always do."

"They've changed it this year."

Sylvia doubted it.

"The directions are right on the voucher, Mom. Open the envelope up and look."

"It's sealed. It will be all right. Let's mail it."

"I can show you the directions."

"Why tear open a printed envelope?"

"I'll show you on the other vouchers."

Ray drove back to Sylvia's house. Sylvia was angry. But she brought out the other vouchers, and Ray pointed to the address. Despite the small print and the late hour, she had to admit she saw through her magnifying glass the words "payable to the '**United States Treasury**'"

—in bold type.

"I have a good way of opening an envelope without spoiling it," he bragged. "Where are your scissors?"

He saw them in a pigeonhole of her desk. Taking her envelope, he slit a narrow strip off the edge farthest from the stamp and pulled the contents out.

"The voucher is all right as it is," he said. He raised his eyebrows as he noticed the amount. "Just write another check."

She had to take out her checkbook from the desk drawer in their presence, but made a mental note to change where she kept it. She tore up the check she had spent so long writing, and began to write the new one, using her magnifying glass to find the line for the date.

"Mom, just let's speed things up. I'll write the check and you sign it."

Against her protests, he wrote the check and pushed it over to her to sign, showing her with his finger where the line was. She wrote her name. It looked like the writing of a very old person. But it was finished. Ray slid the voucher and the new check into the envelope, took the Scotch Tape from her pigeonhole and neatly sealed the slit edge.

Again they were on their way to a pleasant evening. As they approached the post office, their car joined a slow line moving bumper to bumper toward the entrance, where a young woman wore a sign saying, "Hand in Tax Returns Here."

"Give me the envelopes, Mom," Ray directed.

Rita reached back for them. Sylvia could think of no excuse for not handing them over. Ray passed them through the car window and Ray and Rita cheered.

As they drove to the restaurant, Sylvia felt relief that she had done her duty as a citizen. But on the way to that accomplishment, there had been bits and pieces of failure. An accounting firm had picked up some of the failures. Her son had picked up others. The result was success, but with loss—of privacy, of confidence. She could picture herself in the months and years to come. There would be more fragments of failure and fewer of success until finally her independence would be broken to bits and with kindness and some impatience, Young Ray would be picking up all the pieces.

MEMORIES OF AN INSPIRING TEACHER: DOROTHY C. ALLAN

One day in May, 1994, an invitation arrived in the mail that sent me scurrying to my souvenirs and scrapbooks—an invitation to the opening day of an exhibit at the Providence Public Library to celebrate the one hundredth anniversary of *The Rhode Island Short Story Club*. Until then all I had known of *The Rhode Island Short Story Club* was that it is an honor to belong to it, and that three persons whom I knew, who were also members of the Creative Writing Class at Hamilton House, had that honor: Mary Kennedy, Evelyn Doherty, and Dorothy Verte.

The invitation listed distinguished earlier members. A familiar name at the end of the list–"Dorothy Allan, teacher at Hope High, writer of plays published by Baker's Plays"—lighted up in my mind one memory after another, like scenes on a stage in a dark auditorium. I remembered first an autographed copy of one of Dorothy Allan's published plays called *Easter Wings*. A search for this slim volume among my books and memorabilia proved vain, but the memory glowed of the inscription she had written: "To June from her friend, Dorothy C. Allan." Indeed, Miss Allan extended friendship to all her students, but particularly to those whom she was encouraging in the craft of writing.

A second memory was of my acting the part of an impoverished student in her three-act play called *Page the Professor,* our senior class play. Professor Page was a writer serving incognito as a janitor in a girls' boarding school to gain background for a novel he was writing. Of course a beautiful English teacher fell in love with him, and the suspense was whether she should marry this supposedly uneducated workman. From a large box of memorabilia, I dug out the issue of the Hope High School newspaper which told of this play, and my Hope High yearbook, with pictures of the cast and an inserted picture of the author.

Remembering my large copy of the little insert, I ran to my photo album. There, along with photos of several of my classmates, was my copy of the portrait of Dorothy Allan, which she had given me as a member of the yearbook editorial board, of which she was production advisor. We had worked closely all term, in a class entitled "Creative Writing," whose entire assignment was to produce the yearbook.

Outside her classroom, Miss Allan was quiet and reserved; in class she blossomed into a lecturer who held us spellbound. She was like Page the Professor in her play. When she described the audiences in the Globe Theater who came to watch Shakespeare's plays, or the coffee houses in London frequented by Addison and Steele, we were transported to other worlds more real-seeming than the classroom where we sat on the edges of our seats. When she taught *The Rape of the Lock,* she used this mock epic to warn the young ladies in her class against flatterers. The test she gave for a tedious list of punctuation rules was to punctuate a delightful fairy tale of her making, in which the princess won the prince by speaking good English.

In her survey course in English Literature, all her students had to earn their grades by creative as well as correct writing. Her written assignments were a challenge: extract the plot of Milton's "Comus," then write a story with the same plot but new characters and setting! Once I was so stimulated by the assignment to compare the imagery of two Romantic poets that besides writing one paper comparing Byron with Shelley, I wrote an extra unassigned paper comparing the poems of Shelley with the hums of Winnie-the-Pooh. Miss Allan corrected both essays carefully and returned them with a straight face.

The climax of her survey of English literature was the two weeks she spent contrasting Tennyson and Browning. Tennyson, as she presented him, although melodious and regular in meter, was weak and wavering in conviction. Browning, by contrast, rough and irregular in meter and sometimes obscure in diction, was refreshingly confident and forthright. Knowing the evil human heart, Browning wrote fascinating dramatic monologues about murders. Miss Allan taught his *My Last Duchess* with the suspense of a detective mystery, and *Porphyro's Lover* with the effect of a horror movie. But Browning was also the eternal optimist, issuing to all his readers, in the words of his character Rabbi Ben Ezra, an invitation to

> *Grow old along with me!*
> *The best is yet to be,*
> *the last of life for which the first was made.*
> *Our times are in his hand*
> *who said, A whole I planned;*
> *youth shows but half. Trust god, see all, nor be afraid.*

Miss Allan's eyes lighted up when she read these words.

I saw Dorothy Allan herself begin to grown old. Like many of her students whose writing she nurtured, I corresponded with her for several years after my graduation from Hope High. I remember when she told us she was about to retire, to share a house in the country with her writer friend Margaret Stillwell–whose name, by the way, was also listed with former members of *The Rhode Island Short Story Club* on that Centennial invitation. Miss Allan planned to do some gardening, perhaps continue to write. I wondered what could be so good about the last of life, although Miss Allan was as certain as Robert Browning that the best was yet to be. Only recently have I realized what Browning's Rabbi Ben Ezra and Hope High's Dorothy Allan meant by the last of life. Her play Easter Wings should have been a clue. In it the family are watching a butterfly in a large box emerge from its chrysalis, opening its wings. They kneel around the box to get a better view, and one says something like "I can see better on my knees." I also remember her writing on the blackboard a sentence from an early English translation of the Bible as an example of an Anglo-Saxon way of creating words by forming compounds. She wrote, "I am the agenrising and the life." It took us a few minutes to realize that "agen" meant "again," and the word was a truly English rendering of the term for which later English used a word derived from Latin: "resurrection." Miss Allan was looking toward that last and best of life, the life eternal.

The exhibit in the public library was a fascinating display of some of the published writings of Club members through the century, as well as some of their paintings and craft items and memorabilia. Not long after I visited it, Mary Kennedy invited me to attend a meeting of *The Rhode Island Short Story Club*, where the program was to be a reading of two of Dorothy Allan's plays by two Club members who had been actors, Everett Kartum and Ellen Burchard. I was awestruck to be invited during this meeting to apply to join this historic club. After my three sample writings were approved and I was accepted, I gave my photo portrait of Dorothy Allan and a program I had saved from our class production of *Page the Professor* to the archives of the Club, which are kept in the Rhode Island Historical Society Library.

Just as Dorothy Allan clearly accepted Robert Browning's invitation to grow old along with him (for his outlook on life was her constant companion). I also feel that in a sense I have accepted Miss Allan's

invitation to grow old along with her. During my twelve years of
membership in this Club, of which she was once president, I have
been accompanied by her influence as well as the memory of her
devotion to writing and her cheerful outlook: "Grow old along with
me. The Best is yet to be."

If Eve Had Known

If Eve had known
What wages would be earned
By her quick picking of the fruit forbidden,
And biting it, and giving Adam some:
If she had seen,
Peering into the future,
Abel's blood upon the ground, Cain banished, both her children;
If Eve had squinted into the years ahead and seen
Samaria besieged, a king with sackcloth under torn kingly garments,
   A woman pulling at his feet and crying,
"We ate my child and now she won't kill hers!"
Would Eve in horror have withdrawn her hand?
Had Eve been told
Her little deed would lead in later years
To prophets chained or stoned,
To To walled Jerusalem in flames, the temple vessels snatched,
God's people stripped and whipped to Exile;
Had she foreseen
Her own Creator born in human flesh
And that flesh torn upon a cross;
And in the latter days
The subtle serpent, grown to mammoth size,

Ruling the famished earth, mouth open wide,
Devouring children of the children Eve had borne—
Would Eve have then believed
What she had known,
Or heeded what she saw
Or gasped when she was told
Her little disobedience could make great wars,
Absalom hanging by his long hair from an oak,
Judas from a rope,
They, Eve's own children's children—
Would she have refrained?
Or would she still have said,
"How could a little bite of this delicious fruit
Bring ruin to my offspring?"
And, disbelieving, still have bitten it
And given to her husband, that he eat?

Yellow Rooms

Mother, Daddy, and I sat at a round table.
Over the sideboard hung a framed
cottage at twilight
windows yellow, snow on roof and ground.
Daddy would say
"Doesn't it look cozy!"
He'd say, "Jimmy the Elf keeps house under the bridge."
I'd think Jimmy would want to be inside
those yellow rooms.
At twilight in the back seat of our '36 Chevrolet
I'd search lighted windows of passing houses

dreaming of a life inside happier than mine.
Today I stand outside
the house that had the cottage in it
dining room windows squares of yellow light
and I imagine three at a table where
a father tells his family stories
of a pictured house with rooms
inside cozier than their own.

An Apostrophe to Opportunity

"Opportunity knocks, Aunt Opal says, but it doesn't always wait for you to answer the door." —Burton Hillis, "The Man Next Door," Better Homes and Gardens, October, 1993

Opportunity, you knocked. I did not know your knock.
I was slumped in my wing chair, reading *Better Homes and Gardens.*
I heard a rap. Was it a Girl Scout?
I'd already ordered cookies.
Was it two Jehovah's Witnesses come to witness,
or a neighbor who had the heart to canvass for the heart fund?
I lifted my feet from the hassock
heard footsteps leave my door, cross my porch, step down my steps.
I peered through mini-blind slats,
saw you stride across the street,
rap your allegorical fist on my neighbor's door.
She let you in.
Opportunity, you knocked again.
I was in the basement running washer and dryer.
When their roars paused, I heard "tap," faint, repeated.

I raced up stairs to the back door.
No one there. I hurried through
kitchen, dining room, living room.
The porch door creaked.
You hastened through it, tossing your
mythological locks of hair beyond my grasp.
One day you knocked again.
I was in the yard
raking heaps of leaves
red on yellow on brown
marveling how the clothes of summer had been blown ragged.
I never heard your knock. I
dragged a leaf-full bag to the curb for city compost,
saw you flee my front steps, hasten up the hill
your garments swirling in the winds of time.
Opportunity, don't be like the repairman who scribbled on his card
he'd rung but no one came.
Phone before you come, leave a
message on my answer machine like
"I will knock exactly at 3 p.m. Wednesday the 27th
answer the door promptly
I cannot wait."
Opportunity,
I'll have water boiling for tea at 2:55
cookies on a plate.
At 2:59 I'll stand in the open doorway—
only mention in your message
which door.

STELLAR STOVE

My mother's stove was the lode-star of her kitchen.
Not for nothing was she named Estelle.
Her stove gleamed
celestial white with gray trim. Its tall
legs, curved like a greyhound's,
lifted its body to meet its mistress's hands
raised its oven door breast high lest
the efficient homemaker, as had her mother,
have to heave baking pans with bent knees.
Mother drew out custard cups on their watered tray
her posture regal; the kitchen reeled
with scent of nutmeg; I fed my eyes on the creamy egg;
The broiler, under waist-high burners, sizzled silver lightning.
Herbert Hoover was president. My father had taken a voluntary
    cut in pay.
What choice had he? Teachers must set an example.
Besides, the city would repay it in prosperity.
Mother at her stove was prosperous already. Her sink, clad in
    white enamel
drank water dripped from clean dishes on a drainboard enamel-white.
My mother and my father loved what experts recommended
infants fed on schedule; children spoken to in standard English
children called by their given names (June, not Junie or June-bug);
step-saving triangles of sink, ice box, stove
cupboards utilizing wall space, cabinets straddling sink
because Mother's mother had borne nine children and Dad's
father worked in overalls and sang
Shall 'e go here and shall 'e go there,
and shall 'e go all-be doll-be?

He made his son's wife rich by enclosing her sink pipes
within new cabinets at small cost.
The played-back tape of remembrance turns
my grandpa's carpentry into concerts,
while Mother steps so high her toes never touch the linoleum.
Soon into her twinkling queendom will walk
an aproned empress, Elsie, sister-in-law, law-giver
who will declare, "It will be blue of course no other color will do."
"Veni vidi vici," Mother will think sarcastically of her conqueror.
But she will not contradict Ralph's sister.
The stove will cry, "Gray would be better. Gray would match me."
A few years later the dear stove will be carried out like a dead pet
displaced—not replaced—by a narrow stove with knee-high oven
discarded from the high school's cooking class.
Then the weight of roasting pans will
bend Mother's shoulders
metal dishpans will gouge her sink
its cast iron will show and rust
her glass door cupboards will become old-
fashioned and return to fashion again
their top shelves grown too high to reach
a ladder forbidden to her broken hips.
Still she will see with sparkling eyes her
father-in-law tapping with his hammer, singing near the sink
and the tall stove glimmering where it used to stand.
Ikey pikey sikey dikey
shall 'e go 'long with a doll-be?.

Ruth Stabenfeldt

Ruth has been writing for a long time. She is not only a loyal *Short Story Club* member, but a constant with the *Hamilton House* weekly writing group. Her portfolio overflows from her many years of observing and witnessing life.

Short Stories
    The Reality, The Dream
    A Dog Named 'Breezy'
    My Small Friend
    Stark Fear

THE REALITY, THE DREAM

The tall man, with the grey eyes and the dark hair, walked across the dance floor and, with a slight smile, asked Maria for a dance.

Maria, just eighteen, just out of high school, looked curiously into those compelling grey eyes and instinctively felt a burst of delight mingled with an indefinable apprehension.

Maria, tall, with a beautifully developed body and long, slim legs, was accustomed to being noticed, being flattered, being attractive to the young men of her generation. This tall, serious man was someone new, obviously older. His quiet, self-assured manner put her off a little, but she was intrigued nonetheless.

They danced to the jazzy 1930s music played by a college band at the old inn on Cape Cod. Every Saturday night the young people flocked to the Inn for a night of music and dancing.

Favorite pieces played by the band were *Whispering, You're the Cream in my Coffee,* and always ending with *It's Three O'clock in the Morning.*

Maria went off to college in the mid-West. Robert went on with his career in law. They exchanged letters.

The following summer when she returned to old Cape Cod full of anticipation, she found her summer suitor subtly changed. He was casual, cool, self-assured and talked vaguely of "What might have been."—referring of course to "their love affair." Her young heart turned over in pain and with bewilderment. They met occasionally and her hopes would be rekindled. He still loved her, she felt in her heart and soul, but she was too young, too poor. He was moving on and up in his profession and was very ambitious.

The apprehension she had felt vaguely when they had first met was now fully understood. They were no longer so close. Deep in her heart and soul that young love would always remain—a secret buried in her heart for the rest of her life.

Both went on to different worlds, different lives—marriage and children.

In mid-life, 30 years later, they met accidentally, and the electricity between them was still there. They stood holding hands and talked about their lives and their children and grandchildren. The deep pain of unrequited love was gone from Maria's heart, but a gentle glow remained and would always remain. "What might have been" still held pain.

A Dog Named 'Breezy'

As David and Sarah gently lifted their lab, Breezy, into the rear seat of the car their hearts were heavy. Breezy, just a few months before, had been stricken with cancer and this was to be her final journey to the veterinarian.

It seemed like a long drive, although it was only five miles. They began to remember when they brought a young, golden brown puppy home fourteen years before. She was plump and had short, fat legs and the most appealing expression in her bright, dark eyes. The boys, Chris and Tony, fell in love with her on sight.

With rueful smiles, they remembered her puppy-hood and the usual quota of chewed slippers and torn magazines. But, because of her loving nature, she was comparatively easy to train.

As the months flew by, Breezy grew apace. Her short, fat legs grew long, her body filled out and her lovely head grew large and distinguished. But it was her beautiful disposition that made her such an outstanding pet. She loved her family and all their relatives. She reveled in holidays when the whole family would gather. The Fourth of July was not one of her favorites, as she was terrified of the fireworks and would tremble and try to find a safe place to hide.

She had her favorites, and I like to think that I was one of them. When I would visit, she followed me from room to room, upstairs and down, and waited patiently for our daily walk. When she was still relatively small, she would often crawl into bed with me, but when she reached her full size settled for the other twin bed in the guest room.

She was protective of her loved ones, barking fiercely at strangers in the driveway. Although she never hurt anyone, I'm sure she would have done anything to protect her home and her family.

Her tolerance of the multitude of cats that were part of the household during her lifetime was legendary. In her last year she outlived three of them. I think she missed them when they were gone. She was interested in other dogs, but not very sociable if they found their way onto her property. She'd bristle and bark and the wanderer would slink away.

When they finally arrived at the veterinarian (an old friend, after years of taking care of their menagerie) they carried Breezy into the building. They were kindly ushered into a private room where Breezy was lifted onto the examining table. Dr. Eric came in and told Sarah and David that he would leave them alone with their beloved pet for a while. When they were ready, he would come back to administer the final injection.

My Small Friend

Yes, she is tiny—her top weight has never been more than seven pounds. She has a black mask of a face, highlighted by two twinkling blue eyes and two pert, upright little ears. Her graceful legs are black, as is her narrow tail. But her coat, ah! Her lovely coat is the color of coffee, heavily laced with rich cream, a beautiful soft beige.

She is now sixteen years old, which is pretty aged for a Siamese cat. But she is still quite lively and is very vocal at times, filling the apartment with loud yowls. I have been her mistress and adoring slave for fifteen years now.

Presently, now that I am a lone widow, she fills a big definite need. And she does it gloriously. She follows me from room to room and sits in my lap and watches the TV news and any program that I find interesting or amusing. She listens when I talk to her and if I cry, she cries in sympathy. As the months have flown since Larry's demise, I cry less frequently, but she is always there to comfort me and she surely does.

She is not critical and only demanding at breakfast time when she expects me to go down promptly to the kitchen and fix her breakfast and fill a bowl of fresh water for her. She expects me to do this morning chore before I wash or dress and gets very angry if I make her wait.

She likes to cuddle beside me when I stretch out on the sofa to listen to my interminable talking books. At night she cuddles beside me in my big lonesome bed, so soft, so warm, so comforting.

When company comes, she joins the party and if there is a man present, she invariably ends up in his lap. She likes men!

She has always been a warm and friendly personality in our home, and now that I am alone, she tries very hard to be my poor companion. She certainly succeeds in her effort. I thank the good Lord for my small and blessed furry friend.

STARK FEAR

It all happened so quickly. He dove into a cresting wave to ride up to the beach, as he had so many times before. But this time it was different. He was thrown on his back in the ebbing water, when to his horror he realized that he could not move his legs. His immediate fear was that he would drown, since he was completely helpless in the oncoming rush of waves.

At first no one noticed his plight. But suddenly his sister, her husband and their friend looked out at his bobbing figure and knew something was terribly wrong. While his sister and his wife sped to the lifeguards for help, the other two men raced into the water to his aid. Rather than chance his drowning, they elected to drag him from the surf, knowing that they could be causing more damage to his body.

The lifeguards rushed over to administer whatever help they could, while a crowd rapidly clustered around the young man. One man, announcing that he was a doctor, warned them not to move the young man until the emergency unit, which was summoned by the Park Rangers, arrived and took charge. The unit arrived rapidly, and in no time at all they were carrying him on a stretcher up the steep staircase from the beach to the waiting ambulance. His young wife, terrified by the situation, leapt into the ambulance with him. With a blare of sirens they sped off to the hospital, twenty-five miles away.

With his wife holding his hands and murmuring consolingly, he stared at the roof of the ambulance, in shock at the terrifying suddenness of this frightening paralysis in his limbs. It was a nightmare ride, one of stark, raw fear.

In the emergency room, a neurosurgeon examined him and quickly decided on a course of action to reduce the swelling in his spinal column. As his family, sister, mother, brother-in-law, and father arrived at the hospital, each voiced their fears to one another, but vowed to be strong and encouraging to their beloved young man. While the family desperately tried to conceal their fears, he lay there with eyes dark with foreboding and helplessness. The stress of raw emotions of all would linger for a long time.

After months in the hospital with intensive therapy, and some experimental operations, he was able to return to his home. With heavy braces, special shoes and crutches, he could take some halting steps. He was upright, although he spent most of his time in a wheel chair. To keep his legs strong and useful, he exercised at least an hour each day with braces and crutches, wearing a rut in his basement floor as he paraded across it.

Over the years he has remained strong and active. He drives a car (sometimes great distances, with hand controls), established a successful business, plays golf, bowls, swims, and has become a very active member of spinal cord injury organizations. With his wife and now two daughters, he leads an active and inspiring life.

He is my six foot three son, and today there is no fear in him. He has faced his destiny with dignity and strength. He has embraced his life to the fullest. His fears have been replaced by faith, courage and determination. My son's story is one of victory of body, soul and mind over what could have been a devastated life.

MAREA STAPLETON

Marea Stapleton graduated from Manhattanville College and received her Masters Degree from Bryant College. Later business courses from Columbia University led to a career with the Coty Perfume Company, where she wrote advertising and their sales manual. She began writing at an early age. Marea has belonged to the *RISSC* since 1965.

SHORT STORY
> Application for Warrant Officer

POEM
> I Hitched my Chariot to a Star

Application for Warrant Officer
A Vignette from Stories my Husband Told Me

We didn't know it—and he didn't either—but Adolph Hitler was losing the war. In a staggering feat of daring, or self-delusion, he had sent 200,000 troops and the last of his armor, his field pieces and fighter planes into the Ardennes to punch a hole through to Antwerp and divide the allies.

Eisenhower had sent the Third Army to contain the bulge on the southern flank. With the army went the Twenty-Sixth Division. And with the Division went the 104th Infantry Regiment. Its senior officers were National Guard and Officer Reserves; its junior officers were OCS and battlefield-commissioned. Its men were draftees. Its one Regular Army officer had been evacuated and had died of his wounds. It was short a thousand replacements.

My leave in Paris had been abruptly ended by the emergency and I returned to find I was now a Captain, a Company Commander of an under-strength rifle company, surrounded on three sides by a battalion of German infantry and the most beautiful mountains to be found north of Munich.

The Company was centered on the winter resort town of Esch-sur-la-Sur in the Luxembourg Alps. Two days of snow gave it the look of a storybook Tyrolean village. The fine construction of the buildings indicated that it had been more concerned with tourists than farmers.

The Command Post was in the cellar of the rectory of the town church. The building was substantial and the cellar appeared to have been used before as a small unit headquarters by the Germans. The building faced the town square, which it shared with the church and the Town Hall. The cobblestones of the square, the style of the fountain, and the facade of the Town Hall were part history and part contrived.

It was dusk when I arrived and had started to snow again. The Executive was in command. He was a twenty-three-year-old officer newly a First Lieutenant. The Company was half strength. Except for the small headquarters group, the men were dug-in in a wide perimeter along the foothills around the village. They were in contact with the Germans and under intermittent but heavy artillery fire. Our link with Battalion was a small bridge over a mountain stream. It was shelled several times during the day and night. Although it was never hit, the scars of artillery in the snow pockmarked both sides of its approaches. It was expected that the Germans would envelop the village by morning having pounded it with rockets and shells. It was not expected that the Company could successfully withdraw.

The small company headquarters staff were strangers to me excepting the messenger and orderly and the driver I had brought down from my job as assistant Regimental S-2 — Intelligence. The First Sergeant was the most unusual of the lot. He was about thirty-two, had been born in Alsace, spoke German with fluency, although he had come to the United States at the age of fifteen. He was tremendously resourceful and more stable than his tiny Charlie Chaplin mustache and clownish expressions would imply.

I checked the roster, the list of the missing and the dead for the last twenty-four hours, and several wounded in the corner of the room. We hoped they would be evacuated before sun-up.

I thought it advisable to tell the Executive and First Sergeant that I had been a staff officer since our landing in Normandy and my last experience as a platoon leader was in pre-embarkation maneuvers in Tennessee. It seemed desirable not to tell them that the experience had been less than successful. The Executive replied that six weeks ago he had been an anti-aircraft officer assigned in the States to a coast artillery detachment. The First Sergeant had arrived a week ago from a prison camp where he had been a surplus interpreter.

I finished a c-ration, passed around the last of a whiskey ration I had carried from Paris and laid out my sleeping bag in a corner shadowed from the lamp. I intended at first light to go with the Executive to visit each of the platoon command posts dug into the hills. With considerable difficulty in attempting to forget our unlikely circumstances, I went to sleep. The First Sergeant and the orderly were on duty and three guards were posted in the courtyard.

Sometime after midnight I abruptly awakened by the sound of vehicles and the voices of soldiers. Boots were scraping against the cobblestones, punctuated by the sound of crashing metal, too light to be a tank or artillery, and too heavy to be hand weapons. It was an effort to recollect where I was. When I did, I was absolutely convinced that a combat patrol of Germans had broken through our position and were about to overrun the Command Post. I took my pistol and belt from under my field jacket, which I had rolled up to use as a pillow. The First Sergeant and messenger were already on the way up the stairs, followed by the Executives. The only order I gave was to tell my driver not to go pulling the pin out of the grenade which he was fumbling in hand, at least not while we were still in the cellar.

Before I finished, the First Sergeant had returned, his little mustache twitching with a nervous smile.

"There are two truck loads of replacements," he reported. "The racket is the band—the band instruments to be exact, particularly the bass drum."

Specifically, our replacements had arrived. They were ASTPs including the band from the University of Maine.

We all knew something of the Army Student Training Program. Its ostensible purpose was to develop and preserve special skills for the pursuit of the war. Its actual purpose was to placate the professional educators and keep open the colleges and universities. It attracted boys who qualified by scoring 120 or over in the Army Classification

Tests and who thought it a more prudent choice than OCS and a commission in the infantry. It was developing a vast surplus of ersatz Russian, German and Japanese interpreters and military government specialists. The Army, the foot soldier and I resented its existence.

By now, Adolph Hitler's high and desperate strategy was whirling the ASTPs right into the ground forces. Frightened public opinion could not object. In twelve days only, these from the University of Maine were now in Europe, in the infantry, in the theater, in the Bulge, in the regiment and in my Company in the middle of enemy territory. The band would have been hard to explain anywhere except in an army at war. It might have been planned by the I. and E. Division; it might have been an army psychiatrist's idea of soothing combat fatigue on the spot. More likely, it just happened, and in the army everything including death, is expected to be accepted without explanation. So here they were: thirty bandsmen AND instruments, forty interpreters and military government non-commissioned specialists and one badly directed technical sergeant specially trained in Japanese psychology.

I instructed the First Sergeant to have the replacements quartered in the Town Hall. The senior Non-Com was to be placed in charge, a guard posted and maintained, and the instruments were to be stacked in the corner of the basement to remain there until peace or the German Army would free them. The men would be assigned to the perimeter defense by the platoon leaders in the morning.

Before I could return to sleep, the First Sergeant came back. His little mustache was twitching, this time more with displeasure than humor.

"One of the recruits wishes to speak to the Company Commander."

"Do you know what about?"

"About a transfer, sir."

With more irritation than I intended, I pointed out that there wasn't anything I could do for the recruit, or for that matter there wasn't much I could do about the Company's position or my own. However, I agreed to see him.

He reported in with a nervous sharpness and saluted somewhat awkwardly. He was short, healthy but slightly built. His field gear hung on him like that of a 3-day recruit in a reception center receiving his issue for the first time. He had dark eyes behind government-issue glasses.

For a moment, he represented all the men who, caught up in war, will insist to themselves that knowledge and intelligence have got to prevail, even in the army. The pleasant atmosphere of the college campus in uniform had assured this conviction. Each experience in the last twelve days had diminished it. Now it was nearly dissolved, ended with a rifle, a foxhole, artillery fire and the enemy.

The soldier had a request. Could he be permitted to make application for Warrant Officer? I felt very depressed. I told him he would be given the information if we were eventually successful in our present position. He saluted and I returned the salute. He left and I rolled up my jacket for a pillow and placed my belt and pistol underneath and attempted to sleep.

Two days later, the First Sergeant reminded me of the incident. He said we didn't have to bother about the application. He said the soldier had been shot in the throat while moving to his position in the perimeter. He died within minutes. It was not possible to remove his body, which was now covered with snow.

March 4, 1969

Marea Stapleton

I Hitched my Chariot to a Star

T'was on a day when I was young,
I hitched my chariot to a star.
And while stepping from a rung—
I said,
"I'll try to keep it up that far."
But as the years came and time rolled by,
spattered mud the turning wheels did mar.
The reins were up, and not so high,
but still my chariot was
hitched to a star.

1935

ANN PELLETIER STRONG

Ann Pelletier Strong has been writing poems and stories since she could walk. A former President of *The Rhode Island Short Story Club* and winner of the *Blaisdell Award*, Ms. Strong is a nationally published writer of non-fiction. Her work has appeared in *Yankee*, *Women's Day Specialty Publications*, and *Better Homes & Gardens*. She thanks *The Rhode Island Short Story Club* for their camaraderie and support. She lives with her family in Barrington, RI.

POEMS
    Breakfast
    Backstrap Loom

Breakfast

What is the perfect way to make French toast?
My husband would have it battered with egg and cream
then patted firmly into a bowl of coarse, brown sugar.
I would delicately dip my bread in egg whipped with milk
and a dash of nutmeg.
We both agree that the skillet should be hot and
heavy with butter.
What is the perfect way to make French toast?
It was a conundrum that we revisited every Sunday
until our eight-year-old son advised, "Make pancakes!"

Backstrap Loom

Backstrap loom,
easy traveler for
a thousand years.
In the Andes mountains,
shepards wove colorful cloth
as herds of llamas roamed nearby.
From so simple a tool
came intricate patterns
of sun, moon, stars,
lowlands, mountains, clouds,
mothers, fathers, children,
life, death.

CHARLANN WALKER

Charlann Walker is the mother of twins and grandmother of two grandsons. She is an Ordained Interfaith Minister and holds a Masters Degree in Communications from Fairfield University. She produced many in-house videos and an award-winning documentary, *Survivors of the Streets*, which focuses on success stories of formerly homeless persons. She is a published author and program creator on spirituality and ceremonies. Her recent book, *Developing a Spiritual Partnership*, leads couples through the flurry and excitement of wedding planning by providing tangible suggestions for bringing spirituality into their lives. She enjoys being a docent at RISD Museum. Charlann is a grateful member and the Vice President of the *RISCC*.

SHORT STORIES
> Remember When*
> Sacred Circles, Sacred Women
> Tick Tock*
> In Love With Me*

POEMS
> Paper
> Miracle or Faith
> What Goes Down, Comes Up?
> Simple Pleasures, Loving Pleasures

Blaisdell Award

REMEMBER WHEN

It never fails. I decide to do my laundry. I throw in my garments, socks, whatever into the washing machine. One half-hour later, I transfer the clothes to the dryer and wait the necessary time. When it is finished I go upstairs to sort out the items. It never fails. I am always missing one or more socks from the matched pairs. I end up with a couple of single socks. I look around the room, under the bed, go downstairs again and check the washing machine. No socks! I roll the dryer tumbler around so I can be sure they are not stuck. They are not. I look in the space between the dryer and the washing machine. There are no socks, only missing single lonely socks.

Whatever happens to those wayward foot covers, never to be found again. They need each other and one without the other is just not good. The lone sock eventually ends up being thrown away, tossed and forgotten.

These single socks are like the stories in our lives that are lost and never re-told or re-remembered. These stories about our personal times and places that fill our past and thread throughout the years. These stories of who we are and what we did to mark our own individual pages in history. These stories are missed, lost and most times forgotten. But in order for them to be re-remembered, they need to be paired up with our friends and relatives, with times and with places.

You know what happens when you meet an old friend—someone you have always enjoyed being with. You sit down and have lunch and the first thing you usually say is, "Remember when we..." and then gales of laughter fill the air. Going back in time to those remembered incidents is so wonderfully heartfelt. It is good to do this. It is good to fill our hearts and our cells matching up good feelings by remembering the good times with the people we enjoy.

I had not seen this particular friend for many years. She turned up at a local business meeting. We spotted each other from across the room and smiled joyfully with recognition. A few seconds later, arm-in-arm we chucked that meeting and sped off to a local restaurant where we sipped delicious margaritas and filled our tummies with yummy Indian food. We talked about the time when we went to San Francisco for a fun-filled weekend that cost us practically nothing in dollars. We howled remembering the day we tried to go down a cavern near Yosemite Park and I almost fainted because I got claustrophobia. We roared about the near death experience we had in the Grand Canyon. Of course, this is an exaggeration since neither of us came close to the ridge we were traveling on. Three hours later we still had more, "remember when's" to share and arm-in-arm we vowed to return to that special restaurant within that month.

On my home after my unexpected luncheon, I drove through a secluded avenue of trees and I noticed swarms of birds gathering together on the tree limbs, the telephone wires—just about all around. There were so many that the surrounding trees become alive with their little bodies. The noise of them filled the air. What were they saying? What messages were they telling each other? Were they giving each other directions to head south? Were they telling each other to get to their destination safely? Were they reminding their children to stay close? They were all talking at once in lively bursts of tweets and twitters.

But maybe, just maybe, they too, were "remembering when." Maybe they were talking about the summers past events and the fun-filled times they had together. Maybe they were telling each other of their experiences and their feelings. Their chests seemed to burst with song. Their bodies resonated with good feelings and the freedom that they were alive.

So how do we regularly access those tweets and twitters of our past that need telling? Do we set up a regular régime with friends and neighbors? Maybe we can meet on a once a week basis sort of like the AA meetings. "Hi, my name is…and I remember when."

I set about planning an evening of "remember when's" with my Women's Group. The meeting was framed around ritual, song, sharing and spiral dancing. The women came to me after the meeting was over and they said they felt so good about recalling their past times. One old timer exclaimed, "I am so glad we shared this way because I had forgotten so many things we have done together."

Sharing our past stories plumps up our spirits and inflates our moods. With re-telling the good stories about what we are doing is something good for our minds, something good for our relationships and something good for our health and our bodies. Even when there are sad or unhappy memories to relate, at least there is someone to share them with. Many times a new awareness of the story may change a down feeling.

I remember when I was a young woman—not yet married and still residing at home with my parents. I lived in Long Island and commuted to work on the Long Island Railroad. The train ride took a long time to get into the final stop in Brooklyn where I then trudged almost one mile into a department store work environment. It was Christmas time and they called it "iron days" because the shift lasted from 9:00 a.m. to 9:00 p.m. This did not include my hour-plus each way traveling to work. So you could imagine how exhausted I was by the time December 29th rolled around. Not only was I exhausted, but also I developed a severe stomach flu that was accompanied with all the grunts and groans of what usually happens with this kind of sickness.

I holed up in bed for the usual 24 hours and then slowly, very slowly made my way up from the depths of hell finally surfacing again with my head above the blankets. The moans were turned into small sighs and I knew I was going to live. Later in the day my mother walked into the bedroom with a bunch of new crayons and a coloring book. Imagine this. I could not believe that she actually went out to the store to buy these children's toys, but by the end of the day, she and I were having the time of our lives sitting in bed and coloring together. Our laughing and our coloring had us recalling all the different "remember when's" that essentially were stored in the recesses of our minds. We talked about the yesterdays of years gone by and the yesterdays of just yesterday.

The thing about it is that this feel good experience was recalled every time one of my children got sick. I would go out and buy a new box of crayons and some new special coloring book. Just about the time when they were feeling better, I would come up and sit with them on the bed and we would color together and talk about times and places that were dear to us.

There are so many ways we can bring in the "remember when's" into our lives. Then, by acknowledging this time with a special something and maybe even with food and even some tweets, I know good will and happiness will be delivered.

Oh, incidentally, guess what happened just the other day. I was searching my bureau drawer looking for a "you know what" and I actually found two single socks that joined together into a pair of matched socks. This is a sure sign from above and beyond that I had better go off today and connect with a dear friend so we could recall our personal "remember when's."

Sacred Circles, Sacred Women

Circles are smooth, round and complete. They do not contain any sharp points. They do not have any straight lines. Sitting in a circle invites all that are within it to talk equally and to be at one with each other. No sharp points. Women of all ages form these circles and dedicate them to different reasons.

I joined a woman's circle about six years ago when I moved to Rhode Island from Connecticut. I had been a part of women's groups in the past, but this one is different. This one continues to move my soul and helps my growth in new and different ways.

The group started about 12 years ago by Kay, a schoolteacher. She discovered the world of the Goddess, wanted to explore it with women, thus charging the group with a mission. The women sleuthed out different Goddesses, their messages and used seasonal rituals to honor them. When I first joined, this idea of honoring the Goddess appealed to me. In the past I placed women in a passive role—you know, sort of one step behind a man. No more shall I think that way. I honor women in all that they do.

Supportive is what this group of women is all about. We call each other and come to the aid of those who are in need. Right now we have a young women who is closing the doors on life because of cancer. Beth has been with the group since its inception. She is a young mother—I think in her late 40's with three children and a husband and for the past three years, she has been fighting a strong battle. Beth has also been a strong member of our women's groups and takes on many of the meetings and the rituals.

Three times a year we gather together for potluck and planning. We plan the meetings through for the next season. I picture Beth standing at the easel writing our ideas down as toss out our suggestions. We are each allotted three votes. Beth places the total votes next to each idea. She tallies them and the ideas with the highest number are slotted into the available dates. Since this group runs as a shared leadership, whoever wishes to may opt to lead an evening. Beth keeps us organized and at the same time having fun. I do not think Beth will make this pot luck and planning. I do not think she will make it at all. As a group we are already in mourning.

I remember I once heard her say, "Sometime we have a tendency to push women aside when we have trouble and that would have been the worst thing for me. But I would have been cuckoo without these women. They are a gentle foundation. There was a respect for my needs. It was exactly what I needed."

We also have an eminent birth in the group. Karen, the daughter Marie who has been a member in the group for a long time, is pregnant. Last year we celebrated Karen's wedding with a ritual honoring her new life. So many of these rituals include singing, readings, and presentations of good thoughts. This year it looks as if we will be honoring Karen with the birth of her first child.

> *"Be like a bird, halting in it flight*
> *On a limb so slight, that it gives way beneath her*
> *Yet sings, sings, knowing she has wings*
> *Sings, sings knowing she has wings."*

This is one of the many songs we sing during our times together. I love this song because its words encourage me to be a strong woman. Before coming to this group, I felt that women held their own in their own way. I was comfortable, but accepting. This is not an option for me any longer. *"Sings, sings, knowing she has wings."*

Marie and I have been close since I first came on board in the group. Marie is a vascular nurse at a local hospital. She and I have organized many of the events and we also spent private time together—me going to her home for walks and lunch and vise versa. Last October she and I made a two-week trip to New Mexico, the Painted Desert in Arizona and Mesa Verde in Colorado. You always hear tales about friends going on vacation together and not getting along, but this was not the case with us. We clocked in 1200 miles on our car and busied ourselves with enjoying the scenery, the life, the food and the being together. We seemed to connect at all turns of the road, even when we locked the car keys in the trunk. Or there was the time when a deer almost ran us over.

I am glad Marie is my friend, along with all the other 25ish women. Friendship and community are so important in life. And sitting in a circle is sacred. A circle is safe and everything said in the circle is said in confidence. We talk, but our circle is not a time for bitching, male bashing or complaining. It is time for centering, gathering together, honoring each other and being in ritual. We gather in circle every Thursday night. There is usually an altar table set up in the middle decorated with candles and whatever we wish to add for a particular ritual.

One of the seasonal ritual the Winter Solstice honors the Pagan goddess Brigid. This is one of my favorite goddesses who is perhaps one of the oldest goddesses of Celtic Europe still recognized and worshipped. She is a triple goddess. One aspect of Brigid is of poetess and muse, goddess of inspiration, learning, poetry, divination, witchcraft, and occult knowledge. A second aspect of Brigid was as goddess of Smithcraft, carrying a famous cauldron for this purpose. The third aspect of Brigid was that of healer, goddess of healing and medicine. These three aspects were united through the symbol of fire; thus calling her the fire goddess. In various places she was also know as goddess of fertility, the hearth, all feminine arts and crafts. This ritual honors the divine feminine, the spiritual feminine.

In honoring the feminine spirit one weekend a group of us visited the Brooklyn Museum where there was an exhibition on the works of Judy Chicago's, *The Dinner Party*. This is an art expression that forms a physical portrait of woman of significance. They are either actual or mythical, ranging in date from prehistory to the modem era. The art form is a dinner setting with symbols and words and designs.

The goal of the Dinner Party, which is a symbolic history of women in Western Civilization, is two-fold. First to teach women's history through a work of art that can convey the long struggle for freedom and justice that women have waged since the advent of male-dominated societies. And second, to break the cycle of history that the Dinner Party describes.

The Dinner Party is triangular in configuration, 48 feet on each side, that employs' numerous media, including ceramics, china painting, and needlework, to honor women's achievements. It is an immense open table covered with fine white cloths and is set with 39 place settings, thirteen on a side, each commemorating a goddess, historic personage, or important women. The Dinner suggest that these female heroes are equally worth of commemoration, as are those hundreds of other 999 whose names are inscribes upon the Heritage floor. I, for one, have heard about the work years ago, but never had the opportunity to see it except in pictures.

A few of us did feel the need to want to know more about the women Chicago choose and then try and relate their lives to where we are today. But first we had to present this idea to the group for their vote at a potluck and planning session. After approval, five of us met about six- times over the summer to plan the curriculum for the following semester. Our planning meetings proved fruitful because we always had food and wine as part of the evening.

We decided to copy the Chicago exhibition, by creating our own personalized ceramic plate and to create our own personalized runners. The highlight of our conceived program was that each woman who wanted to participate—would select a woman in history to research and portray. They would dress up in the garb of their choice of woman and sign on for an evening to share that person's life.

We had 18 people sign up and their presentations were assigned over four different weeks. I selected Dorothy Day, a crusader for the homeless. The other women portrayed included: Virginia Wolf,

Trotula, Hypatia, Annie Smith Peck, Elizabeth R., Sojourner Truth, Anna Garland Spencer, Elizabeth Cady Stanton, Elizabeth Blackwell, Judy Chicago, Anne Hutchinson, Eleanor of Aquitaine, Caroline Herschel, Petronilla de Meath, Sacajawea, Theodora and Artemesia Gentileschi. The finale took place one evening when 50 invited guests viewed our "Dinner Party" set with our ceramic plates, clothe runners and to hear about our experiences.

One thing about this group is that we seem to honor each other's ideas and never try and to negate our expressions of creativity. I think Judy Chicago's work is a monument to womankind. But I think that what we did here was a rich and worthwhile portrayal of the voices of the past interpreted by the voices of the present. We learned, we created, we crafted and most of all we had fun.

And our creativity continues with our annual weekend retreats held in another state at a lovely old home. Our weekend is filled with activities and of course, good food. Again, a planning committee organizing the events for the weekend and each year something different happens.

But for me there is another message here. Throughout history women and their accomplishments have been misunderstood, maligned and ignored. But I guess that through thick and thin, each one of us may want to take up our gauntlet and keep on trying. Don't give up and do not be hurt by the harsh words of others. If you have something to say, something to portray, something to do, then the best thing is to keep on trying and do it. As Eleanor Roosevelt said, "You must do the thing you think you cannot do."

I am an only child. My parents lived together in-tacked. I have no brothers or sisters. During my youth I remember missing that inclusion of siblings. I had friends, but at the same time, still felt myself a loner. I had husbands, but sill felt single all the time. I do have two children—twins—now grown and they make me feel together, almost.

But generally throughout my life I have felt onto myself. I missed those hugs and huddles, secrets and giggles.

I nurtured relationships and friendships with women throughout the years and some of them developed into longer and stronger ties. I also belonged to some groups—women's groups, prayer groups, book groups, and they were all satisfying, but not quite. I never possessed the kind of relationships or was involved in groups that were sustaining and rich.

I read about women who maintained their childhood relationships throughout the years and they grow with each passing incident. They had ups and downs, but they continue to skip along in life with love and affection. I never possessed this fascinating long term linking of arms with another.

Or maybe it is that "sisterhood" of women that one can find so nourishing and soothing that I have missed all my years. Maybe it is the fact that so many women out there have discovered the experiences of being in a woman's circle early in their years. Women's groups, women's circles provide the opportunity to share—to tell your story. But they do more. They help you to grow in your perspective. They turn on feelings that can be shared about woman's worth.

Women's groups that work together benefit each other. We are at a time in history when the reviving of rituals is reasserting itself and proving to be powerful. But I did not know this until I walked through the doors of this vital women's group which changed my thinking and changed my life. There is no "woo woo" here. There is a mighty thrust toward developing personal empowerment by holding seasonal rituals, studying and promoting feminism, nurturing personal spirituality and experiencing programs on social justice. We are a group of women who are innovative, educated, and in love with our femininity.

In this group of strong women there is a feeling of goodness and togetherness. Yes, it may be the people in the group. Yes, they may be cohesive, but there is more to this group. We listen, we are open and we hear each other. When entering through the doors, I discovered for the first time that I really understood the ways of women and their needs. Can this be duplicated in other groups? Maybe, maybe not, but it is the staying power that makes a strong circle. Through the healing powers of circles of women, our culture is sure to turn around.

The following poem heralded in big bold script letters was displayed at the entrance to the *Judy Chicago Exhibition* at the Brooklyn Museum:

"And then all that has divided us will merge.
And then compassion will be wedded to power.
And then softness will come to a world that is harsh and unkind.
And then both men and women will be gentle.
And then both women and men will be strong.
And then no person will be subject to another's will.
And then all will be rich and free and varied.
And then the greed of some will give way to the needs of many.
And then all will share equally in the Earth's abundance.
And then all will care for the sick and the weak and the old.
And then all will nourish the young.
And then all will cherish life's creatures.
And then all will live in harmony with each other and the Earth,
And then everywhere will be called Eden once again."

TICK TOCK

I had to have it. It was there and it was staring at me. I get these urges and they must be fulfilled right away. I walked through the open doors. I could not resist the temptation. The urge was so clear and uncompromising. I quickly reached for my handbag. All of a sudden, as though it had a mind of its own, my charge card popped out and leaped across the counter to the salesclerk. I had to have it, so I bought it.

Let me tell you about it. It is not sleazy. It is a bit garish. It is pink and plastic and it has a big face, which is what I like. I like to be able to see what I am looking at. You know as I get older, my eyesight is not as good as it used to be.

Anyway, you may think I am silly—I mean who needs 20 watches. But I do. And this one was different. It has character and it has a duel purpose. It was not only a watch that tells time, but also it was going to be my "Florida Watch."

A few weeks ago I decided to drive by myself to Florida. My intention was to visit a friend in Crystal Beach, which is near Tampa. It would be more than 2800 miles round trip and I have always wanted to drive across country. So instead of going horizontally I would travel vertically. Up and the down the coast I would go and I would stop off at different intervals.

What a dream and I had my Florida watch to accompany me. It is bright pink with geometric designs on the plastic strap. I am sick of these dark colors that I live in during the winter. Lay it on me. Lay on those yummy yellows and bright blues. I need sun and soft warm breezes—and pink.

Peace

I had a couple of weeks to spend on this trip and I wanted to be at my destination within five days. I wanted to be at Crystal Beach for five days and then it would take me four days on the trail homeward bound. It was tough driving especially the first day because I made it all the way from my house in Rhode Island to the top of Virginia. I did not stop too much either. I found it hard to pull off the road in Baltimore and in Washington. I just had to keep moving. The best thing I did was to pack my car with a case of water and a bag full of apples, pears and cheese. And yes, I remembered the knife. What a healthy way to start this trip.

From then on I covered at least 300 miles a day. I would stop in the afternoon and spend some time traversing selected locations. My favorite stop was in St. Augustine, FL. There I spent the afternoon and then a big part of the next day at this lovely spot in heaven.

The town was chock full with shops that tantalized the senses and the pocketbook. Oh no, there goes the charge card again. But the best part was the fresh, clean, warm air and watching the water bank its waves on the shore. So many snowbirds fly south for the winter. I did that once a long time ago and I found I did not like Florida at all. The traffic is just brutal. But this time the warmth and the sun healed my soul.

But that continual driving, driving, driving was hard. Is this the way I spend all my days of my life? I continually have things to do and places to go. There seems to be no space in between for breathing. Sometimes I stop before I start in the morning and do a meditation. I get up at around 6 a.m. and sit in my chair and light a candle. I select a reading for the day and then enter into a 20-minute silence. Many times it is hard for me to settle down and quiet my thoughts. I struggle with a daughter relationship and my mind continually goes over the, "what ifs." Finally, I am able to settle in and when I reach that center place of silence, I find peace.

Attaining peace is a way of resolving conflicts, which may be self imposed or found in the accumulation of old residue. How to attain it sometimes is allusive. I wish for it and I am envious of others who seem so content. But this trip allowed me the opportunity for a contentment that I have never known before. I do not know how I arrived at this centered place, but it surfaced and I was happy and proud.

Gratitude

It was a spur of the moment decision -this trip to Florida. My friend called and invited me down to stay in her little house by the beach. I would rent it and have her friendship—but not all the time. She would be in her own place and I would be in mine. It was a tiny house. All cute—and I almost said—pink, but no, it was white and just three blocks to the beach. I would be on my own to walk the path and to listen to sounds of the new surroundings. I delighted in my rented abode and in my new life. I found myself bursting at the seams with song and smiles. And the birds serenaded me every morning with their song as I gave thanks for my blessings.

I find I do not feel these gratitude feelings all the time when I am at home. Even when something good happens I sometimes just pass it off as nothing. Oh sure, I do feel filled with thanks some of the time, but it is this constant recognition of the good things that I want to envelope.

I usually walk every day, but this cold winter drove me inside and instead of briskly setting the pace, I sniveled inside with a blanket and hot chocolate. I need that walk and that brisk air to clean out my thoughts and ideas. My walk flushes me and gets me going. I used to do the, "A, B, C's" when I walked. I would start with A. I would think of things that I felt filled with gratitude for, which would begin with the letter, "A." Ann (my mother), arms, ankles, and the list would on until I could not think of anymore. Then I would start with the letter, "B" and so on until I arrived home.

This is a wonderful exercise and I would find it to be so gratifying. Sometimes my mind wandered, but I would regroup and find a letter and then fill in the blanks. "W"—water, wishes, walking.

Pilgrimage

On my path in Crystal Beach where I walked every morning, I discovered new things, new places. It was a paved walking path that stretched from St. Petersburg to Tarpon Springs. Of course that was too long of a distance for me to walk, but I did do a part of it and took a different turn every day. One day I met this man and inquired about the distance from where I was to the next break in the path. He suggested I should investigate this special spring, which was a detour a mile up the road and then turn left. I did just that and came across a lovely setting that multiplied itself throughout this area which turned into a park. I expected to see the spring bubbling up from the ground, but it looked just like a normal shallow pond. Evidently in the past, thousands of people made pilgrimages to this spring known for healing properties.

I love to take other roads and discover what is happening in other places. I always wanted to walk the El Camino in Spain and last summer I almost did it. I would not walk the entire length, but just that idea of a pilgrimage would be glorious. I love that word—pilgrimage. Thousands of people have accomplished that hard trek and for different reasons. Some for religious reasons, some for healing, others because they were prisoners and had to walk off their prison sentences. But for me I would walk just do it. Maybe this September would be my time to walk the Santiago de Compostello El Camino.

Perhaps it is good to think of life as a pilgrimage and set each day with an intention. The intention can be varied and it could change and develop. Say, for example, you could start out with the intention of "feeling comfortable" with everything you do. Then it could change to feeling comfortable with a specific thing. Perhaps I need to set an intention when I do the El Camino. But no matter what, I would definitely wear my Florida watch. And I would not rename it.

This trip to Florida was a pilgrimage. I was alone and I was completely in charge of making my own decisions. I am good at meeting people and making friends. I am not afraid of dallying into unknown places. I love to find secret pathways to unforgettable parks. I love pilgrimages.

Time

In Thoreau's book, *Walking*, he talks about a person who just picks up his bag and sets out, without any destination, no time constrictions, he just goes. He meanders on different roads wherever his feet lead him. He saunters, rather than walks. But for me, unfortunately I was not a saunterer. Time kept ticking away at me and even if I was on a pilgrimage, I still had to get home.

I missed my cat and I worried about her. Mimi is a calico cat and she is about 14 years old. She is pretty and spritly. Mimi is very friendly and this was the first time I had been away for such a long time. I felt good about the new cat sitter, but I still felt the hands of time ticking and calling me to come home. I kept looking at my watch and being delighted in having the time reflected back to me in pink, but homeward bound I had to go.

It is funny how we impose ourselves with so many time constrictions, which can be personal, business or just whatever. For me, it is time to get rid of that tightened feeling and spread my timeless qualities. I think I will use my Florida watch all the time. Yes, even though I will probably end up putting on my dark colors again to finish out the winter, the heck with it. My pink Florida Watch stays. I will remember the times I spent on my walks, in my tiny house, my side trips and that fresh warm breeze that touched my shoulders and made me happy.

In Love With Me

One of the rules of life is to never marry a man that you think you may eventually divorce. Even my long-term relationships with different men ended up in a divorce of sorts and I knew each one would even at the beginning of our sex filled starts.

One of the worst problems about being in relationships that do not work is that they do not work. I used to wait for the first husband to come home and to serve him his dried up dinner. Dried up because it sat in the oven too long-waiting. This happened for years and I wonder now when was I ever going to get it that I did not have to do this.

I am happy and foot loose now in my—yikes—older age. Some advanced thinkers do not like to be in this age, but I am in love with it.

I am in love with being free. I am in love with the ability to be on my own. I am in love with the idea of getting up when I want to and delving into the chocolate of life. I can even be sick if I want to. I can curl up with a book in bed and not feel a bit guilty that I did not shower yet- or even brush my teeth.

Both husbands were organized, "squeeze and roll-up from the bottom" type of toothpaste handlers. As for me, I am a "squeeze in the middle and forget to put the top on" type of gal. And I love it. I look at the toothpaste and proudly I say to myself, "I lovingly created that sculpture." And I walk out of the bathroom, leaving the light on and not closing the door.

Judging from this insight into my character, you might think I am a bit slovenly with my household duties. Bah. I may not be a neat-nik, but I am organized. I know what is in each one of the piles on my work counter and the piles on my desk and on the bedroom bureau and on my work table downstairs. I can find anything at the drop of a hat. I know where everything it and I love my organizational skills. Oh, darn it, "Where is that tax form that I need right now?"

The problem with this age is that I cannot see. I cannot read those tax forms or anything else that I may need to read with those silly 8 point fonts that are even on vitamin pills, or on aspirin bottles. How do I know if it is to be taken 3 at a time or once in the morning? And just when I need my glasses, I cannot find them.

I bought about 8 pairs of those reading glasses that were on sale at Job Lot. I supplied each room with one or two pairs and now I cannot even find any of them. If I were married, I would be able to blame one of those husbands. Ah, but I am still in love with my single life and the ability to make my own decisions. Even though I cannot see them.

The other day I sat at my desk and I noticed an envelope peeking out from underneath the piles of paper on my right. It looked as if the envelope was unopened and I snatched it free from the confines of its quarters. Low and behold it was an envelope—an unopened smaller envelope. You know the type, the kind of smaller envelope that contains a card. I tore it open and it was a card—a Valentine's card.

Golly, what date is today? Is this still February or are we in March? Oh no, maybe we are in April. Oh well, a few months late does not matter, as I gaily rip open the envelope. My heart does not sink because it is not from a man. I do not need a man in my life, remember? It is from my dear traveling woman friend and the sentiment behind the note is heartfelt.

Traveling is very important to me. I love to be on the go. This year I am scheduled to spend the entire month of December in Mexico. I am house switching with a friend who lives in San Miguel de Allende. But before I go, I must lose some weight. I have said this before, but the older I get, the harder it is. I seem to pack on those pounds no matter what I do. I eliminated bread, chocolate, butter, spruced up coffees, and I do not drink alcohol. I cut out donuts, other sweets, and sodas. I have tried Weight Watchers, LA Weight Loss, Nutra-Systems. I have tried all the different weight loss pills. I swim at least three times a week for 60 laps each time. I go to yoga classes twice a week. I am back to walking. Oh no. I just got on the scale again and I have gained 5 pounds.

I say to myself, "The heck with dieting and worrying about seeing." I do not want any part of kisses, or cozy late night dinners. I love my life and the freedom that I have when I want to do something that is pleasing to me. "Hum, what would I love do right now?"

PAPER

Paper—I love paper
I buy it and covet it
I turn it around and trim it
And twirl and fold it

What is it about paper?
The texture so revealing
Be it smooth or rough
I feel that feeling

The colors are varied
Yellows, blues, reds, greens
From plains to speckled
How many of you are paper fiends?

Paste away to create
In a special way
Crumble and crease
To pass the time of day

Draw or write
Jotting down dreams
Calling on logarithms
Whichever way it seems

Save it for scrap
To use for a later time
Whenever you need it
To write a rhyme

Paper for shopping notes
Paper for prayers
Paper for new ideas
Paper for cares

Whatever way it is used
Even to burn
Paper is for those
Who are ready to learn.

But what I like best
Is paper in my pocket
That is green and rectangular
With big numbers on it.

MIRACLE OR FAITH

Faith or miracle
Maybe not "or" but "and"
Maybe not "and," but "neither."

Neither miracle nor faith
Neither faith nor miracle
What is the path?
To the depths of the soul.

Instead of just wishing
Instead of just wanting
Be strong and stalwart
Create with the mind.

Don't wait for the unexpected
It will not fall from the sky
Don't hope and whine
It will just say goodbye.

Courage and conviction
Take up that gauntlet
But there is more to it
So stir your convictions.

It is all in the mind
What we think we get back
What we pray for is revealed
It is all in the making.

Do not leave it to whim and whimsy
Do not procrastinate the unknowable
But plan and conceive
And speak your desires.

Be clear and concise
Draw on the real.
Dig into your heart
Up pops realities.

Miracle or faith
Neither-nor
But spin you life with your own dreams
And up pops realities.

Charlann Walker

What Goes Down, Comes Up?

Autumn is here
Cool air so clear
Light jackets are worn
Thanksgiving brings a new morn

Falling down
From green to red, gold and brown
Leaves that feed
From seed to seed.

Squirrels dashing to and fro
Busy hiding their acorns to sow
Gazing out the window I giggle
There is a squirrel trying to wiggle.

He goes up the tree
And—oh my gosh, what do I see
His mouth full of leaves of brown
Dropping them in a branch he then zooms down!

Down to the ground
He looks till more are found
Those confounded leaves are falling
While he is upward hauling.

Oh, why did I wait to rake?
that darn naughty little fake.
With his leaves upward bound,
And my leaves still on the ground.

SIMPLE PLEASURES, LOVING PLEASURES

Eyes searching out the newness of the day
Gazing out on a single moment in time
Ducks move in unison
Every day a fresh day
From snow to rain to sun to green—I see.

Hands slipping over soft and tickle-e things
Velvet smooth against my skin
Whiskers brushing against my hand
Fingertips touching in prayer-like pose
Slipping in between clean and soft sweet smelling sheets. I feel.

Ears tuning to the magic of the stillness.
Listening to quiet and soothing noises
The whisper of snowflakes gently falling
The thump, thump of a car over a wooden bridge
Music of the 50's. I hear.

My mouth savors that special satisfaction
The edible delicious smooth chocolatly taste
A crunchy apple, tart yet sweet
Wet and cool Pistachio ice cream
Well deserved special treats. I taste.

My body moving and stretching
Striding with the dogs pattering beside me
Walking next to pines
Swimming in the water above and below
Bending into a yoga pose releasing stress. I move.

My mind yearning for understanding
Learning the mystery of the why
Molding words on a page in ways that speak
Creating ideas desiring to be free
Making sense from gobbledygook. I learn.

My insides working in masterful ways
Blood beating with percussion sounds
All parts resonating in right patterns
Life is accepted and digested to rightness
I take in and I take out. I am.

My eyes, my ears, the touch, the moving, the flowing,
    the understanding
All in synchronistic togetherness and in gratitude
Making life a sparkling crystal pattern
Of unity and human-ness
Blended and formed with infinite patience. Ah, I love.

MARY C. WHEELER

Mary C. Wheeler was born on May 15, 1846, in Concord Mass. to Harriet and Abiel Wheeler. She was a prominent artist and educator and will well be remembered as a creative genius with a kindness of heart, always advocating that education was meant for everyone. It is noted that Miss Wheeler understood the four primary needs: to live, to learn, to love and to leave a legacy, and for those who followed her inherited her spirit. She officially founded The Mary C. Wheeler School in 1889 in Providence, Rhode Island, surrounding herself with lovely Braun photographs of Corot's landscapes, and Botticelli's *Spring,* and charming bits of old-world pottery and copper to add to the artistic whole. Mary C. Wheeler was one of the first women to sit in at the first meeting at Fanny Purdy Palmer's house, founder of *The Rhode Island Short Story Club*, of which Miss Wheeler was a member for many years.

Mary C. Wheeler died on March 10, 1920, at the age of 73. She was buried in the Wheeler family lot in Sleepy Hollow Cemetery in Concord, where she lies as she desired with her beloved family, near her friends of childhood, the Thoreaus, the Hawthornes, the Alcotts and the Emersons.

PAINTING
Girl Portrait, *oil on canvas*

GRADUATION ADDRESS

Mary C. Wheeler

Girl Portrait, *oil on canvas*

Courtesy of: *The Wheeler School, Providence, Rhode Island*

FROM A GRADUATION ADDRESS
Written and given by Mary C. Wheeler

"And now in view of what I have told you, of the natural connection between school and family and society, of the same training fitting for all, of the need of a vital interest, of the necessity of qualities of heart to animate all, I will give you the key to unlock the door of what is before you, namely, the power of the Will. The best life to lead is of a two-fold nature: constant self-development by some purely individual pursuit, and the cultivation of great heartedness or unselfishness. If we have these, then we have as a matter of course a deep interest in the pursuits of the lives of those about us, a true and not affected interest, and all life will be to us as an open book."

Taken from: *Mary C. Wheeler Leader In Art And Education*
Written by: *Blanche E. Wheeler Williams*

Douglas Phillips Whitmarsh

Douggie was the incoming president in 1995 after having worked hard toward the Club's successful centennial celebration in '94. She considers it an honor to belong to a club with such a long history and distinguished membership. Douggie, whose mother was a published writer and poet, comes by her talents naturally. Writing is also a release for her from the stresses of life. She has recently been voted to be an Honorary Member as her busy life of caring for her invalid husband for the past thirty years keeps her from active membership.

Short Story
    The Wings of the Morning

Poem
    50th Reunion

The Wings of the Morning

If anyone ever had said I would fly to Fairbanks, Alaska from Sakonnet, Rhode Island in a very small plane, in three days at age 62, I would not have believed him.

If I had said I would like to take a trip like that, they wouldn't have believed me.

So when I was offered the chance to do that before spring arrived this year, I seized the moment and left. With a knapsack full of photography gear, my wallet, and wearing layers of coldest-possible-weather clothing, I was ready before dawn for the first leg of my Adventure.

Six hours after take-off, we made our first stop, for fuel and a stretch, in Saginaw, Michigan. My friend, and pilot, Bob Venusti, was disappointed we only had got that far. It seemed his Piper Comanche was capable of averaging 140 knots through the air, which is roughly equal to 175 miles per hour on the ground, but we were experiencing strong headwinds.

Even so, our first day we zoomed over Connecticut, New York, Michigan and Wisconsin, and landed at a small town near Rochester, Minnesota, which meant we had crossed two Great Lakes and one Time Zone. This took a bit more than 9 hours in the air—air of breathtaking clarity all the way.

The Finger Lakes south of Rochester, New York, where I grew up, had brought back memories. This was my father's country. This was his airspace, too. When I was a child, his stories of the early days of flying fascinated me. Sitting in his corner of the old tan corduroy sofa, or at the dining room table, he would reminisce:

"It was so basic then. Push and pull the throttle and the 'stick,' left rudder pedal, right rudder pedal. Flying by 'the seat of your pants.'"

He demonstrated what these motions would do in terms of nose up and down to climb and dive, left wing tipped and banking, right wing the same, loops and rolls.

"Barnstorming Days. I remember one guy who specialized in jumping meets, parachuting down to a big target painted on the ground. He stood out there on the wing of my bi-plane, and when he had figured the right moment, he signaled and just fell away backwards, grinning and thumbing his nose at me!" My father chortled at the audacity.

High above Cayuga's waters, I recalled the stories of his "salad days," as he called them. He and Mutt Townson would go down to a house party at someone's summer cottage on Canandaigua Lake, and taxi his seaplane right up to the dock. The girls were impressed.

Edgar Phillips was a dashing young man. I knew from his pictures and his old "flames." He was such a raconteur, he held us in thrall with early aviation stories, even we had heard them for the "umpteenth" time. He had known a lot of early aces, like Eddie Rickenbacker.

When the Florida development era was a "boom," Dad went down to design some really exciting houses in Miami Beach—a change from somber, rock-solid Rochester. Thirties contemporary and Spanish styles...he had a flair and was in demand...with rich clients and the ladies.

My mother was a writer and horsewoman. They met, married, honeymooned in Havana, and partied on yachts. Then came the "bust," and it was back to Rochester and no more high-flying of any kind.

Raising two children through The War, when his office was closed while he did Defense work, meant his most creative years in architecture were thwarted, and he never could get back to his first love ...flying.

But he passed it on to me. I mean I could never afford to take lessons, although I was always crazy to go aloft—in anything, any time. Big planes, little planes, balloons. Never a trip like this. His kind of flying.

The second day of my dream trip dawned cold and exhilarating. A tail-wind hurried us all the way to Fort St. John up near the border of northern Alberta and British Columbia in 10? hours of flying time, with two "pit stops," one of which was for Canadian Customs.

We finished off Minnesota, skirted the northeast corner of South Dakota, cruised across North Dakota, and came to a brief rest in Glasgow, Montana. Before landing at Lethbridge, Alberta, for clearance, we plainly saw the demarcation line of the 49th Parallel. The Border is kept carefully cleared. All that in 4 hours, taking in the view and lots of information. Another Time Zone zapped meant more daylight to travel. So, onward and upward...North to the Yukon!

At this point, we left behind the flooding waters of the Mississippi and the Missouri, the 20,000-plus lakes, the beautifully tilled fields of Mother Earth's patchwork quilt. The eastern side of the Rockies, still covered in snow, glistened and beckoned.

One mishap only: Leaning across my companion's lap, to try to take a really clear picture without windows in the way, we opened the small porthole, and the suction snatched my camera right out of my hands.

How could I have forgotten? When Dad died about ten years ago, my brother and I had a rare reunion for his memorial service in Rochester. What to do with his ashes? Dad had occasionally joked about spreading his ashes around some of his favorite places. It seemed appropriate that Tony and I go for our only plane ride together in remembrance of our father and what he gave up for us, and carry out his idea. Ray Hyland had been an old flying buddy and was still at it. His aeronautical school provided us with a pilot and a plane about the same size as the valiant Piper Comanche.

We circled around, looking for a likely spot. Out over Lake Ontario, where Dad had sailed with Bill Calkins? No, there...where the lilacs bloom near the Lakeshore. The pilot fitted a hose to the porthole and put the other end of the box that contained the physical remains of one dear soul. They were gone in a blink of a misty eye. Like my camera.

Luckily, I had another, better camera, and it was time for black and white pictures of winter in the Rocky Mountains anyway. By then I had had some turns at the controls, steady enough to give Bob a chance to twiddle the myriad dials on instruments that come with even small planes in the Nineties. Edgar Phillips would be amazed at what LORAN can tell you. A push of a button indicates exactly where are you are, miles to your destination, the nearest tower, speeds, ETA, etc., etc. An array of backup communication and navigation aids, and plane function displays, plus excellent charts and source books, made for reassurance, crossing so many miles of uninhabited terrain.

Bob was very cautious, also patient teaching me things that could help him. At least he was kind enough to make me feel useful, especially approaching a landing place; looking for the runway and other planes, remembering when it was time to change one of the four gas tanks.

We sighted Calgary and Banff and picked up the Alaska Highway, then pretty much followed it the rest of the way: a spectacular pass through the Ranges into Alaska, not to mention a handy place to set down in an emergency.

Refueling in Whitehorse, Yukon Territory, I sent postcards to my grandchildren. Dad had been called "Poppy by his grandchildren, Mimi, Bobby and Lucy...another connection which occurred to me when we were talking to control towers. The old Able, Baker, Charlie names have changed since World War II. Our N9030p number, shortened to "30 Papa," or "30 Pop," crackled back and forth dozens of times. It brought me up sharp each time. I would think, "Here I am, Pop, winging Northwesterly, and with an architect, too." How pleased he would be. I sensed his presence keenly again. I felt his joy, his soaring freedom, the control of his life. At the same time, I realized how very sad for him to have had to pack it all in.

At one of our stops, a marvelous character appeared out of the sky. A veteran of flying planes to Russia from Alaska in World War II, he was still instructing at age 85. Still bristling with vigor, he was living proof of never giving up what you love.

The third Time Zone and the third day away from home brought the exciting finale. We overtook clouds that were sending snow showers down into the valleys and onto the peaks, mottled with patches of sunlight. We passed through a "front" with hardly a wobble, as we climbed to 8500 feet. Our cockpit was snug and warm, as was our reception back in the U.S.A., in a customs stop called Northway. The cut-out Alaska/Yukon border is easily visible way up there, too.

Average winds had made for 8 hours of flying. We arrived at our parking place in Fairbanks at 5:50 p.m. Alaska Time, with four more hours of daylight to spare, in mid-April! The area looked like a huge shopping mall for airplanes: there were easily 100 small craft. Alaska is a pilot's heaven.

Four thousand seven hundred miles in three days. Twenty seven hours of the sixty-hour trip were in the air. Eight take-offs and landings. A thrill a minute. Memories old and new.

To use some terms that have crept into the language, Life can be as Dad's was...often "touch and go," or in a frustrating "holding pattern." But if you can handle the turbulence, or, if "grounded" too long...stay prepared to lift off when the weather clears. The chance will come to be uplifted.

Four Time zones back in the Easternmost part of our country, where I live at sea level, the waves of the air and sea blend. The surf surges and sighs, rolls and roars. From above, other sounds join in harmoniously; the deep drone of big planes, the buzz of small ones, the whine of jets. Here the pipers peep along the tide line, and the honking of wild geese headed North quickens my pulse more than ever, for I have gone where they are going...and "gladness breaks like morning."

50TH REUNION

When you enter the house, wind-chimes,
tuned to an old chord, softly announce
the harmony dwelling within.
On the stove a kettle murmurs, with dulcet sigh:
it's time for tea and talk.
The heart of the house embraces one,
crossing the threshold.
The preparation and partaking of
food and drink are performed upon the
cat's parade-ground; she purrs a blessing,
moving to her resting place by executing
her soft-pedaled minuet slowly across.
A very grand piano, around which is wrapped
a roomful of accoutrements for attending
the charms of music and the written word.
Harkening back half a century,
a new wine at hand, we hear the echoes
of girlish laughter—and a chorus
of young men's voices dying away.

1945-1995

Ingrid Wild Kleckner

Worked in Germany in the family-owned diamond & precious stones wholesale business; planned, built, & led as Executive Director The Irish Diamond Co. in Ennis that, after her departure, was bought by Winston Jewelers, New York; acted as International Coordinator of Ogilvy & Mather with their 54 offices world-wide; &, for almost 20 years, as Physical Facilities Officer at Brown University Medical School; runs her own company, The German Connection. She writes in both English & German, won many prizes, has been widely published, & her book with stories & poems was just brought out in Germany.

SHORT STORIES
> Misconceptions
> Trick Or Treat
> R.S.V.P.

POEMS
> The Last Ride
> Rolling Thunder
> When The Elephants Dance

MISCONCEPTIONS

"What if our plans backfire?" asked Maura under her breath, surveying the party that had spread out from her living into the dining room and the den.

"Defeatist!" Jill gave her friend, a tall, gray-haired woman in her sixties, a slight nudge.

"Still playing the daredevil," and with a half-amused, half-exasperated smile, Maura glanced at Jill who pointed with her chin across the room.

"Look, it seems almost as if Liane goes out of her way to snub people, especially men," said Jill, a bland smile covering her vexation. Maura returned an equally bland hostess smile. "It not only seems like it, it is so..."

"And what, ladies, is so, and is it necessarily so, or only seemingly so?" With a short bow of his massive body, Mr. Peach joined them, his moist red lips under the forest of mustache and beard still blubbering with delight at this elegant turn of phrase. "I was saying what an interesting group we got together with our invitations, and you have to agree, they're all nice people, aren't they?" Maura was fast.

"None of your parties have ever been dull," and Mr. Peach pressed each woman's hand passionately before ambling toward the buffet. "Especially with all the food," murmured Maura dryly, furtively wiping her cheek where Peach's moist pronunciation had left an unmistakable trace. "God, Jill, I hope our plans succeed. It must be hard living with Liane in her present disposition."

Jill nodded, her eyes following the tall, graceful figure of her daughter who was plunking herself in an easy-chair in a distant corner as if to express her utter disdain with the whole party. "Not that she was ever possessed of a sweet temperament, and she never even really tried, but it has been so much worse this last year since her divorce when she came to live with me..."

"She should be glad to be rid of this cheat, he's an exact replica of her first husband, but I'm afraid it knocked down her self-assurance a notch when he left her. Come on, Jill, help me with my hostess' duties!" and the two women started circling through the rooms where everybody who was somebody in the small college town was tentatively mixing with other invited guests. Shortly before Dr. Hamm, a retired political scientist, was getting ready to start his lecture on 'America's Foreign Policy,' a newcomer arrived whom Maura embraced warmly. She steered him in Jill's direction, his arm around her shoulder, on the way introducing him to various people. "Meet my friend Henry, Jill. I told you that he opened a law office in Hartford now that he is semi-retired, and I hope to see more of him than I have in the past few years!" Henry shook Jill's hand and said reflectively: "It's true, Maura; when your husband was still alive and I wasn't divorced yet, the four of us saw a lot of each other. But I'm glad you invited me. Hartford is still, well, kind of new to me, and when your letter came, I thought 'good for Maura;' here she tries to get together a group of like-minded people for lectures, discussions and excursions—what a great idea!"

"The idea was Jill's," explained Maura. "It was the same thing when we were together at college—Jill planned, she did everything with panache, and I and the others went along."

"But we always had fun..."

"...except when you got us into trouble," interrupted her friend laughingly, and while she was discussing old acquaintances with Henry, Jill looked him over unobtrusively. She knew that he was twice-divorced and had grown-up children. A tall, imposing man in his late forties or early fifties, younger than she and Maura, he radiated integrity and dependability. *And that's what we need,* she thought, strangely pleased, and then the two women tried to get everybody seated for the upcoming lecture which ended in a heated discussion that broke up only when the first people started leaving.

When Jill introduced Henry to Liane, she registered his involuntary start, his eyes opening wide, signs which most men showed upon meeting her daughter, and she felt a tiny stab of regret and, yes, envy with it. She wasn't young anymore and had never possessed this almost flawless, lofty prettiness that Liane carried oh so carelessly, almost contemptuously. She herself had always attracted men and women with her vivacity and warmth, both qualities which Liane lacked. When most guests had left, Maura ambled over and asked: "Liane, would you like to join us? Your mother and Henry and I are going out to have a bite to eat; not that we need it after having nibbled all afternoon," she said, turning to the others, "but it will be fun." Liane declined with a lame excuse, and Jill let out a long breath and felt her shoulders relax. *You're not sticking to your own plan,* she admonished herself; nevertheless, with a surge of anticipation, she got into the car with Maura and Henry and decided to enjoy herself. Over dinner, she and Maura took turns relating some of the escapades they had perpetrated at college, tales which had Henry burst out laughing more than once. "Oh, and then," said Maura, "the time I bought this huge red jalopy that blew smoke like a chimney, Jill at the wheel, careening through the country like a real madcap when we were stopped by a cop. Now by that time, she still had that strong French accent..."

"Why, are you French?" interrupted Henry. "My mother was French," said Jill with a fond smile at the memory. "She met my father, an American, in the foreign service in France, and that is where I grew up until I was 19 and we moved to the States where I met Maura at college. At that time it was still hard for me to pronounce the h, and when I get excited I still skip it nowadays..." and then Henry wanted to know what the women had planned for the next group meeting, something that really seemed to interest him.

"It will be a musical soirée," explained Jill. "I'm working now at the layout of the invitation which I have to get to the printer. I bought this new computer, also because Liane, my daughter, will start next month working at a travel agency and they want her to be 'computer literate,' but neither of us ever worked with these darn machines, and when I tried to do it on my own and put together that first invitation for today, I almost wrecked the computer. So now we both are going to enroll for classes at the college."

"Oh," said Henry, "there's not need for that. I don't know whether Maura mentioned it, but computers are my hobby. I can help you with the invitation, and being semi-retired, I have time, and if you'd like, I could tutor both you and your daughter, in exchange for—" and he grinned expectantly, "—some coaching in my very rusty French, and some guidance how to negotiate with the people there." And he explained that he was representing a large American distributor who tried to form an alliance with a French winemaker. "Oh great," said Jill, "if it wouldn't be too much bother for you..."

"Not for me," protested Henry, and while the two of them were still exchanging polite assurances back and forth and then started talking about at what times they could meet, Maura shot a triumphant glance at Jill, who looked back innocently and demurely.

Her first computer lesson went extremely well; Henry could explain the most difficult problem, was patient and had a refreshing sense of humor. Even Liane, whose lesson was next, seemed to lose some of her brittleness, and at one point she even laughed, an easy, happy laugh that went through Jill like a stab. *For heaven's sake, get a hold of yourself,* and chin raised angrily, she marched to the other side of the house, closing the door behind her. But the invitation she and Henry worked on for the next week turned out to be both professional and witty, the musical soirée was a great success, and they started planning for an opera night in New York, with Henry, as if it were a matter of course, as part of the planning committee. He also managed to take care of some problems still pending since Liane's divorce, set up a trust for both of Jill's children, Liane and her brother Bernard, and soon it seemed as if Henry had become part of their lives. On rainy or cold days, they played board games or cards and talked, they had dinner at Maura's or Jill's house, and other nights and weekends Henry took the two friends out for dinner and concerts, sometimes including Liane. But it was Jill who came up with the ideas of visiting a country fair, festivals here and there, amateur plays and others, and arranging the events of their local group which seemed to be thriving.

"He seems to be spending more time here now than at his office or home," remarked Maura one day. Jill nodded. "You know what's funny? Liane seems to be loosening up in his company. Now that she's working, Henry helps her with the travel programs on the computer, and whenever she starts getting disagreeable, he becomes stiff and formal and breaks off the lesson, and that's what she needs, a stabilizing element in her life. I think he really likes Liane."

"I wouldn't be so sure," said Maura and looked at her friend out of the corner of her eye, "I have the feeling that Henry is around more because of the mother than the daughter."

"Don't be silly," said Jill with a vehemence that was unusual for her; "gentleman that he is, he includes us in everything."

"And all the time he spends with us or you while Liane is working?"

Jill seemed nonplussed. "Oh, he wants to stay in our good graces, yours and mine..."

Maura just shook her head.

On one of their excursions late at night, Henry had gone in the wrong direction. "Just cross over to the other side," advised Jill who sat in the back. "This is a secondary highway, and the police is never around."

"Well, I don't know..." Henry was hesitant. "Ah, come on, be a sport," and at that, Henry reluctantly turned around to the other side of the road, going back the way they had come. A few minutes later, a police car passed them by. Henry didn't say anything, but Jill saw him looking at her in the rear-view mirror. "Look, we were lucky," she said brightly, "I've never been caught."

"Neither have I, and I don't intent to now," but he was grinning. The next weekend, the two women took Henry for a walk, "one of our favorites," they said. They left the car at the side of a small forest road and walked on. When they came to a sign, Private Property, and a sturdy fence blocking the road, Henry stopped. "We have to turn around!"

"Oh no," said Maura complacently, "we always climb over the fence. Jill has explored this path—nobody lives here—and it's really wonderful." And Henry, with amazement, watched the women high-stepping as graciously as dancers over the looming fence, and there seemed to be nothing left but to follow suit. From time to time, he was looking around as if any minute he expected to be stopped by a game warden. But nothing happened, or rather, a lot. A deer broke through the undergrowth on their left; a fox, bushy tail high, crossed their path; bird calls Henry had never heard before tripped from the trees, and the air was aromatic and so still that even their conversation stopped. He breathed deeply.

That night, Jill examined long and critically her strong, Gallic features and her once pitch-black hair that now, cut short and graying, lay around her face like an elegant helmet, until she gave herself a vigorous jolt and turned away from the mirror. Resolutely, she began cleansing her face that, as Henry remarked a few days later, was apparently so clear and fresh because of her crazy ideas. They had spent a couple of hours at the computer, and Maura was to join them later in the day for dinner. Jill pointed outside where the rain came down in torrents. "Let's go for a rain walk!" Henry looked at her sideways, with a hint of incredulity. "I've never gone for a rain walk."

"Oh Henry, you missed so much, and it's so invigorating," said Jill encouragingly, returning a short while later with her slicker, pants, rain boots and southwester, and the same outfit for him in large. "From the time we had the boat," she explained, and Henry, to his astonishment, felt a thrill when they stepped out into the rain storm. They walked along a small country lane, a lone car passing them, the rain drumming on their gear, everything hidden behind a gray veil, exchanging a few words now and then. "It smells so fresh," said Henry once, and Jill nodded happily. When they came home and told Maura about their excursion over a drink, Henry looked at Jill and said, shaking his head in wonder: "A rain walk—this woman makes me do things I've avoided doing my whole life!"

"But you seem to enjoy it, Henry," said Maura, and at that, he laughed.

It was autumn when Henry and Jill strolled through town looking for a go-away present for Maura who was going to visit her son in Chicago for a couple of weeks. They stopped in front of an antique store when Henry said: "Oh, Jill, I haven't told you yet, I'm supposed to go to France and see that winemaker, representing the American distributor. Would you care to come along? We could rent a car and you could show me some places and sights that an ordinary tourist usually never gets to see."

"But Henry," there was a trace of irritation and admonition in her voice, "Maura won't be here at all, and Liane is still new in her job, she couldn't get away..."

"Well—" Henry seemed to ponder this. "I hadn't exactly planned to make this a threesome and..."

"But," here Jill seemed to lose some of her customary self-assurance, "Liane is—I mean—she is so much younger and prettier...I didn't think..."

Henry studied her intently. "Younger, yes; but age doesn't really matter. Prettier—no. You are beautiful, Jill, not pretty. And I don't mind helping you as long as you think you're responsible for your daughter, but I didn't intend to take her along on our vacation—that is, if you would like to go..."

Jill was still looking into the window where the two of them were mirrored at an angle, like a transparent image superimposed on the display. Now she turned around, linking her arm through his, and said happily: "Oh, and then we could rent a houseboat for a few days and cruise down the Seine—it's so beautiful there in the autumn..."

Henry looked down at her, eyes laughing, and said: "See what I mean? When you made me climb that fence, I knew there wouldn't be any more dull moments, and my life would never be the same again!"

Trick or Treat

"Trick or treat," he says in a deep, scratchy voice, and with an exaggerated shriek, she jumps, saying fearfully: "You're such a terrible monster, don't hurt me—here, I'll give you some really good candy, it's made in Holland..."

"Ha, fooled you again," the boy cries happily, whirling around once, "it's me, William!"

"My, I wouldn't have recognized you, William—you have grown, haven't you?"

"Yes, you can see it, can't you? I'm now the third-tallest boy in my class, and I used to be so small, remember?" Wistfully, she nods, handing out treats automatically to all the other kids approaching her door to get them out of the way just so she can talk with William again. William whom she has met three years in a row now, always and only on Halloween, whose real face she has never seen, whom she wouldn't recognize in the street (or would she—just by his gait, his vivacity and, yes, by his voice?) but whose life story she knows inside out, to get updated every Halloween when he appears in a new costume, naturally unrecognizable, to frighten her to death. His father left them when he was a baby, his mother died shortly thereafter, and he, having no other relatives, has been brought up by his grandmother, Mrs. Bellotta, whom he loves deeply.

Mrs. Bellotta lives a few blocks away, in a neighborhood of small, neat cottages, and cleans houses so she can send her grandson to private schools. It was easy to find all this out. She drives by there from time to time just to make sure everything is all right.

"William, you said you like to read—perhaps you'd like this book before I throw it out—I don't need it anymore—it's about all kinds of discoveries, geographic, scientific..."

"Oh great," he cries, happily stuffing the book into his shopping bag. "You know, you should come and have your car washed now and then down where the baseball courts are—every afternoon except Sundays—we try to earn money for a field trip to Redwood City in California—oh, I hope I'll make it!" There is a longing in his voice that rends her heart. She puts her hand on his ear, the only piece of his head left uncovered, what with the horned cap and the black, grisly face mask. "Oh you will, William, you will—I know it!"

"Thank you, see you next year, and then I'll tell you all about my trip, O.K.?" And he gives a slightly skewed military salute and runs down the driveway. She salutes back, half-heartedly, shuts the door in the face of a couple of new arrivals and switches off the outside lights and the bell. In the kitchen, she picks up a tall glass of orange juice and a gin and tonic in which the ice cubes have almost melted and walks into the living room. Her son sits slumped over in his wheelchair, secured by chest-, stomach-, and legbelts. Spittle has dribbled onto his sleeves and hands. She dries it with a nearby towel and gently pushes his head back. Even in the soft lighting, the color of his eyes when he opens them, even after all these years, makes her breath stop. They are pure purple, and of a touching gentleness. "Mommmmommm," he mumbles, letting his arms drop like dead-weights around her shoulders, drooling on her sweater.

"Michael, sweetheart, look what I brought you," and she dangles a battery-operated flashing light with a bell in front of his face. "Hovhovhov," and with greedy hands, he takes the gadget, pressing and shaking it, his spittle flying all over. It crumbles in his strong grip, the lights extinguished, the little bell's clapper imprisoned and mute in the squished metal form. He howls like an animal, awk-wardly hurling the ruined plaything at her, and then he collapses in his chair, bent over double, racked by frenzied convulsions. She rushes out into the dimly-lit kitchen and leans against the wall, out of his sight, too worn out even for tears.

All the love and care she has given him, and all the costly medica-tions and treatments—some of them excruciating—have not improved his condition. "He will not get better, his condition will probably get worse and he'll die at an early age," is the general diagnosis of every doctor who has seen him. He is as old as William. Wearily, she walks back into the living room, carefully lifting up his now quiet body, leaning it against the backrest.

"Tricker treat, Michael," she says brightly, "come drink this," and she puts the glass with orange juice against his lips. "Onge, onge," orange juice, he exclaims happily in his own garbled language that has gotten better over the years with all the speech therapy, but even she has sometimes difficulty understanding him. While he is slurping it, she cradles the back of his head with her free hand. "You'll sleep so well, my love, and you'll be happy."

Michael gives her that guileless look of love that only children and young animals have when they are still trusting. Her body goes rigid but she forces herself to relax. After a while, Michael's eyes close and his breathing becomes quiet and slow. She puts the empty glass to the side and looks down at her son. Nobody should have to live like this.

She goes to the wooden cabinet, unlocks one of the drawers and takes a handwritten note out which she puts on the dining table. With the now lukewarm gin and tonic, she sits down in the chair next to her son and drinks in thirsty gulps. As the head pharmacist of the regional hospital, it has been easy for her over time to hold back just one strong pill every so often from a prescription of 10, say—how many people count their pills?

She sets her glass down, drowsy already, puts her ear to her son's open mouth. Nothing. And no pulse beat. Content, she sinks back into the chair, emptying her glass. She glances at the table, the note for the day nurse to inform her lawyer. Her last will and testament will leave everything to William and his grandmother; oh yes, he'll be able to go on the California field trip and to many others. Her letter of explanation will state, not excuse, why she took this course, and, her last glance falls on her son—why nobody should have to live like this, and why nobody should have to die like this.

R. S. V. P.

"Vivie!" Even before turning around she knew who was calling her. She had expected Mark to be there, but would have recognized his voice anywhere. After 20 years, it was still a bit husky, and nobody pronounced her name the way he did. "Vivie."

Across one of the long tables set out for the class reunion, they faced each other, and the same thing happened that had brought them together 40 years before: A charge, an electric spark fluctuated between them. Their eyes locked, and there were only the two of them in this large hall. With an effort, Vivian touched Gregor's sleeve, leading him to the end of the table where Mark waited, Barbie clinging in a kind of desperation to his arm.

"Gregor, meet my divorced husband, Mark Bethany." She had never been able to talk or think about him as the "ex..." It sounded cheap, and final. And then, like an afterthought: "This is Barbie Bethany. Gregor Carstens." She had not said: Barbie, Mark's wife, and she would never say it. With a jaundiced eye, she surveyed the other woman while the men were shaking hands and talking small. Dumpling was still the correct name for Barbie; she had even gone more to fat than in the past. Her face had become kind of lopsided, the tip of her long nose now bent toward her mouth which gave her a witch-like appearance. How this sweet, helpless madonna image had changed. Vivian drew herself up, nose straight in the air, while Barbie looked up at her, head angled. "And how're you doing..." *If she calls me Vivie, I'll slap her in the face...*"Vivian?"

"I'm fine, thank you, Barbie." *And if you think I'm asking you how you are—I will not.* At this moment, the men turned to them, Gregor enthusiastic. "Vivie, Mark is doing photography on a big scale, he even won several contests..." Mark looked at her. "Do you still do it,—Vivie—?" And again there was this charge he could give to her

name, and his gray eyes seemed to envelope her. "No." She shook
her head ruefully. "No, you were too good at it, Mark—I didn't want
to compete with you, not even later on."

"A pity," he said, and again his eyes did not leave her, a welcome,
expected, and at the same time disturbing sensation. "Vivie, Vivie..."
Several of their classmates descended on her with most of whom
she had stayed in touch. Some had visited, with others she had gone
on vacations over the years, and there was a lot of hugging, happy
exclamations, embracing the spouses, introducing Gregor to the
ones who had not yet met him, and finally they all settled down at
their tables. Mark sat at the small end of theirs, just a few seats
away from her. Whenever she looked in that direction, his eyes met
hers. "You both still love each other," Sybil, her childhood friend,
whispered into her ear. "I know," she whispered back, almost crying.
"I could kill the bitch."

"So could I," corroborated Sybil, and with moist eyes, they clinked
their glasses, blond (touched-up) head touching dark (touched-up)
one. "She is so dumb," said Sybil, in undertones, her voice grating,
"as far as anybody knows, she sits in front of the TV all day, loves
soap operas, and that's all she does talk about."

"That's all she could talk about then," Vivian snapped, and, as if
for comfort, gripped her friend's arm.

"Be honest, Vivie—with hindsight—would you leave Mark now?"
Sybil put her hand over Vivian's, hard, and reassuring. Vivian stared
into the distance and slowly shook her head. "No, I would stay with
him. Pay for that bitch until the baby was born and then adopt the
child—which would have been her first choice anyhow, she said a
child would be such a bother and would disrupt her whole life—or
pay her child support."

"And what good does it do you now?"

"I don't know, Syb," said Vivian with a sideways glance, and then talked to Gregor on her left, her right hand still clasped in Sybil's who, with her husband, had also visited her in Chicago. But she had never been back to the small city where she graduated with them all. Her parents, both dead now, had moved west, and after she had left Mark, there was no reason to return to what had become to her the scorched-earth place of the universe, the very same place where she and Mark had started after graduating.

Vivian had some money from her grandparents and an immense intellectual curiosity and drive. Mark had inherited money, too; he had less ambition but an inimitable manner to please, market himself and his product convincingly, and make cold calls—which was not Vivian's strength. After graduation, they became engaged, half a year later married, forming the marketing and advertising agency R.S.V.P., branching out all over the mid-west in time.

They held on to each other at night, lost themselves in their embraces, giving redoubt to the world in the morning, fortified by their warm mutual regard and this strange affinity that jolted them every time they locked eyes or touched. Twenty years. And in spite of Mark's occasional flings and Vivian's one and only, they had survived and forged a stronger relationship over time, something they thought nothing could destroy.

"So what did destroy it in the end?" asked Gregor that night in the motel room which Vivian had insisted on renting, never mind all the invitations from her friends. "You never told me any details about your life here, your marriage afterwards in Chicago and the death of your second husband—was he the reason for the breakup?"

"God no." Vivian was indignant. "It was the dumpling."

"The...dumpling?"

"Well—you met her. The present Mrs. Bethany. She got that

name when we were in our teens, and it just stuck to her." Vivian had moved to the window, staring out over the river into which the moon had dropped a cold bar of light. "We were all in the same school, went to college together, partied together, it was..." her voice became raspy, "it was such a good group. Mark and I were already going steady at the time. We all took excursions, motorcycle and boat trips—we all knew each other..." and now she started crying. Gregor switched off the small bedside lamp and moved behind her, encircling her in his arms. Vivian leaned back into him. "When the dumpling was younger, 40 years younger, she had this madonna-face, and her mother who was as stupid as her daughter, used to say *Our Barbie is so beautiful—nothing is good enough for her. Oh, she'll make her way in life.* Well, she did. Moved away with a cad, no-good, no-job, no-consideration, with whom she had two children, now grown-up. He left her, and I had the bad luck to run into her in the mall here when she returned. Fatter than ever, madonna-looks skewered, but whining like always. Once, she had been part of our clique—although nobody had kept in touch with her for which she blamed everybody else but herself—and I felt sorry for her. Our longtime secretary had had a heart attack, so I offered her a job. Which she grasped immediately, and messed up badly. Like my life.

Mark traveled a lot, mainly visiting and trying to acquire potential clients. By that time, we had 15 employees—account executives, and admin and creatives, something I am good at, and Mark and I both tried to keep it running. We just complemented each other. I also did much of the copy writing and producing for our accounts, spending a lot of time at TV stations getting the commercials going. One day I returned to the office instead of going directly home, and there were Mark and the dumpling having sex on the carpet. With him I dealt later, and harsher. At her, I screamed. 'You slut! Get out of here and never come back!' I could hardly control myself. Barbie whined as she usually does, sniffling that she was lonely and unhappy, but she left. When I asked Mark for how long this had been going on, he was devastated. "It just—it just happened today..." because Barbie was so unhappy and lonely and had been crying on his shoulder every time I was out of the office—I—the biggest idiot ever—I brought it on myself—I had hired her!" She banged her fists against the window. Gregor tightened his arms around her waist. "We all do stupid things."

Vivian turned her head back and forth, like a caged animal. "No, this time it was different. During the 20 years we were married, Mark had several affairs, and I had a serious one—a Canadian from one of our client companies—I was even ready to leave Mark for him—but something—we thought we belonged to each other— always made us reconsider—and we stayed together..."

Gregor put his cheek against hers. "What was different this time?"

Vivian went rigid. "I asked Mark to sleep in the guest room for a while. We had hired a temp to take care of the office work and thought that slowly we were getting our life together again. And then the dumpling called one night, telling me that she was pregnant. Mark and I had wanted children, had been trying all these years—we had even thought of adoption—all that was still in flux—and there is whining dumpling, pregnant, as she claims, with Mark's child, something I never accomplished—dumpling, catholic, deeply religious, or so she claimed, but not religious enough to prevent her sleeping with a married man, already tainted by her husband's deserting her, now pregnant out of wedlock by a married man. She was going to kill herself. This bit I did not tell Mark. I asked him to give me some time to think it over, and after half an hour, I came out of the bedroom and told him I would divorce him and he was to marry Barbie and raise their child. It was not easy. We were up all night. The times in the past when we went our own way were different—but— I couldn't get over the dumpling and the child."

"But were you sure it was Mark's child?" Gregor saw her face like a pale blur in the window. Her voice was muffled. "That's what everyone of my—our friends said—that in her usual vein, she had slept around with various men. Nowadays, we could establish the father's identity, but then—I just couldn't deal with it anymore. I wanted out of it. Mark and I split everything. I asked him to keep the company without ever making Barbie a beneficiary or letting her work there—not that she wanted to work—and pay me out—a clean break. Since he refused to convert to Catholicism (I think she had had her first marriage annulled), they had a civil ceremony. Barbie lost the child in the seventh month and Mark wrote me that he was divorcing her. I called him, told him to stop it, I would never marry him again. He called from time to time. I did not want to talk to him, but every month he sent me a sizable check. I met my second husband in Chicago where I worked already then in publishing. We had many things in common, but it was never a...passionate relationship. We were compatible...the same..." and here Vivian turned around in Gregor's arms, facing him in the dark:..."the same as we are—compatible, and..."

"Is that why you won't marry me? We are compatible but not passionate?" Gregor pushed her away from him, trying to read her face in the dark. In a tired gesture, Vivian put her arms around his neck, looking over his shoulder. "I don't know, Gregor, I don't know. It's also that for some time now, I've been independent. We see each other when we both feel like it..."

"I more than you..."

"Granted. But when we spend time together, it's not because I have to because I'm married to you, but because I want to be with you, and I enjoy it, and I do not want this to change."

"But it is also because you and Mark are still in love?"

"Perhaps." And in the dark, all he could see in her eyes was a glint. For the next day, a boat trip had been planned. Everybody was there except Barbie who didn't like boats because she said she got seasick. "I think that's why Mark planned it," said Sybil, giggling. Arms linked, the two friends meandered to the upper deck, saying hello here and there until Vivian got snagged by Carl who was running a horse ranch. "You and Gregor should come visit—I'll take you through the mountains—it's beautiful..." Vivie laughed at herself. "I haven't sat on a horse for years, Carl!"

"Look..." and he was showing her pictures when Mark approached who was on the planning committee. "Are you two buying lottery tickets? We have great prizes. Oh, and...what are you having for dinner later on, Vivie—chicken or fish? R.S.V.P.!" he said lightly. Vivian blushed and looked at him sideways. R.S.V.P. was the name they had given their company, but it had also been their private way of saying: I love you. Just as lightly she said: "I'll have the fish, and ask Gregor to give you ten dollars for lottery tickets. I left my purse with him. He's downstairs talking sailing with Rob."

"See you later," and Mark went to the next group. Vivian looked after him. He had gained weight, but he was tall and held himself erect, and he still had a full head of gray hair. "It's good that you two are talking," said Carl. Vivian shook her head, thoughtfully. "We didn't, not for a long time," and she picked up the pictures again.

It turned out to be an enjoyable trip; the weather was nice, the food good, there were games and a whole lineup of performances, some of them amateurish but all given and received in a cheerful and generous manner. "I didn't know you had so many talented friends," joked Gregor when he joined Vivian and a group of others who were singing sea chanteys, interspersed with a lot of good-natured ribbing and 'God-do-you-remember-when.'

After dinner Gus, having been appointed DJ, played some modern tunes but also the old melodies to which they had danced years ago, and Vivian, laughing and happy, danced with friend after friend. When Rob brought her back to her table, somebody touched her shoulder from behind. She smiled to herself. "Would you like to dance?" said Mark, and he seemed to be a little unsure of himself while walking back to the dance floor. They held each other, moving easily and comfortably, not talking much. After the third dance Vivian said hesitantly, "Mark, I should get back to my table..."

"Don't worry; Gregor didn't sit out a single dance, he enjoys himself. And I wanted to...I mean, well, next month I'm going to Canada for two weeks, business, and I was wondering—would you come and join me? I'll send you the ticket and we could do some sight-seeing and exploring and..." His voice trailed off. They were moving very slowly now. Vivian looked up at him, her face serious.

"I might," she said. And then she smiled. "I just might."

THE LAST RIDE

One last deep breath
to leave this world behind,
my awkward body chaining me to life—
and then I can ascent
to places unbeknownst to man,
become part of the Universe,
ride, for a thousand years, the light of stars
dead for 10 million,
jump off and slip into a nebula,
its spiral arm much like a carrousel,
start dancing with the shooting stars
and let the last big riddle,
unfathomable black hole
devour me.

Just to experience the blackness,
nothingness
between the stars,
explosions of unknowable, clear light—
and then expand forever
and forever
with whatever
makes up the Universe.

Ingrid Wild Kleckner

ROLLING THUNDER
Vietnam Memorial
Washington, DC
May 28, 2001

America—
what happened
to your Vietnam Veterans?
You sent them to war; they were killed and tortured and caged
so you who stayed home
would be safe.

America—
the ones who returned
got booed when they got out of the plane
by the ones who stayed home
and were safe.

Today the ones who returned
came by the thousands on their motorcycles,
wearing their old insignias on their biker's gear.

They walk along their memorial in the rain,
wiping their fingers over a friend's name who didn't come back.
And they weep.

They huddle together,
arms around each other,
and the rain blends with the tears on their faces.

Ingrid Wild Kleckner

Two steady a comrade
who can't walk or talk,
only weep.
What invisible baggage are they carrying
after all this time,
America?

People put flowers and letters
and souvenirs at the foot of the wall,
search the book for the names of the dead and missing in action,
and they weep.

But tomorrow the Vets will be rolling.

Ingrid Wild Kleckner

Washington, DC
May 29, 2001

The sun has come out
for the 14th Annual Rolling Thunder Motorcycle Procession.

250,000 bikes assemble at the Pentagon.

Now the police clear their way,
stop the traffic in the city,
and the Vets ride for their memories
and for their friends.

Wave after wave
they roar through Washington
where people line the streets.

They give the thumbs-up and the power sign,
throw flowers, wave,
and they weep.

But the Vets roll on.

Ingrid Wild Kleckner

WHEN THE ELEPHANTS DANCE AT NIGHT

When the elephants dance the jungle is still
and over the steppe lies a hush.
The news travels over mountain and hill,
through the plains where giraffe and wildebeest mill,
and flits through forest and brush.

Nobody said so, but everyone knows—
the birds interrupt their flight,
the herds assemble and turn around,
all animals are eastward bound:
The elephants dance tonight.

When the elephants dance, no animal hunts,
and the law of the jungle is mute.
All creatures for once live together in peace
their fierceness and mauling and cruelty cease—
they cannot be savage and brute.

It only happens once a year
and when the moon is full.
The call goes out in every way,
the animals cannot delay
and follow Luna's pull.

The grass bows where the tiger walks,
the hippo trots in his wake,
from branch to branch the monkeys swing
and every bird is on the wing
and the fish come up in the lake.

Where the animals march the earth vibrates
and rhythmically thunders the ground.
They travel together, an army so vast,
and as long as they travel, the peace will last.
Not one of them utters a sound.

And lion and zebra walk side by side,
hyenas slink awkward along.
Rhinoceros stomps slowly behind;
the animals know that it's almost blind
so they guide it amidst their throng.

Some have been on the hoof for days
but still they're plodding on,
and as they walk their numbers grow,
toward east is where they have to go,
where others have since gone.

The jungle takes them in its arms
and leads them deep inside;
on hidden paths, through forest's maze,
it leads them to the sacred place—
a clearing, huge and wide.

They all know that they have arrived
and settle down to wait.
Old enemies sit side by side,
a hare rests on the cheetah's hide—
nobody is afraid.

They populate the trees around,
the ones who climb and fly,
and spiders, ants, and frogs and toads
have put on others' backs their loads—
they really are not shy!

And when at last the sun goes down,
a sigh heaves from the crowd.
They have achieved their goal at last,
their times of hardship in the past,
no enemy about.

The swish of footsteps can be heard,
approaching, soft and slow;
they drum the earth, large bodies sway—
the elephants are on their way,
the rising moon aglow.

And as it rises, huge and warm,
its orange turns to white,
and in its finely woven sheen
the gray colossi can be seen
assembling in the night.

The clearing fills; the babies first,
so well-behaved and quiet;
none of their usual friskiness,
no jostling and rambunctiousness—
they keep their measured stride.

Ingrid Wild Kleckner

A long trail forms, row after row,
they all have to line up;
while winds sweep clear the nightly sky,
they press each other, awed and shy,
the calves, pup after pup.

The females follow close behind;
they lead the herds, they reign.
They are related or close friends,
take up in need the group's defense,
protecting their domain.

And lastly all the rogues appear,
the giant bulls are here.
They don't live with their families,
have no responsibilities
and roam alone, but near.

And here they stand, an army bold,
tiered after size and rank.
The glade is filled to overflow,
there is no other place to go—
the spell has taken hold.

The moon is climbing up the trees
and then swings overhead;
its otherworldly globe of light
is bathing everything in white.
The elephants start to tread.

Ingrid Wild Kleckner

A sea of bodies, silver-gray,
moves back and forth like waves.
They move as strong as flood and tide,
nobody pushes them aside,
the elephants, the braves.

They think as one and move as one,
the old ones and the young.
They strut and dance the minuet
in following the etiquette
which cannot come unstrung.

They balance forward and they bow
as graceful as they can,
they face each other, coming close,
they bent their heads and point their toes—
the fun has just begun.

The watching beasts are spellbound, fixed;
they sit as in a trance.
So many trunks move with a hum,
so many feet the ground make drum—
and on the elephants dance.

They form a string that spools around
and then unwinds again;
their legs which are like jungle trees
pound up and down; they bent their knees
and shape another chain.

Ingrid Wild Kleckner

For all the animals around
the genial giants dance;
they dance with dignity and pose,
by turns are solemn and jocose,
they strut and pace and prance.

Until the time when dawn draws near,
the moon turns pale and sad.
All animals share in the pain
for something they will lose again,
for something they just had.

Outside the jungle, on the plain,
appears the sun's first blush,
and while its tickling fingers dig
through brush and trees, so dense and thick—
the whole world seems to hush.

The elephants face outward now,
their flappy ears alert.
They raise their heads and trunks up high,
prepared to give their warrior's cry—
the likes is rarely heard.

A vast, tremendous trumpet blast
resounds into the air;
The elephants receive the day,
the sun's first disenchanting ray:
You animals, beware!

Go back now, over is the dance
and at an end the peace.
We, as the kings of animals
will call you to the same locales
which are one night for lease.

Now steppe and jungle will awake,
the creatures' lives go on.
They all get up with hesitation
and look around with trepidation:
The sacred place is gone.

Like shadows leave the elephants,
the kings of strength and might.
And all that's left is memory,
a shared and treasured jubilee:
The elephants danced last night.

Present and Past Members
of the Rhode Island Short Story Club

PRESENT MEMBERS

Clara I. Rivera Banchs

Carolyn Bray

Bernadette Conte

Patricia J. Gerstner*

Elaine Kaufman

Eleanor McElroy

Frances L. O'Donnell**

Edna Pannagio

Earl F. Pasbach*

Lisa A. Proctor

Marie C. Russian

June Smith

Ruth Stabenfeldt

Marea Stapleton

Charlann Walker

Douglas Phillips Whitmash*

Ingrid Wild Kleckner*

*Past Presidents

**President

Frances L. O'Donnell, President

Patricia J. Gerstner, Past President

From left to right, top row: *Earl F. Pasbach, Charlann Walker, Marie C. Russian, Frances L. O'Donnell, Patricia J. Gerstner, Ruth Stabenfeldt, Marea Stapleton, Lisa A. Procter* Bottom row: *Douglas (Douggie) Phillips Whitmarsh, Ingrid Wild Kleckner*

From left to right: *Edna Panaggio, Carolyn Bray, Clara I. Rivera Banchs*

June Smith

Past Members

Abraham, Joseph
Allen, Dorothy C.
Allison, Anne Crosby Emery
Appleton, Marguerite
Armington, Justine K.
Armington, Francis Bowen
Austin, Katherine H.
Bailey, Margaret Emerson
Baker, Lucy E.
Banks, Miriam A.
Barney, Mrs. J. K.
Bates, Louise Prosser
Bird, Dr. Grace E.
Blanchard, Edith Richmond
Bonticou, Mrs. Frederick
Bosworth, Mrs. Orrin
Bowen, Lieselotte
Boynton, Griswold
Boynton, Mrs. Rae
Bradbury, Harriet B.
Bradshaw, Marjorie
Branson, Elsie S.
Brayton, Susan S.
Briggs, Caroline
Brown, Mary Louise
Brown, Edna
Bruns, Lucille
Bucklin, Lorraine P.
Burchard, Ellen

Campbell, Anne E.
Cappelli, Amy Spencer
Catton, Virginia Conroy
Chandler, Sarah
Chase, Phoebe B.
Clough, Elsie Lustig
Coburn, Marjorie
Colcleugh, Emma Shaw
Collins, Mrs. Clarkson A. Jr.
Comstock, Alice
Cooke, Abigail W.
Couch, Mrs. Herbert N.
Covington, Mary
Davis, Blanche N.
Demopelos, Frances
DeWolf, Louise Henry
Doherty, Evelyn
Driggs, Nancy
Ducasso, Mabel L.
Dudley, Mary
Durand, Edith Cook
Easton, Mrs. Frank T.
Elliott, Maud Howe
Emerson, Margaret
Evano, Mary Frost
Fansler, Mrs. Dean S.
Faulkner, Joan
Field, Gertrude Rugg
Fletcher, Mrs. Henry

Fountain, Jean
Frye, Mary
Galo, Maria G.
Gardner, Abbie
Gaslin, Lucy Hale
Gleason, Dr. Marion A.
Gleeson, Alice Collins
Goodwin, Frank J.
Green, Mrs. Joseph W. Jr.
Greene, Miss M. A.
Griffith, Mrs. W. O.
Guyol, Louise H.
Hallett, Saida
Hammond, Jane
Hanson, Emily
Hart, Mrs. Bertrand K.
Hart, Mrs. Henry C.
Hazard, Caroline
Hopkins, Sara F.
Howe, Julia Ward
Huffman, Carolanne
Hunt, Debbie
Irons, Mrs. Walter Stokes
Kaula, Edna
Kartum, Everett
Kelley, Leona
Kendall, Elizabeth P.
Kennedy, Mary H.
Kirby, Chester

Kittredge, Eleanor H.
Knight, Mrs. C. Prescott
Koisch, Mary
Laney, Annie L.
Lansing, Martha C.
LeRoux, J. H.
Linn, Harriet
Loomis, Mrs. Ralph
Lustig, Mrs. Alfred L.
Mackenzie, Louise
Mason, Barbara B.
Mason, Mrs. Barbara
Matteson, Rose
McCann, Mrs. Kathleen
McCarron, Mary
McCarton, D. Gloria
McQuade, Mary Ann
Metcalf, Anna
Miner, Lillian B.
Miner, Susan F.
Monserrat, Jane Graves
Morse, Emily
Neikirk, Mabel E.
O'Neil, Aileen A.
Palmer, Fanny Purdy
Palmer, Henrietta
Pamel, Mrs. Samuel
Pardee, Jill
Pardee, Alice

Partridge, M. E.
Patterson, Adelaide
Perry, Mrs. James DeWolf
Perry, Nora
Pheiffer, Sally
Pierce, Katherine
Powel, Mrs. Samuel
Powell, Elsa
Pratt, Dorothy
Pratt, Mary
Putnam, Dr. Helen
Reynolds, Mrs. F. A.
Richardson, Miss H. P.
Richmond, Margaret
Riggs, Doris R.
Root, Mary E.
Sanderson, Alan
Sands, Mrs. Harold
Sanford, Mr. (Jack) Elton
Sherwood, Grace
Shulman, Mrs. Charlotte
Sisson, Pat
Slocum, Grace L.
Smith, Eliza
Smith, Emma L.
Spencer, Rev. Anna Garland
Stearnes, Elsie
Stevens, Ada Borders
Stewart, Nancy M.
Stillwell, Miss Margaret B.
Stone, Esther

Strong, Ann Pelletier
Talbot, Mary A.
Tallman, Marianna M.
Thomas, Jane
Thurber, Mrs. Dexter
Tillinghast, Charlotte
Tucker, Katherine Patricia
Van Schalkwyck, Cindy
Verte, Dorothy
Walter, Mrs. Herbert S.
Walters, Alice Hall
Watts, Pamela
Weeden, Miss Ann
Wheeler, Mary C.
White, Elizabeth Nicholson
Wholey, Mrs. Gerry
Wilder, Prof. Magel C.
Wilson, Sally D.
Wilson, Mrs. George
Woodward, Mabel
Wyman, Lillie Chace